The Church of England and Divorce in the Twentieth Century

Attitudes toward divorce have changed considerably over the past two centuries. As society has moved away from a Biblical definition of marriage as an indissoluble union to that of an individual and personal relationship, secular laws have evolved as well. Using unpublished sources and previously inaccessible private collections, Holmes explores the significant role the Church of England has played in these changes, as well as the impact this has had on ecclesiastical policies. This timely study will be relevant to ongoing debates about the meaning and nature of marriage, including the theological doctrines and ecclesiastical policies underlying current debates on same-sex marriage.

Ann Sumner Holmes is Associate Dean of the Ogden Honors College at Louisiana State University.

The Church of England and Divorce in the Twentieth Century
Legalism and Grace

Ann Sumner Holmes

NEW YORK AND LONDON

First published 2017
by Routledge
711 Third Avenue, New York, NY 10017

and by Routledge
2 Park Square, Milton Park, Abingdon, Oxon OX14 4RN

Routledge is an imprint of the Taylor & Francis Group, an informa business

© 2017 Taylor & Francis

The right of Ann Sumner Holmes to be identified as author of this work has been asserted in accordance with sections 77 and 78 of the Copyright, Designs and Patents Act 1988.

All rights reserved. No part of this book may be reprinted or reproduced or utilised in any form or by any electronic, mechanical, or other means, now known or hereafter invented, including photocopying and recording, or in any information storage or retrieval system, without permission in writing from the publishers.

Trademark notice: Product or corporate names may be trademarks or registered trademarks, and are used only for identification and explanation without intent to infringe.

Library of Congress Cataloging-in-Publication Data
Names: Holmes, Ann Sumner, 1951– author.
Title: The Church of England and divorce in the twentieth century : legalism and grace / by Ann Sumner Holmes.
Description: 1st [edition]. | New York : Routledge, 2016. | Includes bibliographical references and index.
Identifiers: LCCN 2016030685 (print) | LCCN 2016033077 (ebook) | ISBN 9781848936171 (hardcover : alk. paper) | ISBN 9781315408507
Subjects: LCSH: Divorce—Religious aspects—Church of England. | Church of England—Influence. | Divorce—England.
Classification: LCC BX5149.M3 H65 2016 (print) | LCC BX5149.M3 (ebook) | DDC 261.8/358908828342—dc23
LC record available at https://lccn.loc.gov/2016030685

ISBN: 978-1-848-93617-1 (hbk)
ISBN: 978-1-315-40850-7 (ebk)

Typeset in Sabon
by Apex CoVantage, LLC

Printed and bound in Great Britain by
TJ International Ltd, Padstow, Cornwall

For Wendell
Forever

Contents

	Acknowledgments	ix
	Introduction	1
1	The Church of England and Divorce Reform, 1900–1914	5
2	The Interwar Years: Church and State Diverge	28
3	Till Death them do Part: The Church and Divorce, 1945–1960	60
4	*Putting Asunder*: The Church and Divorce Reform in the 1960s	92
5	Remarriage in Church after Divorce: In Pursuit of Consensus	127
6	Remarriage in Church after Divorce: Each Case is Different	162
	Index	191

Acknowledgments

I have been studying the subject of divorce in England for quite some time, and many individuals have helped me with my research. In England Lord McGregor of Durris (formerly O.R. McGregor), Cyril Glasser, and Stephen Cretney met with me, recommended sources, and advised me. I am grateful to Stephen Cretney for sharing his own research and for explaining the intricacies of English divorce law. In the UK, also, I would like to thank the staffs of the libraries at Durham Cathedral and Lambeth Palace for their assistance. Dr Rachel Cosgrave at Lambeth has been especially helpful. Quotations from the Henson diaries appear by kind permission of the Chapter of Durham Cathedral, and Lambeth Palace Library has granted me permission to cite the sources that I found in their archives.

I can never adequately express my appreciation to Helen Oppenheimer. She graciously welcomed me into her home and shared her personal papers and memories with me. As a member of various Church of England commissions that explored questions regarding divorce in the 1960s, 1970s, and 1980s, Lady Oppenheimer was a valuable source of information. She has granted me permission to quote from her papers and from our conversations, both in person and through correspondence. Lady Oppenheimer also read the entire manuscript, when it was much longer than it is now, and her comments and advice have been invaluable to me. She emphasized the significance of the role of Gordon Dunstan in the debates over divorce. His son, the Very Reverend Gregory Dunstan, has kindly granted me permission to quote from his father's papers, both in Lady Oppenheimer's collection and in the archives at Lambeth.

I am grateful to Louisiana State University for granting me two sabbaticals to travel to do research and to write. Two successive Deans of the LSU Honors College—Nancy Clark and Jonathan Earle—have encouraged and supported me in this project. In years past several undergraduate assistants helped me with the collection of documents for my research. I would like to thank Sarah Perkins Reid, Leslie Bourgeois, Tommy Jacobi, Ryan Gregoire, and George Holmes for their help in this regard.

I am grateful to friends and colleagues who have offered helpful advice and suggestions. They include Alisa Plant, Paul Freedman, Martha Vicinus,

x *Acknowledgments*

Ed Henderson, Ann Loades, Lee Ann Lockridge, Anne Loveland, and Bill Worger. I am especially grateful to Meredith Veldman for her valuable comments after she had read the manuscript. The kind hospitality of John and Virginia Noland made my research trips to London very comfortable indeed.

The support of my family has been essential to my work. My two sons, Sumner and George, have enriched my life immeasurably and taught me the meaning of unconditional love. I could never have completed this project without the patience, selflessness, unwavering support, and encouragement of my husband Wendell. A lifetime is not enough to express my love and appreciation to him.

Introduction

In April of 1895, spectators disrupted a wedding at St. Mark's Church, North Audley-street, London. The groom, Theodore Brinckman, had been identified as the guilty party in an undefended divorce suit. When the engagement of Mr. Brinckman to Miss Linton, the stepdaughter of Lord Aylesford, was publicized, several 'Churchmen' petitioned the Bishop of London not to allow the ceremony to take place in a church. After the Bishop of London declined to reply to those petitions, representatives of the English Church Union decided to stage a public protest. Father William Black, the most vocal of the group, protested when the bridal party took their places at the chancel. When the Reverend Ker Gray, who was officiating, said 'If any man can show any just cause why they may not lawfully be joined together, let him now speak', Father Black attempted to read a statement that 'one of the parties has his canonical wife living, and . . . therefore his marriage with any other person is contrary to the law of God and to the doctrine and discipline of the Church of England'. The interruption caused a commotion and evoked expressions of sympathy for the bride. The Reverend Ker Gray stated that he had the Bishop's mandate, and concluded the service. Police outside the church controlled the crowd, but the protesters were loudly hissed as they departed.[1]

Remarriage after divorce in the Church of England was once controversial enough to evoke such public protest. Guided by the injunction in the Gospel of Mark, 'What therefore God hath joined together, let not man put asunder' (Mark 10:9), the post-Reformation Anglican Church, through the ecclesiastical courts, enforced the view that marriage was indissoluble. That position, however, became more difficult to maintain after the Divorce Act of 1857 made divorce available in English secular courts. Although the statute clearly indicated that marriages could be legally dissolved, the Church continued to define marriage as a lifelong union.

Nevertheless, a wide diversity of opinions among bishops, clergy, and theologians made it difficult for the Church of England to establish an official position on divorce. The bishops in the House of Lords were able to accept the 1857 Act because the statute provided that only adultery was a ground for divorce, a provision that the New Testament appeared to justify. According

2 Introduction

to what was known as the Matthaean Exception, 'Whosoever shall put away his wife, saving for the cause of fornication, causeth her to commit adultery' (Matthew 5:32). By the time that a Royal Commission on Divorce convened in 1910, however, higher criticism of New Testament texts had brought the authenticity of the Matthaean Exception into question. Some theologians therefore argued that the Marcan prohibition of divorce was absolute, while others insisted that the injunction in Mark should be interpreted as an ideal rather than a rule. Arguments based on Biblical texts ranged from the interpretation that marriage was indissoluble under any circumstances to the assertion that adultery should not be the only ground for divorce.

When arguments based on Biblical texts proved inconclusive, representatives of the Church of England frequently opposed divorce as a threat to social stability. The traditional response to reformers who wanted to enable unhappy spouses to end their marriages was the legal maxim 'Hard cases make bad law'. No matter how great the suffering in individual cases, marriages should be maintained to foster the welfare of the community. In 1889, in an extreme statement of the argument, the art critic and journalist Harry Quilter wrote:

> The purpose of happiness is really no part of the purpose of marriage. . . . Marriage is what it is through the necessities of society. . . . So long as society has the same necessities, and finds them fulfilled by marriage, the institution must be considered to be a success, though every married man and woman in the world were unhappy.[2]

Clerical opponents of divorce reform sometimes used similar reasoning to reinforce arguments based on Biblical references. They encouraged self-sacrifice among the hard cases.

During the twentieth century, changes in social expectations regarding marriage undermined arguments against divorce reform based on the welfare of the community rather than the personal happiness of the individual. As married women gained a legal and economic identity apart from their husbands, they began to function more clearly as individuals in an egalitarian marriage rather than as dependents in a patriarchal relationship. The unit portrayed in the Biblical 'They two shall be one flesh' was no longer an accurate description of marriage. As a Commission appointed by the Archbishop of Canterbury to study the Christian doctrine of marriage noted in their report in 1972:

> Marriage has . . . come to be thought of, less in terms of its function, what it is for, than in terms of what it is. Thus many people have felt that, child-rearing apart, the only bond left to the married pair is their personal bond. . . . If this bond fails, then there is 'irretrievable breakdown' of the marriage; there is no reason why it should not be dissolved, for it is without social function either.[3]

A 'broken' marriage served the interests of neither the individual nor the community. When a marriage was identified more clearly as a personal relationship, rather than an institution solely defined by Christian principles or by its social value, then restrictive divorce laws and inflexible ecclesiastical rules appeared untenable.

Secularisation, the decline of the significance of religion in British society, also challenged the Church of England in the attempts to maintain permanent marriage. Although the dating and scope of secularisation are controversial, most scholars agree that religious decline is characteristic of the twentieth century.[4] As Hugh McLeod has argued, when a shift occurred in the way that people understood the religious identity of their society—from 'Christian' to 'pluralist', 'post-Christian', or 'secular'—then 'laws which purported to be based on Christian moral principles might no longer be appropriate'. McLeod specifically identified divorce as a 'contentious issue' on which there was no consensus.[5] Without consensus, the Church of England found it increasingly difficult to defend the strict definition of marriage as a lifelong union. Additionally, secularisation meant that the Church was struggling to maintain traditional Christian standards at a time when membership numbers were declining.[6]

Despite the growing secularisation of society, divorce reform still evoked strong opposition. The reluctance of British governments to sponsor controversial divorce legislation is evident in the fact that two of the major bills passed during the twentieth century—one in 1937 and the other in 1969—were introduced by private members. Throughout the twentieth century, the Established Church continued to play its traditional role in influencing the formulation of secular legislation involving what were seen as 'moral' issues. If the Church of England officially opposed a particular divorce bill, it was difficult for either the government or a private member to guide the legislation successfully through Parliament.

With the extension of the grounds for divorce in 1937, the laws of the State clearly diverged from the doctrines of the Church. The Church responded by seeking to maintain its definition of marriage by a strict discipline that prohibited remarriage in church after divorce. By the second half of the twentieth century, however, the increasingly dominant view that marriage is a personal relationship and not a social institution challenged the insistence on the indissolubility of marriage. The shift in understanding compelled various Church Commissioners to recognize the qualities that made each marital relationship distinctive. Charged with addressing questions related to divorce, Commissioners began to argue that marriages should be indissoluble, but not all unions achieved that ideal.

In 1981 the General Synod voted to accept remarriage in church after divorce in certain cases, but disagreements continued about the procedure for determining which individuals would be allowed the use of the Prayer Book Service. Continuing debates on that question revealed widespread disagreement within the Church and an institutional inability to resolve the

4 Introduction

disagreements. The complicated and controversial issues tested the authority and effectiveness of the Archbishops of Canterbury and of various ecclesiastical assemblies. An overwhelming difficulty that the Church confronted was the impossibility of maintaining the strict definition of marriage as a lifelong union. No matter how determined the Church was to give meaning to the words 'till death us do part', marriages did break down, couples divorced, and divorced Anglicans wanted to remarry in church.

In 2002 the General Synod passed a motion stating that a divorced person might be married in church under 'exceptional circumstances'. The parish priest was to determine which cases were 'exceptional'. After a century and a half of debate, the Church of England officially acknowledged that divorce cases could not be judged indiscriminately. As the House of Bishops proclaimed in 1999, 'Each case is different'. Human behavior, especially in such a personally intimate relationship as marriage, could not be governed by inflexible rules based on Biblical texts and social utility. Punishing divorced persons by denying them remarriage in church did not preserve marriages nor enhance the sanctity of marriage. The Church did not abandon the definition of marriage as a lifelong union, but the recognition that not all unions achieved that ideal enabled the clergy to respond to divorced persons more compassionately. For centuries the Church had been restricted in its response to divorce by the Biblical injunction 'What therefore God hath joined together, let not man put asunder'. During the twentieth century, however, the reality of human experience compelled the Church of England to look beyond the Bible and Christian tradition in the formulation of guidelines regarding divorce and thus to move from legalism to grace.

Notes

1. 'Extraordinary Scene at a Wedding', *The Times* (29 April 1895):6.
2. H. Quilter, ed., *Is Marriage a Failure? A Modern Symposium* (Chicago and New York: Rand, McNally & Company, 1889), p. 10. Quilter's daughter Gwendolyn married A.P. Herbert in 1914. Quilter had died in 1907 and never knew his son-in-law, who, as a strong advocate of divorce reform, sponsored the 1937 Matrimonial Causes Act.
3. *Marriage Divorce and the Church: The Report of a Commission Appointed by the Archbishop of Canterbury to Prepare a Statement on the Christian Doctrine of Marriage* (London: SPCK, 1972), p. 47.
4. See C. Brown, *The Death of Christian Britain: Understanding Secularisation 1800–2000* (Routledge, 2001; 2009); S. Green, *The Passing of Protestant England: Secularisation and Social Change, c. 1920–1960* (Cambridge, 2011); H. McLeod, *The Religious Crisis of the 1960s* (OUP, 2007); and Grace Davie, *Religion in Britain Since 1945: Believing without Belonging* (Blackwell, 1994) among others.
5. McLeod, p. 2.
6. G. Machin, *Churches and Social Issues in Twentieth-Century Britain* (Clarendon Press, 1998), p. 210.

1 The Church of England and Divorce Reform, 1900–1914

Historical Background

Divorce, the legal dissolution of a marriage, was central to the creation of the Church of England. In the well-known story of Henry VIII, the King of England wished to rid himself of a wife who had failed to provide him with a male heir. He desperately wanted to marry another woman who would, he hoped, be able to bear a legitimate son. Henry's Queen, Catherine of Aragon, had been married briefly to his brother Arthur. After Arthur's death, Catherine had married Henry. Of six children born to them, only one daughter, Mary, survived. On the basis of the Biblical prohibition against marriage to a brother's widow, Henry claimed that his marriage was cursed and asked the Pope for an annulment. The Pope, who could not afford to offend Catherine's uncle, the Emperor Charles V, refused. The King then turned to Parliament, which passed a statute prohibiting appeals from English courts to Rome in ecclesiastical suits. The Archbishop of Canterbury's court could then declare Henry's marriage to Catherine null and void. After 1534, when the Act of Supremacy recognized the King as the head of the Church in England, the Pope no longer had legal authority there.

Despite its origins, the new Church of England was not sympathetic to divorce. The Anglican Reformation had abolished the jurisdiction of the Roman Catholic Church in matrimonial cases. When the courts of the Church of England assumed that jurisdiction, they continued to enforce the canonical view that marriage was indissoluble. While Continental Reformers in the sixteenth century generally agreed that divorce could be allowed in cases of adultery and malicious desertion, Anglican Church courts refused to grant divorce *a vinculo*, one that severed the marriage bond and gave each party the right to marry another person. These courts granted only decrees of nullity and divorces *a mensa et thoro* (from bed and board), which were similar to judicial separations and did not enable the parties to remarry. Canons passed by Convocation in 1603–4 stipulated that parties so separated must each provide a bond of £100 not to remarry during the lifetime of the other spouse.[1] By 1603, the official position of the Church of England had been clarified: Divorce with the right of remarriage would not be granted in English church courts.

6 Divorce Reform, 1900–1914

Since ecclesiastical courts continued to maintain plenary jurisdiction in matrimonial cases, it was almost impossible to end a marriage and remarry legally in England. Wealthy spouses who were unhappy in their marriages gradually devised a procedure to circumvent the restrictions of the system. Those who desired a divorce could petition Parliament for a Private Act to end a marriage. The process of obtaining such an Act was complicated and expensive. According to Standing Orders passed in 1798, the House of Lords passed the Acts as judicial proceedings. In order to obtain what became known as a Parliamentary divorce, a party had to secure a divorce *a mensa et thoro* from the ecclesiastical courts and to prosecute successfully an action of criminal conversation, which was a husband's suit for damages against a person accused of committing adultery with the husband's wife. Parliamentary divorces were expensive. The cost of ending a marriage by this procedure was estimated at between £700 and £800 in 1853.[2] Although only the wealthy could hope to obtain such a divorce, over 300 Private Acts were passed before 1857.[3]

Parliamentary divorces complicated the issue of divorce for the Church of England. The rejection of divorce *a vinculo* after the Reformation was not based upon a consensus regarding the indissolubility of marriage. The Anglican clergy disagreed on the issue. Some believed that marriage was absolutely indissoluble, while others held that divorce *a vinculo* could be granted on the ground of adultery. Innocent parties in such cases could be allowed to remarry. This position found expression in the ecclesiastical recognition of Parliamentary divorces. The bishops in the House of Lords rarely raised objections to the Private Acts that ended marriages. Further evidence that the Church of England accepted Parliamentary divorces is found in parish registers that indicate that some individuals were remarried in church after their marriages had been dissolved by an Act of Parliament.[4] Officially, then, the Church of England would not recognize divorces *a vinculo*, but bishops accepted Parliamentary divorces, and some clergy remarried individuals whose marriages had been ended by a Parliamentary Act. Since the parties to a divorce *a mensa et thoro* had posted a bond to an ecclesiastical court that they would not remarry while the other spouse was living, bishops and clergy found themselves in a difficult position indeed.[5]

When the Lord Chancellor introduced a Divorce Bill in Parliament in May 1856, the bishops in the House of Lords were forced to take a stand on the principle of the indissolubility of marriage. The Matthaean Exception enabled the Archbishop of Canterbury, John Bird Sumner, to support the Divorce Bill. During the debates in the House of Lords, Archbishop Sumner said that he subscribed to the view that marriage was indissoluble 'saving for the cause of unfaithfulness'. Since the 1857 Bill recognized only adultery as a ground for divorce, Sumner could accept the proposed legislation. Although the passage in Matthew mentioned only a husband's divorcing his wife, Sumner argued that 'by parity of reasoning, it would be lawful for a woman to put away her husband'.[6] The 1857 Act did not entirely reflect that

Divorce Reform, 1900–1914   7

'parity of reasoning' in that, while a wife's adultery was a sufficient ground for divorce, a woman could divorce her husband only if his adultery had been aggravated by another matrimonial offence.

The Bishop of London, A.C. Tait, who later became Archbishop of Canterbury, was the strongest clerical supporter of the 1857 Bill in the Lords. He reminded the House that the clergy had confirmed recognition of Parliamentary divorces by marrying the parties so divorced to new partners. Tait felt that the Bill merely constituted recognition of existing practices and that the proposed Divorce Court was preferable to the 'haphazard legislation' that had previously governed the dissolution of marriages.[7] Their acceptance of the Divorce Bill in 1857 indicated that the Archbishop of Canterbury and other bishops did not believe that marriage was absolutely indissoluble.

Once the principle of indissolubility had been breached, the Church confronted the troublesome question of the remarriage of divorced persons. Archbishop Sumner based his opposition to remarriage on a Scriptural text when he argued in the House of Lords, 'Whosoever shall marry her that is put away committeth adultery'.[8] Bishops might recognize the State's dissolution of the legal bond, but some believed that a spiritual tie remained. Accordingly, there could be no remarriage as long as one of the spouses was alive. The 1857 Act did offer some relief to the clergy by providing that no clergyman would be compelled to solemnize the marriage of a guilty party. If a member of the clergy refused to marry a divorced person, however, he was obligated to allow another clergyman to perform the ceremony in his church.[9] Such an arrangement could only aggravate disagreement within the Church regarding the remarriage of divorced persons.

Increased attention to Biblical criticism contributed to the controversy over divorce within the Church of England because theologians continued to look to the Bible for guidance in defining Christian marriage. Charles Gore was an influential theologian and bishop who played a significant role in the debate over divorce reform. In 1896 he addressed the question of Scriptural references to divorce in *The Sermon on the Mount*. According to Gore, 'Our Lord proclaimed, as a prominent law of His new Kingdom, the indissolubility of marriage. And for us as Christians it is perfectly plain that not all the parliaments or kings on earth can alter the law of our Lord'. Gore denounced any remarriage after divorce, regardless of whether the parties were innocent or guilty of a matrimonial offence. He stated unequivocally, 'Beyond all question, for the Church . . . it is absolutely out of the question to regard those as married who, having been divorced, have been married again . . . during the lifetime of their former partner'.[10]

Although he maintained an extreme position on the indissolubility of marriage and the impossibility of Christian remarriage after divorce, Gore did accept the Matthaean Exception. Stating that 'it is a law of interpretation that a command with a specific qualification is more precise than a general command without any specific qualification', Gore acknowledged that the words of Jesus as recorded in Matthew 'would seem to sanction, or, more

8 *Divorce Reform, 1900–1914*

strictly, not to prohibit, the re-marriage of an innocent man who has put away his wife for adultery'.[11] Yet, within fifteen years after publishing *The Sermon on the Mount*, Gore had abandoned his adherence to the Matthaean Exception. New Testament criticism influenced his decision. Biblical scholars, especially in Germany, came to recognize the priority of the Gospel of Mark to that of Matthew. Since the verses concerning divorce in Mark contained no exception to the indissolubility of marriage, theologians began to doubt that the verse in Matthew represented the original text.[12] Biblical criticism thus reinforced the Marcan prohibition against divorce. In *The Question of Divorce*, published in 1911, Gore stated that he had decided that the words constituting the Matthaean Exception were 'probably interpolated glosses which really misinterpret the original utterances'.[13] By bringing into question the authenticity of the one possibility of divorce attributed to Jesus, Biblical criticism ultimately strengthened the case for indissolubility.

While Gore was certain about the indissolubility of marriage, other theologians and clergymen were not. The Church of England could not settle the debate by establishing an official position regarding divorce and remarriage, mainly because the organization of the Church did not provide the machinery necessary to issue an authoritative statement. The Archbishop of Canterbury was not a Pope who could issue encyclicals. Representative ecclesiastical assemblies did exist, but those bodies did not seek to establish Church policy regarding social questions. The Convocations of Canterbury and York, which had emerged during the Reformation, were silenced by the King early in the eighteenth century and revived only in the middle of the nineteenth century. They rarely discussed social policy. Church Congresses, which met annually after 1861, did debate social issues in relation to theological and moral questions, but these assemblies were unofficial. The first Lambeth Conference, an international gathering of Anglican bishops, met in 1867. Meeting approximately every ten years, the bishops discussed theological and social issues. Their resolutions, although influential, were only advisory; the Lambeth Conferences could not establish official doctrines for the Church of England.[14] As Biblical criticism influenced Anglican theologians to reaffirm the principle of the indissolubility of marriage, the institutional Church could not respond by establishing an official position on the issue.

Amidst doctrinal uncertainty, the Church confronted a growing demand for divorce reform that was strengthened by significant social and legal changes. The legal emancipation of women was one such change. Historically, in English common law, the marital relationship had resembled a guardianship more than a partnership. The husband, as guardian, was responsible for his wife's protection and maintenance; the wife, as ward or subordinate, owed her husband obedience and submission. During the nineteenth century, women began to attain a legal identity apart from their husbands. Married women gained the right to own property and no longer served as mere conduits for the property of men. Marriage came to resemble more clearly a contract between equal partners rather than a guardianship that governed the transfer of property. The possibility that either partner could petition to terminate the contract began to appear more reasonable.

Reformers who wanted to extend the grounds for divorce beyond adultery found support in the literature and shifting social attitudes of the 1890s. Authors such as Thomas Hardy, George Bernard Shaw, John Galsworthy, and H.G. Wells frequently presented marriage as repressive; they criticized laws and social conventions that stifled the individual. At the same time sexual theorists challenged Victorian attitudes by questioning the belief that marriage was the only legitimate context for the expression of human sexual desires. Havelock Ellis and Edward Carpenter were among those who criticized divorce laws that forced unhappily married individuals to remain legally joined to one another. This emphasis on individual happiness contradicted the traditional argument that 'hard cases make bad law'. As long as the family was seen as the foundation of society, as it was in Victorian England, then divorce threatened social stability. The potential conflict between the happiness of the individual and the welfare of the community would be central to the debate over divorce reform throughout the twentieth century and was certainly apparent in the testimony that was heard before the Royal Commission on Divorce appointed in 1909.

Archbishop Randall Davidson and the Appointment of the Royal Commission on Divorce

Randall Davidson, who became the Archbishop of Canterbury in 1903, played an influential role in the selection of members of the Royal Commission that convened in 1910. Davidson operated from a Victorian background that did not limit the leadership of the Archbishop of Canterbury to ecclesiastical affairs. He had served as Chaplain and Private Secretary to Archbishop Tait and had married Tait's daughter Edith. When Tait died in 1882, it was Davidson who sent Queen Victoria an account of the Archbishop's last days, and he subsequently developed close ties to the Royal Family.[15] Those connections helped him to develop his political influence. In *Church and Politics in a Secular Age*, Kenneth Medhurst and George Moyser wrote of Davidson:

> He not only made authoritative interventions in the House of Lords but also had ready access to the governments of the day and was quite regularly consulted by senior statesmen. To an extent that was not subsequently true, he felt free to act as if Church-State relationships were chiefly a matter of privately negotiated accommodations between ecclesiastical and secular leaders.[16]

Based on that understanding of his political role, Davidson was determined to participate in the selection of the Royal Commission.

10   *Divorce Reform, 1900–1914*

Davidson had already demonstrated his determination to maintain conformity between the marriage laws of Church and State in the controversy over marriage with a deceased wife's sister. In 1835 Parliament had adopted the sixteenth-century ecclesiastical tables of consanguinity and affinity, which made a marriage between a widower and his deceased wife's sister void. During the nineteenth century the Wife's Sister Bill became a 'hardy annual', as reformers attempted to legalize such a marriage.[17] The Church resisted such a reform, mainly because a marriage within the prohibited decrees was viewed as incestuous.[18] For the clergy, there was not the same ambivalence about marriage with a deceased wife's sister that was apparent with regard to the marriage of divorced persons. The Church of England could present a fairly united opposition to the former while the clergy remained divided over the latter.

A Deceased Wife's Sister's Marriage Bill was introduced in 1907. Despite the strong opposition of Archbishop Davidson, the Bill passed both the Commons and the Lords by substantial margins. Davidson responded:

> For the first time in the history of the Church of England, has the law of the State been brought on one specific point into direct open, overt contrast with, and contradiction of, the specific and divine law laid down in the authoritative regulations of the national church.[19]

The Archbishop's statement reflects his frustration over the inability of the Church to direct reform of the marriage laws. The legislation did, however, take clerical opposition into account. A member of the clergy had the discretion not only to refuse to officiate at the marriage between a man and his deceased wife's sister but also to refuse the use of his church for such a ceremony. Thus, the 1907 Act was more considerate of the clergy than the 1857 Divorce Act had been, since the latter required the clergy to allow their churches to be used for the marriage of divorced persons.[20]

In light of Davidson's strong feelings regarding the passage of the Deceased Wife's Sister Bill, it is not surprising that he was determined to play an active role in the selection of the Royal Commission that was appointed in 1909 to consider reform of the divorce laws. Prime Minister Asquith had hoped that the Commission could concentrate on the legal issues of divorce reform without the hindrance of religious concerns. Davidson's activism, however, made disregard of the Church's position impossible. On 23 July 1909, Davidson wrote to the Archbishop of York, Cosmo Gordon Lang, strongly urging him to accept a position on the Royal Commission if the Government offered it, and on 9 August, Davidson wrote to Asquith recommending that the Archbishop of York and Sir Lewis Dibdin be appointed Commissioners.[21] Dibdin had served as the principal judge of the Court of Arches, the court of appeal for the Archbishop of Canterbury, since 1903. In that position he had gained experience with matrimonial cases.[22] Another possible lay representative was Sir W. R. Anson, a legal scholar who had written several standard works on English law. As an M.P. from Oxford University since 1899, Anson had close political ties with the Church. Although he was a moderate liberal as a young man, Anson split with the Liberal Party over the issue of Home Rule and later became a spokesman for the Tory Party.[23] Lang, Dibdin, and Anson would be strong representatives of the Church of England.

Asquith opposed the appointment of clergy to the Royal Commission apparently because he did not want the Church to block reform. On 13 September, the Prime Minister told the Archbishop of Canterbury that the Government had decided not to appoint any clerical representatives.[24] The Commissioners who were proposed indicated that the Government intended serious consideration of reform. The Chair, Lord Gorell, had served as President of the Probate, Divorce, and Admiralty Division of the High Court of Justice and was familiar with the difficulties of the divorce laws. He had expressed his support of reform strongly from the bench and in Parliament. The backgrounds of other proposed Commissioners indicated that they, too, would favor reform. Lady Frances Balfour, as a colleague of Millicent Fawcett, was a well-known supporter of the cause of women's suffrage. May Abraham Tennant, who had served as an Inspector of Factories, and Thomas Burt, who had served as Secretary of the Northumberland Miners' Mutual Provident Association, were well acquainted with the effects of strict divorce laws on the poorer classes.[25] What the Government proposed was, in effect, a 'reforming' Royal Commission.

The Prime Minister's reluctance to include clerical representatives on the Commission also evidenced the Government's positive attitude toward divorce reform. Asquith opposed the appointment of any bishop, but he specifically objected to the Archbishop of York. He told Davidson that he had heard one of Lang's sermons on marriage questions and thought that his words were 'unguarded and unwise'.[26] Davidson insisted that Lang was the best choice for the same reason that Asquith opposed him—the Archbishop of York would be a strong representative of the Church. He would not sit meekly and allow the Commissioners to decide the issues on their own terms.

On 21 September Asquith's office sent Davidson a list of proposed Commissioners; none could be identified as a representative of the Church of England. Two days after receiving the list, Davidson met with Lord Chancellor Loreburn and told him that not appointing a bishop to a Royal Commission whose purpose was to consider reform of the divorce laws was comparable to 'ordering an enquiry into important Army matters and putting on subalterns and no General'. Loreburn agreed but told the Archbishop that Nonconformist opinion discouraged the appointment of a bishop from the Church of England. In a subsequent meeting with Davidson, Asquith was not as concerned about Nonconformists. Rather, he did not want to appoint a bishop because the Commission's terms of reference were limited to legal issues.[27] Davidson, however, was tenacious in his campaign to persuade the Government to include representatives of the Church, and his

12 *Divorce Reform, 1900–1914*

determination made it difficult for the Government to refuse. Finally, on 28 September 1909, Asquith wrote to Davidson that the Government would offer a seat on the Commission to the Archbishop of York. Davidson replied that 'if the Royal Commission has among its members the Archbishop of York, Sir Lewis Dibdin, and Sir William Anson, I shall take no exception whatsoever to the terms of reference'.[28]

It is not surprising that the Prime Minister yielded to the Archbishop on the appointment of representatives of the Church of England to the Royal Commission. Pressed by the Nonconformist element within the Liberal Party, the Government was already struggling with the Church over the issues of educational reform and disestablishment of the Church in Wales. 1909 was the year of Lloyd George's Budget, the prelude to the debate over limiting the constitutional powers of the House of Lords. The Liberal Government had other, arguably more politically important, issues to debate with the bishops in the Lords. Divorce reform was not a popular political issue, yet the question thoroughly aroused the hostility of the Church of England. The final decision to appoint representatives of the Church to the Royal Commission was probably based upon a desire not to antagonize the bishops. Whatever the reasons for their appointment, the presence of Lang, Dibdin, and Anson made a unanimous report virtually impossible. Indeed the three of them, none of whose names had been included on the original list of Commissioners, signed a Minority Report that opposed the Majority's recommendations for extending the grounds for divorce. The very existence of such a Minority Report made the enactment of controversial reforms difficult. Had Randall Davidson not actively intervened in the selection process, the Government could very well have appointed a reforming Commission with no clerical representatives. His persistence meant that the Royal Commission would not be able to ignore the Church of England.

The Royal Commission, 1909–1912

During the first decade of the twentieth century, Anglican clergy and theologians were divided over the principle of the indissolubility of marriage, but several factors strengthened the Church's determination to resist the expansion of divorce. Politically, having lost the battle over the Deceased Wife's Sister Act in 1907, the Church wanted to lose no more ground with regard to the marriage laws. Theologically, New Testament criticism had weakened arguments based on the Matthaean Exception, indicating that the only ground for divorce that Church and State had accepted in 1857 no longer had clear Biblical sanction. Within the Church, Anglo-Catholics, who tended to be conservative in their views of marriage and divorce, were becoming a dominant force among the clergy. Outside of the Church, as divorce became more common and no longer exceptional, many clergymen advocated meeting the threat with stricter discipline.[29] Noting a 'growing prevalence of disregard for the sanctity of marriage', Resolution 37 of the

Divorce Reform, 1900–1914 13

1908 Lambeth Conference called upon 'all right-thinking and clean-living men and women, in all ranks of life' to defend 'the sanctity of the marriage tie'.[30] The demand for divorce reform that encouraged the Government to convene the Royal Commission was countered by a Church resolved to maintain the permanence of marriage.

Despite the strength of the indissolubilist position, the clergy remained divided on the issue of remarriage after divorce. The Lambeth Conference of 1888 had acknowledged the lack of a consensus regarding the remarriage of an innocent spouse. In 1896, however, the Lower House of the Convocation of York voted unanimously to adopt a resolution stating that the marriage law of the Church of England 'does not permit the marriage of any person separated by divorce so long as the former partner is living'. The adoption of the Lower House's resolution would have represented a decisive break with the laws of the State, but the Upper House declined to take similar action, indicating that the bishops were reluctant to relinquish the distinction between the innocent and the guilty parties.[31] The Lambeth Conference of 1908 sought to resolve the question by stating in Resolution 40 that the Church should not bless the second marriage of an innocent party who had divorced a spouse for adultery. The resolution passed by a vote of only 87 to 84; the close margin reveals continuing disagreement regarding remarriage in church.[32] The diversity of opinion would be evident in the testimony of bishops, clergy, and theologians before the Royal Commission.

Charles Gore, who had become the Bishop of Birmingham in 1905, appeared before the Commission as one of the strongest defenders of the indissolubility of marriage. Despite Asquith's insistence that the terms of reference included only legal issues, the Commissioners devoted much attention to Biblical references to divorce, particularly to the Matthaean Exception. In his testimony, Bishop Gore confirmed his belief that New Testament criticism indicated that the Exception should be viewed as a 'later gloss' to the original text; he insisted instead that 'the mind of Christ himself was for indissoluble marriage'.[33] When the Commissioners noted that the bishops in the House of Lords had accepted the dissolubility of marriage on the ground of adultery in 1857, Gore responded, 'I think that a great number of those people . . . partly on grounds of biblical criticism, are abandoning the position they held, and are regarding that solitary exception as an unworkable exception'.[34] Gore believed that the bishops had erred in 1857. New Testament criticism had restored the principle of indissolubility.

In commenting on the relationship between Church and State with regard to marriage, Gore argued that, even though bishops had voted for the Divorce Bill, the Church had always officially maintained that marriage is a lifelong union. The Prayer Book, for example, maintained a strict view of indissolubility. In 1857 the bishops were speaking and voting as individuals. Since 'the whole corporate life of the Church had been in abeyance' at that time, it was impossible for the Church to issue a definitive statement through a Church body. The Lambeth Conference had passed resolutions based on the

14 Divorce Reform, 1900–1914

distinction between the innocent and guilty parties, but that conference consisted of representatives from the entire Anglican Communion and not just the Church of England.[35] Although the Church of England had been unable to issue an authoritative affirmation of the indissolubility of marriage, Gore maintained that the definition of marriage as a lifelong union remained the official view. If the State threatened that definition by extending the grounds for divorce, the bishops and clergy must be free to maintain ecclesiastical discipline, especially with regard to the remarriage of divorced persons. Such marriages should take place only in a registrar's office. Gore went so far as to suggest that, if the State expanded the grounds on which a union could be terminated, it might be necessary to make *all* marriages civil contracts.[36]

Gore believed that indissolubility was not only Biblically sanctioned but also socially useful. He told the Commissioners that

> my own strong opinion is that on the whole the extension of facilities for divorce would weaken what I am quite sure is still a very valuable social asset, and that is the sense amongst the workers of the indissolubility of marriage. . . . I think there is a very wide feeling that marriage is for ever . . . and that still remains a great social, as well as religious asset.[37]

When asked if he would prefer to base his views 'as to the indissolubility of marriage, not on the practical advantage to society but on the words of Scripture', Gore replied, 'I should not be at all willing to believe that. I think the advantage of society is bound up with the Christian Church, and I think this principle of the indissolubility of marriage is much more than an argument from a single text. It has been the fundamental basis of Christian society'.[38] According to Gore's reasoning, arguments based on social utility did not contradict Biblical passages; both supported the indissolubility of marriage.

Gore's reference to workers pointed to another issue that concerned the Commissioners. The expense of a divorce suit meant, in effect, that the poorer members of society were unable to end their marriages legally. Although it seemed unreasonable to deny a legal remedy to a large part of the population on the basis of expense, Gore did not favor reforms that would have made divorce more accessible to the poor. In his judgment the question was one of not wishing to make a 'bad thing' more readily available. He told the Commissioners that, in general, 'you . . . want all law to be as cheap as to put it at the disposal of every citizen; but if you think a particular law will do more harm than good, you would . . . decline to be a party to extending what you think would do mischief'.[39] The 1857 Act had also discriminated against women by requiring them to prove an additional ground besides adultery in order to obtain a divorce. When Lady Frances Balfour asked Gore if he would support equality between the sexes with regard to divorce, the Bishop replied, 'I do not think you can ask Christianity to have a care for the equal

Divorce Reform, 1900–1914 15

distribution of something which it believes to be bad'. Accordingly, with regard to the differences in grounds for men and women, he would favor 'the equality of allowing divorce to neither'.[40] As long as he maintained the indissolubility of marriage, Gore could not support any extension of divorce.

Hensley Henson, who appeared as a Canon of Westminster and Rector of St. Margaret's Westminster, disagreed with Bishop Gore's claim that there was 'an increasing unanimity of opinion' among communicants that the Church should maintain the principle of the indissolubility of marriage.[41] According to Henson, the concept of *a vinculum*, 'which inheres in the relationship apart from its objects and conditions, is the creature of the ascetic imagination'.[42] When asked about Gore's claim regarding the unanimity of opinion, Henson said that he believed that 'official pressure from above' contributed to the reluctance to disagree with indissolubility publicly, but he thought that there was a substantial group of both clergy and laity who viewed marriage as dissoluble. He stated clearly that 'the mass of English Church opinion among the laity' favored the possibility of remarriage after divorce.[43] To compare the testimony of Henson with that of Gore is to recognize the range of opinion within the Church of England on the question of divorce.[44]

Henson and Gore also differed in their response to a question that became central to the debate over divorce reform in the Church of England: In the teachings regarding divorce as recorded in the Gospels, was Jesus establishing a law or describing an ideal? Christians who accepted the Matthaean Exception obviously felt that Jesus was establishing a firm principle regarding marriage; the only possible ground for divorce was the cause that he had mentioned. Bishop Gore no longer accepted the Matthaean Exception, but he told the Royal Commission that 'on this subject only, or almost only, Jesus Christ seems to have legislated, to have said: Because there lies at the bottom of human life the need for this very difficult precept, therefore I lay it down with all its tremendous severity'.[45] Henson, on the other hand, believed that Jesus was 'propounding a Christian principle and was not giving a specific law, but was leaving it to be effected by the gradual application of this principle which He lays down'.[46] If spouses failed to fulfill the ideal, they had not broken a Biblical law.

William Sanday agreed with Henson that the Biblical prohibition against divorce was an ideal and not a rule. Testifying as Lady Margaret Professor of Divinity at Oxford and a recognized New Testament scholar, Sanday appeared as a witness who was eminently qualified to comment on Scriptural references to divorce. He reviewed the textual criticism of the relevant passages in the New Testament, even citing long passages in Greek, and then he addressed the question of the difference between 'a positive rule and a moral ideal'. He compared the verses in Matthew that referred to divorce to those that prohibited taking oaths and encouraged turning the other cheek. Sanday noted that these teachings could not be literally applied to contemporary society because 'they represent the Christian ideal, the inner

16 *Divorce Reform, 1900–1914*

Christian spirit, not a literal rule of law'.[47] The question of divorce should be considered in the same light. Sanday proceeded to comment on the issue of basing secular laws on these Christian ideals. He said that the precepts in Matthew

> are addressed to the Christian conscience as such. . . . But legislation by the Civil Power is a different matter; and obedience to the Civil Power comes under the head of rendering to Caesar the things that are Caesar's, and does not clash with duty towards God. The individual Christian (whether cleric or layman) is free to apply, and ought to apply, the highest standard to his own conduct; he is free to use, and he ought to use, all his powers of persuasion to induce others to adopt for themselves the same standard. But when it becomes a question of passing judgment upon others and of enforcing that judgment by the arm of the law, the lower standard is the right one.[48]

Sanday's reputation as a New Testament scholar strengthened the effectiveness of his argument that secular laws should not be based on Christian standards.

Two Lady Margaret Professors of Divinity, one at Oxford and the other at Cambridge, appeared before the Royal Commission in succession. Ralph Inge from Cambridge, who would become the Dean of St. Paul's in 1911, believed that the Matthaean Exception was invalid, and thus the New Testament prohibited divorce; but he also noted the context in which that prohibition was established. Inge, like Sanday, referred to other instructions, such as turning the other cheek, to demonstrate that Jesus did not intend to establish rigid rules. Indeed, Inge concluded, 'the doctrine that marriage is absolutely indissoluble cannot, in my opinion, be proved from the New Testament'. His arguments included historical examples of Christian recognition of divorce, such as Paul's acceptance of the dissolution of mixed marriages, the early Church's inclusion of the Matthaean Exception in the canon, and the British Parliament's acknowledgment of private divorces.[49] Sanday and Inge, both respected scholars, agreed that the New Testament prohibition against divorce should be interpreted as an ideal and not as a rule.

Hastings Rashdall, who appeared as a Canon Residentiary of Hereford and a Fellow and Lecturer of New College, Oxford, agreed with Sanday and Inge that Jesus set forth broad principles rather than detailed rules in matters of conduct. In Rashdall's view, Jesus did point to the ideal that marriage is a lifelong union, but he did not establish rules for dealing with marriages that failed to realize that ideal.[50] Accordingly, in designing secular divorce laws, legislators could not be guided by Biblical precepts alone; they had to consider social conditions and human experience and not just abstract principles. Henson and Inge both encouraged that approach. Henson had stated that 'the conditions of divorce are properly to be determined by the State in the light of Christian principle with reference to the actual necessities

Divorce Reform, 1900–1914 17

and circumstances of men'.[51] Inge told the Commissioners, 'The duty of a Christian State, it seems to me, is to legislate with due regard for the imperfections of human nature, while at the same time recognising an imperative obligation to maintain the unique sanctity of the marriage contract, which Christ unquestionably intended to emphasize in the strongest manner'.[52] In 1910, then, Anglican theologians recognized that divorce laws could not be based solely on Biblical precepts. The reality of human experience must also be a consideration.

Rashdall went so far as to say, 'I should find it difficult to regard a saying of Christ as absolutely and permanently binding upon His followers if it were found to be in collision with the dictates of the moral consciousness in the present'. When Archbishop Lang of York inquired, 'Might I ask who is to determine what the moral consciousness of the present is?', Rashdall responded, 'Well, with regard to his own personal conduct everybody must determine it for himself'. Lang then asked, 'Then you would say the only authority that Christ had on the individual or community was limited by whether or not what he said commended itself to the moral consciousness of that person or community?' Rashdall responded, 'Yes . . . so long as it did not commend itself to the individual or community, the individual or community ought not to follow it'.[53]

The value of lifelong marriage to the community was a common theme in the deliberations of the Royal Commission. The maxim that 'hard cases make bad law' encouraged reformers to emphasize the welfare of the community rather than the interests of the individual. From that perspective, society as a whole demanded sacrifice on the part of the hard cases. The Mothers' Union even *glorified* the ideal of sacrifice. Founded in 1876 as a Church of England organization to provide advice and training for mothers, the Mothers' Union had adopted upholding 'the sanctity of marriage' as its first object in 1892.[54] In her testimony before the Royal Commission, the Vice President, Mrs. Evelyn Hubbard, strongly objected to divorce and went so far as to recommend repeal of the 1857 Act. Deploring the current view that happiness, and not duty, appeared to be the central goal in a marriage, Hubbard extolled self-sacrifice: 'We think that the national character is quite as much benefited and raised by the patient endurance of hardships as by loosening the responsibilities of marriage'. Indeed, when Sir Lewis Dibdin asked,

> As I understood your evidence, your point is that there is no injustice to individuals at all. Is it not your point that the self-sacrifice, which is necessary on account of sufferings between the man and his wife, is part of the original contract . . . a part of the 'for better for worse' which they are bound to face?

Hubbard responded affirmatively. As a clear example of the ideal, Hubbard quoted a woman who was married to 'a drunkard in London' as saying, 'He may be a brute, but he is my husband'.[55]

18 *Divorce Reform, 1900–1914*

Some witnesses agreed with Hubbard in admiring self-sacrifice, especially as a feminine virtue, but others saw moral ambiguity in the concept. The idea that women are 'naturally' forgiving and remarkably tolerant of their husbands' faults appeared more than once in testimony. The Right Reverend Pearson M'Adam Muir, Moderator to the General Assembly of the Church of Scotland and Minister of Glasgow Cathedral, told the Commissioners:

> That there are many unhappy marriages is undeniable, but, as a rule, the unhappiness is carefully concealed and the way in which wives screen their husbands' faults and make no complaint of neglect and cruelty, usually arising from dissipation, is most touching and beautiful.[56]

While it may have been 'touching and beautiful' to Muir, Llewelyn Davies, General Secretary of the Women's Co-operative Guild, recognized that self-sacrifice on the part of wives could be based more on economic necessity than on Christian principles. A woman who was totally dependent on her husband for financial support would usually have no choice but to endure his mistreatment. Rather than touching and beautiful, her tolerance of neglect and cruelty could be degrading. Davies testified:

> If divorce is considered a sin, and the patient endurance of degradation and compulsory suffering a virtue, a most serious moral confusion is created. It means that women's self-respect and happiness are sacrificed, and adultery on the part of men condoned.[57]

Davies's testimony provides a striking contrast to that of Hubbard. Both women represented large organizations of married women, and yet their views of divorce were completely different. Hubbard glorified the 'patient endurance of hardships' to maintain a marriage whatever the cost, while Davies described specific examples of what that patient endurance could entail.

Davies told the Commissioners of cases of physical brutality and abandonment that were truly horrifying. A common example of desertion provided by many witnesses was a husband who went to another country and never returned. A poor woman had no way to determine where he was or whether or not he would return. Since desertion was not a ground for divorce, she remained bound to the man. She could be left destitute with children to raise and little opportunity for employment, and yet she could not marry someone else with whom she could establish a new home. With regard to cruelty, no matter how brutally she was treated, a woman had no ground for divorce. Additionally a wife would stay with an abusive husband not only because she was financially dependent upon the man but also because she felt the need to protect and care for her children. Davies also provided examples of the flagrant adultery of husbands, such as bringing another woman to live in the family's home. Yet a wife in such a case could not divorce her husband if she could not prove another matrimonial offence. While the Mothers' Union

Divorce Reform, 1900–1914 19

would encourage self-sacrifice in these instances, members of the Women's Co-operative Guild supported divorce reform.

Davies brought evidence from members of the Guild that indicated that an emphasis on indissolubility did not necessarily reinforce Christian standards of morality. One member of the Guild reported:

> I heard a discussion between two girls in our workroom. The girl that had attended chapel was in favour of divorce, and thought poor people ought to be able to procure it so that their children could have a legal right to their parents' name, but the church girl was most vehement in her protest against divorce—once married, always married. This girl said that she would rather live with a man unmarried than marry a divorced person. I know two of her friends are living with married men, and others of her friends have been friendly with married men, and her married friends flirt with men. And yet they pretend to have such a standard of morality that because you have been married in a church, it is wrong to be divorced.[58]

Such evidence challenged Bishop Gore's statement that the workers' understanding of marriage as indissoluble was a 'valuable social asset'. Even those individuals who viewed marriage as 'sacred' did not always maintain the sanctity of the union.

Witnesses who were well acquainted with the lives of the poor revealed a significant difficulty for the Church in using social utility arguments. When individuals from the working classes could not obtain a divorce, they tended to end the marriage informally. Frequently they formed new 'irregular' unions that produced illegitimate children. Thus, strict adherence to the principle of the indissolubility of marriage could actually create social problems. With reference to those problems, Bishop Gore was asked if evidence based on 'civil or social grounds' would persuade him to accept the extension of the grounds for divorce. Gore responded negatively, saying that 'my view is based on what I feel quite certain is the law and intention of Christ'.[59] Gore, then, would use social utility arguments to oppose divorce reform but rejected similar arguments to encourage such reform. Basil Mitchell describes the difficulty:

> If factual investigation can be appealed to in support of theological insights—if the proven evils of broken homes can be adduced in support of the 'divinely ordained harmony of marriage'—then, were this support to be lacking or were evidence to the contrary to accumulate, the theological position would to that extent be weakened and might, in principle, even be refuted.[60]

As long as Christians referred only to Biblical injunctions, then arguments based on social welfare were unnecessary. When they argued that Christian

20   *Divorce Reform, 1900–1914*

principles benefitted society, however, evidence to the contrary undermined their arguments.

The Church could not rely solely on arguments based on religious considerations, however. As Lord Gorell, the Chair of the Royal Commission, noted, 'It is one of the most striking features of the evidence which has been taken by the Commission that theological difficulties have weighed little with the great mass of the witnesses, and among those who feel them there are differences of opinion'.[61] The Royal Commission sat for fifty-five days during 1910 and heard testimony from 246 witnesses, among them judges, solicitors, barristers, doctors, social workers, and journalists. Testimony based on religious principles constituted merely a portion of the evidence that the Commissioners heard and revealed a wide variety of opinions. Representatives not only from the Church of England but also from the Roman Catholic Church, the Church of Scotland, the Wesleyan Methodist Conference, the Society of Friends, the Greek Church, and the Presbyterian Churches of England and Wales presented evidence on Christian views. Nonconformists differed from Roman Catholics, of course, but also among themselves. The issue of divorce reform did not unite Nonconformists in the same way as other issues involving religion, such as education and disestablishment. Archbishop Lang described their views on divorce as 'slack'.[62] Such a diversity of Christian opinions made religious evidence less effective.

Lord Gorell, however, recognized the importance of the Church of England to the debate, especially in light of Establishment. He was a dedicated reformer who very much wanted a unanimous report, and he feared that opinions based on religious beliefs would make that impossible. Accordingly, Gorell prepared a long memorandum in which he analyzed Biblical texts, scholarly theological works, church history, and witnesses' views in an attempt to determine what religious beliefs should be considered in the formulation of divorce laws.[63] Gorell found no consensus among the religious sources, however, and the diversity of views thwarted his attempts to accommodate Christian principles for the sake of a unanimous report.

Not only differences of opinion among theologians but also an apparent lack of lay interest in religious beliefs limited the influence of the Church of England in the debate over divorce reform. In reviewing testimony before the Royal Commission, Gorell noted that, while clerical witnesses assumed the religious character of questions related to divorce, lay witnesses regarded theological arguments as 'theoretical or academical and not practical'. He wrote:

> It is one of the most striking features of the evidence which has been taken by the Commission that theological difficulties have weighed little with the great mass of witnesses, and among those who feel them there are differences of opinion. It seems . . . that . . . the lay witnesses pass by questions of doctrine as if they concerned theologians rather than the practical legislator.[64]

In line with that observation, Gorell contended that reformers must consider human nature as well as Christian beliefs in the formulation of divorce laws. In his view, events that destroy marriages do occur; maintaining a legal tie that is otherwise nonexistent does not serve the interests of the spouses, their children, or the community. According to Gorell, 'While marriage should be regarded as normally indissoluble, it should be capable of dissolution if the continuity of the relationship has become practically impossible so as to frustrate the objects with which it was formed'.[65] Believing that it was the duty of the State to provide the means of dissolving such unions, Gorell recommended extension of the grounds for divorce.

The Report of the Royal Commission and the Response

The Report of the Royal Commission largely followed Gorell's memorandum in outlining the difficulties of basing recommendations on religious considerations. The Commissioners concluded:

> In view of the conflict of opinion which has existed in all ages and in all branches of the Christian Church, among scholars and divines equally qualified to judge, and the fact that the State must deal with all its citizens, whether Christian, nominally Christian, or non-Christian, our conclusion is that we must proceed to recommend the Legislature to act upon an unfettered consideration of what is best for the interest of the State, society, and morality, and for that of parties to suits and their families.[66]

The Commissioners, in a significant shift in interpretation, argued that 'divorce is not a disease but a remedy for a disease . . . homes are not broken up by a court'. Reform would be socially beneficial: 'If a reasonable law, based upon human needs, be adopted, we think that the standard of morality will be raised and regard for the sanctity of marriage increased'. On that basis the Royal Commission recommended that the grounds for divorce should be extended to include willful desertion for at least three years, cruelty, incurable insanity, habitual drunkenness, and imprisonment under commuted death sentence.[67]

Those recommendations compelled Sir Lewis Dibdin, Sir William Anson, and Archbishop Lang to sign a Minority Report that claimed that there was no guiding principle in recommending the four additional grounds for divorce. Those causes depended upon the court's interpretation with regard to qualification and degree and could be resolved; they did not necessarily end a marriage. Separated spouses could reconcile; the drunkard could reform; and the prisoner could return.[68] The Minority Report sought certainty in familiar guiding principles: 'We must always be on our guard lest the sympathy which cases of individual hardship naturally and rightly arouse should tend to narrow our outlook and prevent a comprehensive

22 Divorce Reform, 1900–1914

view of the whole situation as it affects the welfare of the community'.[69] In short, hard cases make bad law.

The guiding principle in a consideration of divorce laws, the authors of the Minority Report argued, should be the teachings of the New Testament. They wrote that the theological and clerical witnesses who had appeared before the Royal Commission had demonstrated 'absolute unanimity . . . upon the fact and the nature of our Lord's teaching to the world on marriage and divorce. All are agreed that Christ intended to proclaim the great principle that marriage ought to be indissoluble'. The witnesses may have disagreed about issues related to Biblical criticism, especially as to whether Jesus intended to offer any exceptions to the principle, but 'there is no doubt in the minds of any of the theological witnesses as to that ideal itself'. That ideal, according to the Minority Report, provided a better guiding principle in divorce reform than 'ephemeral conditions of the moment, even though enforced by sympathy with individual suffering'.[70] Limited access to divorce was not what caused the suffering. Instead, the three authors of the Minority Report wrote, 'The causes of marriage failure are, speaking generally, the lack of the sense of responsibility in entering the married state, and the lack of self-control, self-sacrifice, and sense of duty in continuing it.'[71] The solution to the problem of a broken marriage, then, was not divorce but self-discipline.

Lang, Anson, and Dibdin opposed extending the grounds for divorce beyond adultery, but they agreed with the Royal Commission's Report in other regards. Disagreeing with Bishop Gore's determination to limit access to a 'bad thing', they stated that 'it is of course incontestable that no one ought to be deprived of his legal rights merely by poverty'. Accordingly they favored the extension of jurisdiction in divorce cases to local courts to reduce the expense of a suit. They also agreed that 'whatever grounds are permitted to a husband for obtaining a divorce from his wife, the same grounds should be available for a wife in a suit against her husband'.[72] The Minority Report would have made divorce more accessible to women and the poor.

Lord Gorell had hoped for a unanimous report, but the views of Lang, Dibdin, and Anson made that goal impossible to achieve. Archbishop Davidson had insisted that representatives from the Church of England be included in the Royal Commission, and their presence impeded the cause of divorce reform. The Minority Report received a great deal of attention. Although *The Times* summarized both reports, the publishers printed the Minority Report in its entirety and circulated it as a free supplement.[73] Such apparent public approval emphasized the differences in the two reports and influenced the Government not to introduce legislation based on the Majority's recommendations. A note attached to the Home Office Minutes of 7 December 1912 described the situation:

> Presumably the Govt. have no intention of tackling this very thorny and contentious subject in the near future—especially after the large measure of support which the Minority Report seems to have received.[74]

Divorce Reform, 1900–1914 23

This assessment indicates how the Minority Report detracted from the accomplishments of the Royal Commission. The Government, already entangled in the complex problems of Irish Home Rule, women's suffrage, and labor unrest, could not respond positively to the Commission's recommendations.

While the Royal Commission assembled evidence on questions relating to reform of the divorce laws, the Committee on Marriage Laws of the Lower House of Canterbury Convocation also considered those issues. Their report in 1910 differed considerably from that of the Gorell Commission. Testimony before the Royal Commission had indicated that spouses who wanted to end a marriage but were unable to obtain a divorce frequently were granted a permanent separation order instead. Reformers had argued that such separations, as opposed to divorce, led to immorality because the separated spouses would form new unions that were not legally recognized. The Committee on Marriage Laws noted that the argument was based on the assumption 'that re-marriage after divorce and the condition of life consequent on it is not immoral'. For the Committee, the remarriage of divorced persons to new spouses was little more than 'legalised concubinage'.[75] The State recognized such unions as valid marriages, however, and the Committee's denunciation of the practice served to emphasize the differences between the marriage laws of Church and State. The distance was also evident later in 1910, when the Lower House of Canterbury Convocation passed a strong resolution calling for the repeal of the Divorce Act of 1857.[76] While the majority of the Royal Commission, unable to ascertain a consensus of religious opinion on the subject, had recommended the extension of the grounds for divorce, the Lower House of Canterbury Convocation attempted to re-establish the principle of indissolubility. In 1857 the bishops in the House of Lords had been able to accept the Divorce Act on the basis of the Matthaean Exception. In 1910, the Church was attempting to regain lost ground.

Belief in the indissolubility of marriage was also evident in the work of the Reverend Thomas Alexander Lacey, who in 1912 published *Marriage in Church and State*, an influential book that became a standard authority concerning the Anglican position on divorce. As a member of the council of the high-church English Church Union, Lacey had been involved in the attempt to reconcile the Roman Catholic and Anglican churches in the 1890s. In 1896 he had traveled to Rome to assist the commission appointed by Pope Leo XIII to investigate the question.[77] In light of his background, it is not surprising that Lacey wrote that marriage was absolutely indissoluble. He described the relationship as 'a natural union, as intimate and indestructible as that of parent and child'. He added:

> If marriage were a mere contractual relation, an artificial partnership, it would be terminable not only by a failure to achieve its object, but even more equitably by mutual consent; because it is constituted in the order of nature, and not only at the will of the parties, it is indissoluble

24   *Divorce Reform, 1900–1914*

except by an event equally in the order of nature; and this can be found only in death.[78]

Regarding the State's divorce statutes, Lacey wrote:

> A law which purports to effect the absolute dissolution of the marriage bond must be unconditionally condemned. It is not so much an infraction of the divine law as an impotent pretence, an attempt to alter a fact of nature. . . . It may be compared with a law which should purport to destroy the kinship of a brother and a sister, of a parent and a child.[79]

Despite his belief that the divorce laws were 'an impotent pretence', Lacey recognized the difficulty of basing secular legislation on ecclesiastical standards. He did not expect the State to maintain the Christian standard because 'not all the subjects of the State are subjects of the Church, and the State legislates for all its subjects alike'. Maintaining that the Church should be free to enforce discipline among its own members, yet acknowledging that 'the State has inherent rights in the matter of marriage and divorce', Lacey advocated a dual system of marriage laws. 'It would be well if the laws of the Church and of the State should coincide', he wrote, 'but it is not necessary'.[80] In Lacey's view, separate secular and ecclesiastical divorce laws appeared inevitable.

Since the Government was reluctant to introduce a bill to reform the State's divorce laws, the introduction of legislation was left to private initiative. Lord Gorell was the obvious person to sponsor a bill based on the Royal Commission's recommendations, but he died on 22 April 1913. His son, the second Lord Gorell, who had served as secretary to the Royal Commission, took up the cause of divorce reform upon his father's death. In the House of Lords, on 28 July 1914, he introduced a Bill whose purpose was to implement the recommendations that were common to both the Minority and Majority Reports.[81] Lord Chancellor Haldane said that the Government looked upon the Bill favorably but noted that it was too late in the session to pass such complicated and controversial legislation. Archbishop Lang, who had signed the Minority Report, supported the Bill, noting that it was based on recommendations common to both Reports. Lang told the Lords, 'I believe that it gives relief, without sacrifice of principle, to many cases of real hardship', and he added that 'there are in the recommendations of the Royal Commission many provisions which I think will make for the good of our common life'.[82] Lord Gorell's Bill very likely would have passed the Lords, but several peers urged the sponsor to postpone consideration of the measure since it was too late in the session for the proposals to pass through the necessary stages. Gorell agreed to withdraw the Bill. A week later, Great Britain was at war with Germany. The First World War delayed the reintroduction of the legislation, and the second Lord Gorell's attempts at reform ended with his death at Ypres in January 1917.[83] When Parliament finally resumed consideration of divorce reform, the world was quite a different place.

Notes

1. A. Winnett, *The Church and Divorce* (London: Mowbrays, 1968), p. 1; L. Stone, *Road to Divorce: England, 1530–1987* (Oxford University Press, 1990), pp. 46–47, 305.
2. O. McGregor, *Divorce in England* (London: Heinemann, 1957), p. 11; C. Davies, 'Matrimonial Relief in English Law', in *A Century of Family Law*, ed. R. Graveson and F. Crane (London: Sweet & Maxwell, 1957), p. 316.
3. Winnett, *The Church and Divorce*, p. 4.
4. *Ibid.*, pp. 1–4.
5. Stone, p. 350.
6. *Parliamentary Debates* (Lords), 3rd series, 145 (19 May 1857):495.
7. *Ibid.*, 532–533.
8. *Ibid.*, 495.
9. 20 & 21 Vict. c. 85, §§57, 58.
10. C. Gore, *The Sermon on the Mount: A Practical Exposition* (London: John Murray, 1896), pp. 68–70.
11. *Ibid.*, p. 71.
12. A. Winnett, *Divorce and Remarriage in Anglicanism* (London: Macmillan, 1958), p. 193.
13. C. Gore, *The Question of Divorce* (New York: Charles Scribner's Sons, 1911), pp. v–vi.
14. E. Norman, *Church and Society in England, 1770–1970* (Oxford: Clarendon Press, 1976), pp. 2–3.
15. G. Bell, *Randall Davidson, Archbishop of Canterbury*, Third edition (London: Oxford University Press, 1952), pp. 41, 53.
16. K. Medhurst and G. Moyser, *Church and Politics in a Secular Age* (Oxford: Clarendon Press, 1988), pp. 93–94.
17. N. Anderson, 'The Marriage with a Deceased Wife's Sister Bill Controversy: Incest Anxiety and the Defense of Family Purity in Victorian England', *Journal of British Studies*, Vol. 31(Spring 1982):67–68.
18. Bell, p. 551.
19. *Ibid.*, p. 552.
20. *Ibid.*
21. Davidson Papers, 'Divorce, 1895–1920', Vol. 416, ff 189–190, 200. Lambeth Palace Library.
22. W. Cleveland-Stevens, 'Dibdin, Sir Lewis Tonna (1852–1938)', rev. Catherine Pease-Watkin, *Oxford Dictionary of National Biography*, Oxford University Press, 2004 [http://www.oxforddnb.com/view/article/32810].
23. H. Matthew, 'Anson, Sir William Reynell, third baronet (1843–1914)', *Oxford Dictionary of National Biography*, Oxford University Press, 2004; online edn, May 2006 [http://www.oxforddnb.com/view/article/30423].
24. Memorandum from Archbishop Davidson reporting a conversation with Asquith at the Grillions Dinner, Davidson Papers, Vol. 416, f 206.
25. A. Holmes, *Hard Cases and Bad Laws: Divorce Reform in England, 1909–1937* (Ph.D. diss., Vanderbilt University, 1986), 81, 84–85.
26. Memorandum from Archbishop Davidson, Davidson Papers, Vol. 416, f. 225.
27. *Ibid.*, ff 223–224.
28. *Ibid.*, ff 235, 237.
29. Winnett, *Divorce and Remarriage in Anglicanism*, pp. 193–194.
30. R. Coleman, ed., *Resolutions of the Twelve Lambeth Conferences, 1867–1988* (Toronto: Anglican Book Centre, 1992), p. 34.
31. Winnett, *Divorce and Remarriage in Anglicanism*, p. 187.
32. *Resolutions of the Twelve Lambeth Conferences, 1867–1988*, p. 35.

26 Divorce Reform, 1900–1914

33. *Royal Commission on Divorce and Matrimonial Causes: Minutes of Evidence* (London: H.M. Stationery Office, 1912), 2:347:21,241. (The references to the *Minutes of Evidence* refer to the volume, the page number, and the number of the question.)
34. *Ibid.*, 2:348:21,252.
35. *Ibid.*, 2:348:21,252 and 2:357:21,422 and 21,426–421,427.
36. *Ibid.*, 2:352:21,324.
37. *Ibid.*, 352:21,329.
38. *Ibid.*, 356:21,394.
39. *Ibid.*, 358:21,455 and 356:21,396.
40. *Ibid.*, 359:21,470 and 360:21,495.
41. *Ibid.*, 2:353:21,341. The disagreements between Gore and Henson were significant because, according to the church historian Roger Lloyd, these two men, together with Archbishop Randall Davidson, were the most influential representatives of the Church of England during the first decades of the twentieth century. Lloyd wrote: 'Every word they uttered was widely listened to, and really counted. . . . Their judgements on all the issues of the day had to be taken into account and weighed, for they would sway the balances'. *The Church of England 1900–1965* (London: SCM Press Ltd, 1966), pp. 77–78.
42. *Minutes of Evidence*, 2:411:22,585.
43. *Ibid.*, 2:408:22,559 and 424:22,866.
44. A comment on the marital status of the two men seems appropriate. Gore never married. Henson married Isabella Caroline Dennistoun, to whom he proposed four days after meeting her in 1902. Henson provided the model for the character of Alex Jardine, an unhappily married bishop, in Susan Howatch's novel *Glittering Images* (New York: Alfred A. Knopf, 1987). M. Grimley, 'Henson, Herbert Hensley (1863–1947)', *Oxford Dictionary of National Biography*, Oxford University Press, 2004; online edn, Jan 2011 [http://www.oxforddnb.com/view/article/33825].
45. *Minutes of Evidence*, 2:362:21,548.
46. *Ibid.*, 2:418:22,752.
47. *Ibid.*, 3:244:38,499.
48. *Ibid.*, 3:245:38,499.
49. *Ibid.*, 3:256:38,677 and 258–259:38,678.
50. *Ibid.*, 3:306:39,306.
51. *Ibid.*, 2:426:22,904.
52. *Ibid.*, 3:259:38,678.
53. *Ibid.*, 3:306:39,306 and 311:39,318 and 39,324.
54. C. Moyse, 'Idolatry and Pragmatism: The Sanctity of Marriage and the Mothers' Union 1876–1976', in *Celebrating Christian Marriage*, ed. A. Thatcher (Edinburgh and New York: T & T Clark, 2001), 441.
55. *Minutes of Evidence*, 2:190:16,925 and 191:16,937 and 192:16,968 and 193:16,996–16,997 and 196:17,087.
56. *Ibid.*, 3:339–340:39,887.
57. *Ibid.*, 3:162:37,006.
58. *Ibid.*, 3:162:37,006.
59. *Ibid.*, 2:352:21,328.
60. *Law, Morality, and Religion in a Secular Society* (London: Oxford University Press, 1967), p. 118.
61. *Minutes of Evidence*, 3:544:109.
62. Letter from Archbishop Lang to Archbishop Davidson, dated 18 November 1912, Davidson Papers. Lambeth Palace Library, vol. 417, f 64.
63. *Minutes of Evidence*, 3:527–548.

Divorce Reform, 1900–1914   27

64. *Ibid.*, 3:544:109–110.
65. *Ibid.*, 3:547:146.
66. *Royal Commission on Divorce and Matrimonial Causes: Report* (London: H.M. Stationery Office, 1912), p. 37
67. *Ibid.*, 95–96, 113.
68. *Ibid.*, 184.
69. *Ibid.*, 176.
70. *Ibid.*, 186.
71. *Ibid.*, 188.
72. *Ibid.*, 189–191.
73. Gorell, 'Introduction', in *John Gorell Barnes, First Lord Gorell (1848–1913)*, ed. J. de Montmorency (London: John Murray, 1920), pp. 16–17.
74. Great Britain, Public Record Office, Home Office Records, HO45/70696-AC/A048355 (231634).
75. Convocation of Canterbury, Lower House, *Report of the Committee on Marriage Laws* (Lambeth Palace Library, 1910, No. 439), pp. 3–4.
76. *Ibid.*, 'Resolutions Agreed to by the Lower House on April 28th, 1910', p. 7.
77. C. Mortlock, 'Lacey, Thomas Alexander (1853–1931)', rev. M. C. Curthoys, *Oxford Dictionary of National Biography*, Oxford University Press, 2004 [http://www.oxforddnb.com/view/article/34368].
78. T. Lacey, *Marriage in Church and State* (London: Robert Scott, 1912), p. 18.
79. *Ibid.*, p. 103.
80. *Ibid.*, p. 223.
81. *Parliamentary Debates* (Lords), 17 (28 July 1914):189–190.
82. *Ibid.*, pp. 206, 214.
83. Gorell, p. 17.

2   The Interwar Years
Church and State Diverge

Postwar Divorce Reform

The First World War produced an increase in the numbers of both marriages and divorces in England. Couples rushed to get married before soldiers were sent to the front. The prewar rate of fifteen marriages per thousand inhabitants rose in 1915 to nineteen per thousand, an unusually high percentage that had not been matched in the preceding fifty years. The marriage rate dropped after 1915 but rose again dramatically to over twenty per thousand in 1920, when men returned home and marriages arranged during the war were celebrated.[1] Many of these marriages did not last, as demonstrated by a comparison of prewar and postwar statistics. The number of petitions filed for either the dissolution or annulment of a marriage increased from 956 in 1912 to 5,184 in 1919.[2]

In 1917 advocates of divorce reform responded to the increase in demand by drafting a bill that would have permitted divorce after three years of separation. Such a reform would have removed the need to prove a matrimonial offence, thereby permitting divorce by mutual consent. Opponents of the proposal used vivid language in their criticism. The *Church Times* proclaimed that the bill 'reduces marriage to the level of concubinage', and Athelstan Riley compared the proposals to 'the social economy of the rabbit hutch'.[3] The supporters of the measure adopted a clever defense of the bill, arguing that the declining birth rate and the war had so depleted the British population that a radical reform was necessary in order to enable separated persons to marry again and have legitimate children. The argument appeared in a circular sent to members of both Houses of Parliament in August 1917: 'When the manhood of the nation has been depleted by the most terrible of wars, it is exceptionally urgent, in the interest of the community and of the Empire, that all unnecessary obstacles to marriage should be removed'.[4] Although the tactic of shifting the emphasis from individual cases of hardship to the welfare of the community appeared shrewd, the 1917 proposal was never formally introduced as a bill in Parliament. Archbishop Davidson had organized a Memorial signed by both Archbishops, Cardinal Bourne, three bishops, five Free Church leaders, and other influential men and women to oppose the measure.[5] In the face of such resistance, it appeared that divorce reform would have to wait until after the war had ended.

In the continuing attempts to maintain consistency between secular laws and Christian principles, the Church of England encountered another challenge in 1917, when five law lords issued a ruling in the House of Lords that undermined the idea that laws should be based on Christian beliefs. In the case of *Bowman* v. *Secular Society*, the next of kin of Charles Bowman challenged his bequest to the Secular Society on the ground that the objects of the organization were unlawful because they promoted the 'secularisation of the State'. The appellants' counsel argued that 'Christianity is and has always been regarded by the Courts of this country as the basis on which the whole of the English law, so far as it has an ethical side, rests, and any movement for the subversion of Christianity has always been held to be illegal'. On the basis of that argument, counsel attempted to persuade the court that 'a society for the subversion of Christianity is illegal and is incapable of enforcing a bequest to it'.[6] Those arguments failed to persuade the law lords. Lord Sumner stated that 'the phrase "Christianity is part of the law of England" is really not law; it is rhetoric'. He added, ' "Thou shalt not steal" is part of our law. "Thou shalt not commit adultery" is part of our law, but . . . "Thou shalt love thy neighbour as thyself" is not part of our law at all'.[7] In the end, the law lords denied the appeal and ruled that the Secular Society should receive the bequest. The judicial repudiation of the maxim that 'Christianity is part of the law of England' did not augur well for those who wanted to base divorce laws on Christian principles.

One of the judges in *Bowman* v. *Secular Society*, Lord Buckmaster, confronted the Church of England more directly in 1920, when he introduced a Divorce Bill in the House of Lords. A former Lord Chancellor, Buckmaster was recognized as one of the leading orators of the time. He was committed to social reform, supporting such causes as improved housing for the poor, birth control, the abolition of capital punishment, and women's suffrage.[8] As a judge in divorce cases, Buckmaster had encountered the miseries and frustrations of those individuals who were unable to free themselves from marriages that had become intolerable. In *The Times* he noted that 'the most competent authority' had denounced the divorce laws as 'immoral and unjust'.[9] He was determined to reform those laws.

Buckmaster moved the Second Reading of a Matrimonial Causes Bill in the House of Lords on 10 March 1920.[10] The proposal included provisions to establish the same grounds for divorce for both men and women, to make divorce more accessible to the poor, and to restrict the publication of reports of divorce cases. These clauses were not as controversial as the proposal of five additional grounds for divorce: desertion for three years, cruelty, incurable insanity, habitual drunkenness, and imprisonment under a commuted death sentence. In introducing the Bill, Buckmaster noted that the legislation was based on the recommendations of the Royal Commission.

30   *Church and State Diverge*

The debates that followed provided an opportunity for the bishops in the House of Lords to comment on those recommendations and to clarify the Church's position on divorce reform. The first of the prelates to respond to Buckmaster's Bill was Archbishop Lang of York. Since he had been a member of the Royal Commission, he was a well-informed speaker. Although he personally believed that Christians should maintain the principle that marriage is dissoluble only by death, Lang recognized the impossibility of imposing that standard on all citizens of the State. Accordingly, he told the Lords that he would base his arguments 'not upon the ground of religious authority, but upon the ground of public welfare'.[11] In his speech Lang established the outlines of the Church's response to Parliamentary proposals for divorce reform after the First World War. He recognized the injustice of the inequality between men and women and between rich and poor, and indicated that he could accept proposals to address those inequities. Lang opposed the extension of grounds, however. Responding to the stories of the hard cases presented by Buckmaster and other reformers, Lang told the Lords that 'principle and the public welfare must govern sentiment and not follow it'. He concluded that, at a time 'when men are more clamorous for rights than mindful of duties', the Lords must remember that 'the object of the marriage law is not to relieve individuals or to promote their happiness, but to protect and safeguard the security and continuity of marriage itself'.[12] Lang continued to claim, then, that hard cases make bad law.

Lord Birkenhead, the Lord Chancellor, appeared as a formidable challenger to Lang's arguments. As F.E. Smith, Birkenhead had established a reputation as a brilliant orator with a biting wit who could be merciless to opponents in debate.[13] Lord Birkenhead's eloquence was evident in his response to the argument, based on the New Testament, that only adultery could be a ground for divorce. Birkenhead challenged the argument in strong terms when he told the Lords, 'I am concerned to-day to make this point, by which I will stand or fall—that the spiritual and moral sides of marriage are incomparably more important than the physical side'.[14] Birkenhead's words constituted a pointed challenge to the Church of England.

The Archbishop of Canterbury, Randall Davidson, had the misfortune of following Birkenhead in the debate. He began with self-deprecating remarks regarding the eloquence of Buckmaster and Birkenhead and did not attempt to address the latter's argument regarding the spiritual and physical sides of marriage. Instead he followed Lang's lead in opposing the extension of the grounds for divorce on the basis of social utility rather than religious principles. Davidson had collected statistical evidence from several organizations to respond to reformers' arguments that there was a great demand for divorce reform, and he devoted much of his attention to that data. He concluded by saying that he could accept the proposals for the removal of the inequities between men and women and between rich and poor, arguing that implementation of these changes would adequately respond to any demand for reform.[15] The speech was not persuasive. Archbishop Lang had argued eloquently against the extension of grounds on the basis of social welfare, but the reformers' case was evidently too strong. The Second Reading of Buckmaster's Bill passed by a vote of 93 to 45.[16]

When the Committee stage on the Bill began in the House of Lords on 20 April 1920, Archbishop Davidson, having had an opportunity to review Lord Birkenhead's speech, did respond to the argument based on the distinction between the physical and spiritual aspects of marriage. Davidson told the Lords that he accepted all that the Lord Chancellor had said

> about the high and ennobling intercourse of soul with soul, under the sanctity of the marriage bond—the inspiring association of memory, fellowship, and hope—and it is because these elevate and uplift, and sanctify what he most inadequately called the purely physical or carnal side, that I am unable to follow him in the wide dissociation which he seemed to advocate between the different obligations of married life.[17]

From this perspective, the physical and spiritual aspects of marriage could not be separated. More significantly with regard to divorce reform, Davidson argued that to allow the legal dissolution of a marriage in cases where only the 'spiritual' relationship was broken would be to permit divorce by mutual consent.

During the Committee stage on Buckmaster's Bill, the reformers won vote after vote on various clauses. With the passage of the Bill as a very real possibility, the need for a clear statement from the Church on the subsequent marriages of persons divorced under its provisions became apparent. On 25 April 1920, Bishop Gore wrote to Archbishop Davidson that the debates on the Bill had not made clear that 'the Church could not recognize marriages, which lie outside what on any interpretation is the will of Christ, either in respect of the use of its churches or ministers or in respect of subsequent Communion'.[18] Accordingly, on 4 May 1920, Davidson moved to insert the following clause into the Bill:

> The marriage of a person whose previous marriage has been dissolved under the provisions of this Act, and whose former husband or wife is still living, shall not be solemnized in any church or chapel of the Church of England.[19]

The 1857 Act had granted the clergy the freedom to refuse to solemnize the marriage of the guilty party to a divorce suit. If a clergyman refused to marry a divorced person, however, he had to allow the use of his church for another member of the clergy to perform the ceremony. In 1920 Davidson wanted to remove any doubt as to whether divorced persons could be married in church by making the prohibition against such ceremonies statutory. Birkenhead objected that the proposal would limit the freedom of a priest to do what he in good conscience felt was the right thing to do in certain

32 Church and State Diverge

circumstances. Archbishop Lang responded that the reformers should allow the Church to be free of any responsibility for the marriages of divorced persons. Such marriages should 'remain within the sphere of that civil sanction which you desire to give them'.[20] At the end of the debate, Davidson's proposal failed by only one vote, 51 to 50. Surely the Archbishop of Canterbury wished that more bishops had been in attendance.

In another attempt to clarify the Church's position regarding the marriages of divorced persons, the Earl of Selborne moved to amend the section of the Bill that stated that a clergyman 'shall not be liable to any suit, penalty or censure for solemnizing or refusing to solemnize the marriage of any such [divorced] person' by adding 'or for refusing to admit to communion'. Lord Buckmaster responded to the proposal by stating:

> The right to receive Holy Communion is established by Act of Parliament, passed in the first year of the reign of Edward VI, and from that time until now by the law of this country every inhabitant of this country, without regard to his religious faith, is at liberty, if he presents himself reverently in Church, to be admitted to Holy Communion.[21]

Archbishop Lang noted that, statutorily, 'open and notorious evil livers' could be refused admission to Holy Communion. Archbishop Davidson added that the Church wanted to pass this amendment partly as a means of avoiding the necessity of labeling divorced persons as evil livers.[22] The debate was heated, with those who opposed Selborne's proposal citing examples of innocent, respectable women being refused Holy Communion, and those who supported the amendment citing examples of clergy forced to admit notoriously guilty parties to the Eucharist. Perhaps the most striking point was Archbishop Davidson's statement: 'The whole subject of Holy Communion is unsuited for Parliamentary debate or Parliamentary division'.[23] That comment emphasizes a crucial aspect of Establishment— Parliament governed the Church. The statute establishing the right to receive Holy Communion illustrates the point. In 1920 leaders of the Church were unable to establish, again by statute, clerical control of admission to the Eucharist. Selborne's amendment ultimately failed by a vote of 87 to 61. With their proposed amendments to Buckmaster's Bill, the Archbishop of Canterbury and Lord Selborne were asking the State to assist the Church by statutorily prohibiting remarriage in church after divorce and protecting clergy who wished to refuse to admit divorced persons to Holy Communion. Their amendments failed, and the issues would remain problematic for the Church for decades to come.

On 22 June 1920 the House of Lords passed Lord Buckmaster's Bill by a vote of 154 to 107.[24] Earlier, on 14 April, Athelstan Rendall, a Liberal MP for Thornbury, had introduced a motion in the House of Commons to give 'legislative effect' to the recommendations contained in the Majority Report of the Royal Commission on Divorce.[25] After a three-hour debate, Rendall's

Church and State Diverge 33

motion was defeated by a vote of 134 to 91. The size of the margin surprised many observers.[26] Lord Birkenhead later noted that the House was small and that the Whips were not put on. There was also speculation that some reformers voted against Rendall's motion because they preferred to wait for Lord Buckmaster's Bill to be sent to the Commons.[27] Rendall wrote to *The Times* that support for the Bill was so certain that many members thought their votes were unnecessary; they therefore felt free not to attend the session. Another member of the House of Commons, G. R. Lane Fox, disagreed with that assessment:

> The movement for easier divorce had not until recently been very seriously regarded by the greater part of those who will be found in opposition to it. Knowing that it had little real popular support they were inclined to underrate its danger. The action of the House of Lords in passing Lord Buckmaster's Bill on second reading opened their eyes to the position, and the vote of the House of Commons on Mr. Rendall's motion was the first opportunity afforded to those who believe in maintaining the permanence of marriage of recording their judgment on proposals that must be the destruction of it.[28]

Fox's assessment supported the argument made by ecclesiastical opponents of divorce reform, who had long claimed that there was no widespread demand to change the law. Whatever the reason for the strong opposition to Rendall's motion, Buckmaster's Bill lapsed after it was sent to the Commons.

The debates on Buckmaster's Bill indicated that, despite the presence of the bishops, the House of Lords was more receptive to the cause of divorce reform than was the Commons. Of course, two of the most eloquent and persuasive orators of the day—Lords Buckmaster and Birkenhead—argued for the proposals in the Lords. Birkenhead also said, 'I have generally been inclined to hold the . . . view that when it comes to matters of social legislation which affect the intimate lives of the people the Lords are apt to take a more sensible standpoint than the Commons, because they have more knowledge and greater sympathy'.[29] Perhaps more significantly, the Lords did not have to answer to an electorate. Although advocates of divorce reform claimed that the opposition to change was limited to a few conservative religious groups, the general feeling that divorce reform was not a popular cause persisted. Birkenhead acknowledged the difficulties that Members of the Commons encountered in responding to their constituencies by noting the strength of Church of England organizations in certain areas. He felt that, if a secret vote were taken, the majority of the Commons would support Buckmaster's Bill. Yet, in commenting on the political reality of the situation, Birkenhead wrote that 'it seems certain to a calculating member that a vote in favour of the Bill will excite many animosities; it is quite uncertain how many friendships it will create'.[30] The perception that there was strong public opposition to the cause of divorce reform reinforced the Church's resistance.

34 Church and State Diverge

Another factor that undermined the efforts of reformers in the early 1920s was the dilemma produced by the Minority Report of the Royal Commission. Since the Royal Commission was divided in its recommendations, reformers had to decide whether to limit proposed legislation to the reforms recommended in both reports or to pursue the wider changes recommended by the Majority Report. The difficulty was apparent in 1921, when the third Lord Gorell introduced a new Matrimonial Causes Bill in the House of Lords. Gorell's Bill would have implemented only those changes which both the Majority and Minority Reports of the Royal Commission had recommended. The Archbishop of Canterbury said that he supported the Bill and hoped that it would pass. Davidson emphasized, however, that he would withdraw his support if the Bill were amended to extend the grounds for divorce. On 12 April 1921, Lord Buckmaster moved in Committee to amend the proposal by inserting desertion for three years as an additional ground for divorce.[31] Although Gorell had no objection to making desertion a ground for divorce, he felt that the amendment would adversely affect the fortunes of the Bill. His object in introducing the legislation had been to accomplish as many changes as he reasonably thought would pass both Houses of Parliament; in sponsoring only limited reforms he was following the pattern his brother had established in 1914. Gorell asked to be relieved of the responsibility for the Bill if the amendment passed. When the proposal was accepted by a vote of 66 to 48, Buckmaster became the sponsor of the new Bill. By the time the legislation passed the House of Lords, however, yet another divorce proposal had failed to achieve success in the Commons, and once again Buckmaster's Bill was allowed to lapse in that House.[32] Divorce reformers would have to wait until 1937 for the extension of grounds.

The Double Standard and the Matrimonial Causes Act of 1923

A change advocated by both supporters and opponents of divorce reform was the removal of the distinction between men and women with regard to the grounds for divorce. The 1857 Act had established a wife's adultery as sufficient cause to end a marriage but stipulated that a husband's adultery had to be exacerbated by another matrimonial offence in order to constitute grounds for divorce. The idea that a woman's adultery was a more serious offence than a man's was based on a double moral standard that was a dominant cultural assumption in mid-Victorian England. One basis for the double standard was the possibility that a wife's adultery could confuse the rightful inheritance of property by introducing another man's child into a family. Samuel Johnson was quoted both in the 1857 debates and before the Royal Commission as expressing that explanation: 'Confusion of progeny constitutes the essence of the crime, and therefore a woman who breaks her marriage vows is much more criminal than a man who does it. A man to be sure is criminal in the sight of God, but he does not do his wife any very material injury if he does not insult her'.[33]

Concerns about the consequences of a wife's adultery were not the only explanation for the inclusion of the double standard in the divorce laws. Another expression of the concept was stated quite simply by a witness appearing before the Royal Commission: 'Women are naturally chaste and men unchaste'.[34] The idea that women lacked sexual desires reinforced the traditional bases of the double standard.[35] A woman's perceived sexual insensibility made her adultery a more serious offence because her 'sin' was unnatural. A man's adultery, on the other hand, could be just a 'lapse', a term used before the Royal Commission to refer to so-called 'accidental' or 'casual' adultery, which was defined as a single act of male infidelity as distinguished from ongoing adultery. Women were expected to be tolerant of their husbands' 'lapses'. Another expression of the double standard heard in Parliament and before the Royal Commission was the belief that women were more forgiving than men. In 1857 the Lord Advocate emphasized this perceived difference between the adultery of a husband and that of a wife when he told the House of Commons that 'condonation on the part of one sex might be amicable, while on the part of the other it would be degrading'.[36] A woman's tolerance was admirable, while a man's was demeaning.

The Church of England did not accept the idea that a wife's adultery was a more serious offence than a husband's. In 1857, the Archbishop of Canterbury argued that, even though the Gospel of Matthew mentioned only a husband's divorcing his wife, 'by parity of reasoning, it would be lawful for a woman to put away her husband'. In 1910 Hensley Henson told the Royal Commission: 'In no respect is the teaching of the New Testament more original than in the emphasis it places on the equality of the sexes'.[37] The testimony of other witnesses also indicated that the double standard was no longer widely accepted. In examining witnesses, the Commissioners would frequently ask, 'Do you think that the grounds for divorce should be the same for both men and women?' Of the ninety-four witnesses who replied to a version of this question, seventy-six replied affirmatively that they would favor granting a woman the right to divorce her husband on the ground of his adultery.[38] That large majority on the issue of the distinction between men and women led the Commissioners to declare in their Report: 'Nothing has been more striking in our inquiry than the agreement amongst the great majority of the witnesses, who dealt with the question, in favour of equality'.[39] The Minority Report concurred in recommending that the grounds for divorce should be the same for men and women.[40]

On a similar note, the Lambeth Conference of 1920 provided evidence of the Church's reasoning in supporting the same moral standards for men and women. The Committee appointed to consider problems related to marriage and sexual morality told the Conference, 'There has been too general an acquiescence in the degrading lie that chastity is not to be expected in boys and men. The single standard for both sexes, before and after marriage,

36   *Church and State Diverge*

must be constantly insisted upon'.[41] From a Christian perspective, when adultery was considered a sin, the double standard appeared indefensible. Social purists in the late nineteenth century had also noted two possible consequences of a husband's adultery that threatened the community: the birth of illegitimate children and the spread of venereal disease. Witnesses before the Royal Commission had argued that a husband could impregnate a single woman or another man's wife and thus cause the birth of children for whom he would not be legally responsible. Male infidelity could also introduce venereal disease into a home. The possibility of infecting an innocent wife and perhaps even children with syphilis or gonorrhea made a man's 'casual' adultery a grievous offence and provided the critics of the double standard with a strong social argument. The Church's advocacy of high standards of sexual morality for men as well as women was based not only on Christian principles but also on concern for social welfare.

In the debates on Lord Buckmaster's Bill in 1920, both Archbishop Davidson and Archbishop Lang had opposed extending the grounds for divorce, but they had supported making the grounds for divorce the same for men and women. By 1923, that particular change in the law was no longer truly controversial. Since Parliament had rejected bills to extend the grounds for divorce as recently as 1920 and 1921, Major Cyril Entwistle was careful to isolate the issue of the equality of the sexes when he introduced the Matrimonial Causes Bill of 1923 in the House of Commons. He opened the debate on the Second Reading by declaring, 'The sole object of this Bill is to give equality to the sexes in the matter of divorce, and it has no other purpose whatsoever'.[42] Archbishop Davidson supported the Bill, telling the House of Lords that 'the law of God' was 'uniform for men and women as regards morality'.[43] The passage of the 1923 Act by votes of 257 to 26 in the Commons and 95 to 8 in the Lords demonstrated the strength of the moral and social arguments against the preservation of the double standard.

The Question of Establishment

While the law lords were repudiating the maxim that 'Christianity is part of the law of England', and Parliamentary divorce reformers were struggling with ecclesiastical resistance to change, the Enabling Act of 1919 and the Prayer Book Crisis of 1927 further clarified tensions between Church and State. Although Establishment provided privileges for the Church of England, it also meant restrictions. Parliamentary control of admission to Holy Communion, as emphasized by Lord Buckmaster in the debates on his Divorce Bill, illustrated the point. Church reformers, who wanted freedom from Parliamentary control in spiritual matters, had long argued for self-government for the Church.[44] That reform was apparently achieved in 1919.

A primary impetus for the Enabling Act was the lack of Parliamentary time to do the work of the Church of England. The Archbishops' Commission on the Relations of Church and State, appointed in 1914, reported that Parliament 'possesses neither time nor inclination nor knowledge for dealing with ecclesiastical affairs'.[45] Since Parliament could not effectively govern the Church, reformers argued that ecclesiastical measures should be referred to a separate legislative assembly. The Enabling Act, which received the Royal Assent on 23 December 1919, created a new Church Assembly to help govern the Church. The new Assembly consisted of three Houses—bishops, clergy, and laity. The Assembly's functions were mainly administrative; the House of Bishops controlled any proposal relating to doctrine or the Church's rites. All three Houses had to approve a motion for it to pass.[46]

The Church Assembly established by the Enabling Act was soon called to action. In 1920, after both Convocations had agreed to proposed revisions to the Book of Common Prayer, Archbishop Davidson formally submitted those recommendations to the Home Secretary. According to the procedure established by the Enabling Act, the proposals were then sent to the Church Assembly for review. In the summer of 1927 all three houses of the Church Assembly passed, by substantial majorities, a measure that authorized the use of a Revised Prayer Book. The vote was 34 to 4 for the bishops, 253 to 37 for the clergy, and 230 to 92 for the laity.[47] The measure was then sent to Parliament.

Feelings ran high regarding revision of the Prayer Book. Historical memories of the Reformation and Civil War as well as personal memories of countless church services contributed to the sense that here was a text almost as sacred as the Bible itself. Despite those sentimental associations, the House of Lords approved the adoption of the new Prayer Book by a vote of 241 to 88 in late 1927. The House of Commons, however, rejected the Church's proposal by a vote of 238 to 205. The vote came as a shock to the leaders of the Church of England, since the Church Assembly had approved the revisions by substantial majorities. In his biography of Archbishop Davidson, George Bell wrote that in one night 'the House of Commons had apparently destroyed the work of more than twenty years'. The debate in the Commons had revealed certain misunderstandings that the bishops thought could be effectively addressed. Yet when they sent a second Prayer Book Measure to Parliament, the House of Commons rejected it by an even larger margin than the earlier vote: 266 to 220.[48]

The exercise of the Parliamentary veto to reject a Prayer Book that had been approved by the bishops, clergy, and laity of the Church of England— to block what was basically a doctrinal proposal—evoked a reconsideration of Establishment. In 1935, eight years after the Prayer Book crisis, the Archbishops' Commission on Church and State favored maintaining the Established Church in a strong statement:

> To many the Establishment is the symbol of the official acceptance of Christianity as the national religion. . . . If England, by Disestablishment, should seem to become neutral in the fight between faith and unfaith in

38 *Church and State Diverge*

Christianity, that would be a calamity for our own people and, indeed, for the whole world.[49]

In a Christian nation, an Established Church enjoyed certain advantages. Leaders of the Church of England thought that representatives of a national Church governed by Parliament should have an effective voice in guiding public policy, especially regarding religious and moral issues. Disestablishment would mean that the Church of England was merely one Christian denomination among many religious groups attempting to influence political decisions. Yet to remain as an established Church meant, as demonstrated in 1927, that Parliament controlled the Church, even in matters relating to doctrine and worship. The difficulty was that leaders of the Church of England wanted freedom from state control while maintaining the Church's political influence.[50] With regard to questions relating to divorce, the Church wanted not only the freedom to enforce its own strict rules but also the influence to persuade Parliament to maintain restrictive secular laws. Establishment survived the Prayer Book crisis, and the leaders of the Church of England would continue to play an influential, but not decisive, role in divorce reform.

In July 1928, following Parliament's rejection of the Prayer Book, Randall Davidson resigned as Archbishop of Canterbury. Davidson said that the Church's defeat in the Prayer Book crisis was not the reason for his resignation. The Lambeth Conference was scheduled to meet in 1930, and Davidson wanted his successor to preside over that assembly. Shortly after the announcement of Davidson's resignation, Cosmo Gordon Lang was designated as the new Archbishop of Canterbury.[51] Davidson had skillfully led the Church through difficult times, but he left his successor with unresolved challenges.

The Law in Action: Tensions between Church and State

One of those challenges was the struggle to maintain consistency between secular laws and Christian principles regarding divorce. The gravity of the matrimonial offence of adultery, which was the only ground for divorce, was central to the debate. In 1920, the same year that Lord Buckmaster introduced his divorce bill in the House of Lords, the Lambeth Conference appointed a committee to consider problems of marriage and sexual morality. In their report, the committee insisted that the Matthaean Exception should not be interpreted as the citing of just one example of a sufficient cause for divorce. Adultery was the *only* ground that Christians could recognize as an exception to the rule of indissoluble marriage because, the committee stated, 'sexual unfaithfulness stands in a different position from any other suggested ground of divorce, since it is the perversion of a special and singular relation which has no proper place outside the marriage tie'. Lord Birkenhead had challenged that emphasis on adultery by telling the House of Lords that the spiritual side of marriage was more important than

Church and State Diverge 39

the physical. The committee addressed that point by reporting to the Lambeth Conference that the physical union is a 'pledge and expression' of the spiritual aspects of marriage.[52] As Archbishop Davidson had argued, the two sides of marriage could not be separated.

The Lambeth Conference of 1920 affirmed the definition of marriage as 'a lifelong union'. Earlier Lambeth Conference resolutions had acknowledged differences of opinion with regard to remarriage after divorce and had only discouraged the practice. The 1920 resolutions did not even address the possibility of remarriage after divorce. The bishops defended strict rules regarding marriage and divorce not only because marriage was lifelong 'according to God's design', but also on the basis of social utility: 'No compassion for present hardships in particular cases can justify the lowering for all of the standard of Christ, which alone insures the welfare of society and of the race'.[53] The Lambeth Conference of 1930 confirmed the 1920 Conference's definition of marriage as indissoluble and stated that 'the marriage of one, whose former partner is still living, should not be celebrated according to the rites of the Church'. Again the emphasis was on social utility: 'To maintain the ideal of marriage is to preserve the social health of the community'.[54] Ecclesiastical opponents of divorce reform continued to argue that basing secular laws on Christian principles benefited all of society.

Such arguments came into question as deceptive practices among divorce litigants became more widespread after the First World War. The 1857 Act provided strict limitations in a divorce suit, as exemplified by the bars of collusion, condonation, and recrimination. In a collusive divorce spouses agreed that one of them would appear before the court as guilty of adultery, the only ground for divorce. Even if neither spouse had committed an offence, one would appear as a guilty respondent. Condonation quite simply means forgiveness. If a husband or wife condoned a matrimonial offence, usually by continuing to live with a guilty spouse, most judges would deny the petitioner a divorce. The court treated a condoned offence as if it had not occurred. Recrimination meant that a plaintiff who was guilty of a matrimonial offence could be denied a divorce.[55]

In a successful divorce suit, then, a guilty party had committed adultery, and the offended spouse was innocent. If the petitioner had forgiven the guilty spouse, if the couple had agreed on a divorce (or even discussed it), or if the petitioner had been guilty of a matrimonial offence, then the judge could refuse to grant a divorce. Faced with such restrictions, couples who wanted to end their marriages frequently perjured themselves in order to achieve their goal. During the interwar years, a popular method of circumventing the law was the 'hotel divorce', in which the husband would send his wife a hotel bill as evidence that he had spent a night with another woman. The wife would then petition for divorce, and her solicitors would collect evidence from the hotel. Servants there would testify that the wife was not the woman who had spent a night at the hotel with the husband. Conveniently, a maid had usually seen the couple in bed together when she served breakfast.[56]

40　*Church and State Diverge*

After 1923, when a wife had to prove only adultery to end her marriage legally, hotel divorces followed a well-established pattern. Even in cases where the wife was having an affair and wished to obtain a divorce in order to marry her lover, the husband would still pretend to commit adultery and the wife would petition for a divorce on that ground. In certain social circles, the husband was doing the 'honorable' thing when he agreed to serve as the respondent in a divorce case, since he protected his wife from the stigma of being branded an adulteress in court. It was apparently more socially acceptable for a man to commit adultery than it was for a woman, indicating that the double standard still held.

The Church was concerned by the possibility of such collusive divorces because the 'innocent' party might really be guilty. The issue arose formally when a Joint Committee appointed by the Convocations of Canterbury and York began to meet on 14 June 1932 to consider questions regarding divorce and remarriage. In order to address legal points effectively, the Committee heard testimony from witnesses experienced in divorce law, including Lord Buckmaster and Sir John Withers, who was both a solicitor with an expertise in divorce cases and an MP for Cambridge with a reputation as a progressive reformer in debates on divorce laws.[57] Another witness familiar with the history of divorce reform was J.E.G. de Montmorency, who had served as assistant secretary to the Royal Commission on Divorce from 1910 until 1912 and who had written a biography of the first Lord Gorell. When the members of the Committee expressed concerns about collusive divorces, all three of these witnesses denied that the practice was widespread. In questioning Withers, Canon Guy Rogers said that when he was in the Army, 'it was a common thing for a man to say that if his wife . . . wanted to break the marriage, he must, of course, as a gentleman supply the evidence that was necessary, and he would go out of his way to do so—because that was his code'. When Rogers asked if judges were aware of the 'code', Withers responded that he had 'heard of the code', but that he had 'never come across a case of that kind'.[58] The Committee was concerned about collusion because the bishops and the clergy had to decide whether or not an 'innocent' party in a divorce suit could be remarried in church. Withers, Buckmaster, and de Montmorency all attempted to reassure their questioners that the practice was not widespread, but their testimony could not completely dispel hearsay evidence.[59]

Another legal question that troubled the Joint Committee was whether or not the clergy could be compelled to perform a marriage ceremony for a divorced person in church. Once a court had ended a marriage, the parties were legally free to marry another person. Archbishop Davidson and most of the bishops refused to allow church services for such second marriages.[60] Since the Church of England was an established Church, many of the clergy were concerned that frustrated couples might resort to legal action to achieve their goal of a wedding in church. Before the Joint Committee in 1932, Lord Buckmaster addressed the question of whether a judge could grant a writ of

Church and State Diverge 41

mandamus to compel a clergyman to perform a marriage service as his public duty. Buckmaster attempted to reassure the Committees by testifying, 'At the present time there is, so far as I know, no power in the secular Courts to compel a clergyman to marry anybody'. The question of admission to Holy Communion was another matter. According to Buckmaster:

> While the right to be married by a priest is not, so far as I can see, a right at common law, the right to receive Holy Communion is established by Act of Parliament. . . . As that is a right established by statute it must be determined by the secular Courts whether or not that right is being refused. It is no longer a matter for the Ecclesiastical Courts. . . . In those circumstances how would it be possible for the Church to say that a lawful cause for refusing the Sacrament was something which the secular Courts had declared was no lawful cause at all?[61]

The prospect of secular courts determining who could or could not be married in church or admitted to Holy Communion was disturbing to the clergy. A precedent that increased their concerns was the case of *Banister v. Thomson* in 1908, when an ecclesiastical court addressed the question of admission to Communion for a man who had married his deceased wife's sister. As the principal judge of the Court of Arches, Sir Lewis Dibdin had ruled that a man whose marriage was authorized by the State did not become 'a notorious evil liver', even though his marriage was condemned by the Church. Accordingly, 'the clergyman was bound to admit him to Communion'.[62]

In another attempt to achieve clarity on questions related to divorce, the Joint Committee requested Bishop Bell of Chichester to send a list of questions to a number of theologians and scholars for the purpose of determining their opinions on the meaning of the New Testament passages. The first question was, 'In our Lord's teaching in the Gospels with regard to Marriage and Divorce, is He stating principles (or ideals) similar to those in other parts of His teaching, e.g., in the Sermon on the Mount, or is he legislating?' From the answers the Committee learned that there was no agreement on the definitions of the terms 'principles', 'ideals', and 'legislate'.[63] Clarity remained elusive.

The Joint Committee issued a formal report in 1935. In the resolutions that they submitted to the Convocations, they stated that marriage was indissoluble and that Christians could not remarry during the lifetime of a former spouse without violating the principles that Christ had taught should govern marriage. Accordingly, the Church should not allow the use of the Prayer Book service for anyone whose former spouse was still living, and those who had remarried after divorce should not be admitted to the Sacraments.[64] The Committees noted that the legal ground upon which the court granted a divorce might not be the real cause of the failure of the marriage. Since the Church could not investigate the facts of each divorce, the clergy could not determine who was 'innocent'. The Committees did recommend

42   *Church and State Diverge*

that bishops should be authorized to review the circumstances of those who had remarried during the lifetime of a former spouse and, if appropriate, to give instructions that they should be admitted to the Sacraments. Truly innocent parties, then, could not be remarried in church, but they could be admitted to Holy Communion with a bishop's permission.[65]

With regard to the Church's relationship with the State, the Committees insisted that, if Parliament extended the grounds for divorce, the Church must be free to forbid the use of its buildings for the marriages of divorced persons and to regulate admission to the Sacraments. They wanted freedom for the Church, but they did not want a complete separation of Church and State. The Committees rejected the possibility of universal civil marriage because they felt that the Church had significant responsibilities in emphasizing the sacred nature of marriage. If civil services initiated all marriages, then marriage could be viewed as an entirely secular matter. In an Appendix, Bishop Inskip of Barking and Chancellor H. B. Vaisey noted a significant financial consideration. The Church at that time collected approximately £25,000 a year in fees for granting marriage licences. The loss of that sum would be a substantial blow to the Church's budget.[66]

The strong resolutions in the 1935 Report were not unanimously accepted. In a Minority Report, Bishop Barnes of Birmingham, Bishop Inskip of Barking, Dean Waterfield of Hereford, and Canon Guy Rogers stated that they could not agree with the unqualified statement that the Church must regard marriage as an indissoluble union. They continued to argue that Christ was describing an ideal and not establishing a law in his teaching on divorce. The signatories to the Minority Report encouraged leniency for the 'genuinely innocent' party to a divorce suit; they were prepared to offer a second marriage in church to such an individual because the failure of the first marriage was due to the fault of another person.[67]

Outside of formal Church committees, theologians continued to debate questions regarding divorce. Kenneth Kirk, the Regius Professor of Moral and Pastoral Theology at Oxford and later Bishop of Oxford, took a strict view of the indissolubility of marriage, but he recognized the futility of insisting that the State maintain that standard. By 1933, when he published *Marriage and Divorce*, Kirk was already recognized as one of the leading moral theologians in the Church of England.[68] In responding to the argument that the teaching of Jesus on divorce represented an ideal and not legislation, Kirk wrote, 'Our Lord never "legislated", in the strict sense of the word: that is to say, He never ordained temporal penalties for those who disregarded or disobeyed His maxims'. Commenting on comparisons of the words on divorce to other Biblical metaphors, Kirk argued:

> Whereas the other instances quoted are genuinely 'picturesque', this one is merely prosaic. . . . The lilies of the field . . . the turned cheek, the camel and the needle—this is the stuff of which poetry is made. . . . A man must be wholly void of literary sense to suggest that the divorce

Church and State Diverge 43

teaching comes into anything like the same category as these others. If *they* are compact of imagination, *its* fibre is wholly . . . matter of fact.[69]

Thus, to say that Jesus was not 'legislating' in the teaching on divorce did not mean that he was merely describing an ideal and not establishing a firm principle.

Although Kirk argued that 'the phrase "till death us do part", and no other phrase, expresses properly the true duration of marriage',[70] he could not and did not ignore the reality of divorce. Since the State granted divorces with the right of remarriage, the Church had to determine ecclesiastical policies toward divorced persons. Kirk noted that Jesus had provided no guidance in this regard. Even if his teachings were interpreted to forbid remarriage after divorce, Jesus had not described sanctions to enforce that rule. Adding to the difficulty was the disagreement within the Church that had been evident in testimony before the Royal Commission and in various theological works. In reviewing resolutions of the Lambeth Conferences between 1888 and 1930, Kirk noted that the Church had been moving in the direction of stricter policies regarding divorced persons, yet no recognizable principle had been established as a basis for those policies. The Church of England, according to Kirk, 'has neither the coherence nor the machinery to enable her to take effective action' in enforcing discipline.[71] Not only could the Church not maintain consistency between secular laws and restrictive Christian principles regarding divorce, the bishops and clergy lacked the machinery both to define and to enforce strict discipline within the Church itself.

The Report of the Joint Committees in 1935 evoked years of discussion in both Convocations. During the initial debate in the Upper House of the Canterbury Convocation, Archbishop Lang stated his disagreement with the Minority Report's view of Christ's teaching: 'I think it cannot be said that He is merely laying down the spirit in which we ought to regard marriage, but that He is laying down a definite standard by which the institution of marriage shall be regarded and regulated'. Since Christ established a 'definite standard' rather than an ideal, Lang did not think that divorced persons should be remarried in church.[72] The Archbishop of Canterbury's view would be especially significant in late 1936, when the King of England wanted to marry a woman who had been divorced twice.

The Abdication of King Edward VIII

The Abdication Crisis began when the Prince of Wales, later King Edward VIII, met Wallis Warfield Simpson in the autumn of 1930.[73] She was an American from Baltimore, and both of her parents came from socially prominent families. In 1916 she had married Earl Winfield Spencer, Jr., whom she had divorced in 1927. In July 1928, Wallis Spencer married Ernest Simpson, who was also divorced. The couple rented a house in London, where Ernest Simpson had been transferred. Two years later, they met the Prince of Wales. During

44 Church and State Diverge

the next few years, the Prince and Mrs. Simpson developed a close relationship, which did not end when the Prince became King upon the death of his father on 20 January 1936. Indeed, although few realized his intentions at the time, the new King intended to marry Mrs. Simpson. One immediate difficulty, of course, was her marriage to Ernest Simpson. After a summer cruise in the Adriatic and the Aegean, the King and Mrs. Simpson returned to England to plan their future. The termination of her marriage was their first goal.

On 27 October 1936, in a hearing at Ipswich, evidence was presented that Ernest Simpson had stayed at the Café de Paris at Bray with a woman named Buttercup Kennedy.[74] Although the case had the appearance of a 'hotel divorce', the court granted Mrs. Simpson what was known as a *decree nisi*. Such a decree was contingent upon certain conditions, and the divorce would not become absolute until six months after the pronouncement of that first decree. During that time, an official known as the King's Proctor could investigate the case to see if there were any reasons why the divorce should not be made absolute. If he found evidence of collusion or adultery by the appellant, the judge might refuse to grant the final decree.[75] Until a judge pronounced her divorce absolute, no sooner than six months after the granting of the *decree nisi*, Mrs. Simpson was not free to remarry.

The difficulty in obtaining a divorce in England was only one impediment to the marriage of King Edward VIII and Mrs. Simpson. The King's position as Supreme Governor of the Church of England meant that Church policies regarding the remarriage of divorced persons would be a serious obstacle to the marriage. Since the Joint Committees of the Convocations had affirmed in 1935 that 'in no circumstances can Christian men or women re-marry during the lifetime of a wife or husband without a breach of the principles by which the institution of marriage is governed according to Christ's teaching', it was unlikely that the Church would bless the marriage of the King to a woman who had been divorced twice. Archbishop Lang was in a particularly difficult situation. The Coronation was scheduled for 1937, and the Archbishop faced the prospect of both crowning and administering the Eucharist to a man who was married to a divorcée who had two living former husbands.[76]

The Archbishop of Canterbury did not have a close relationship with the King. Indeed, Hensley Henson reported hearing that apparently they were barely on speaking terms.[77] Lang had been a good friend of the King's parents, and he had discussed the Prince of Wales and Mrs. Simpson with George V. Not very diplomatically, the Archbishop had made reference to these talks to the new King, shortly after the death of his father. Lang felt that Edward VIII was 'somewhat set against me by knowing that his father had often discussed his affairs with me'.[78] During the weeks preceding the Abdication, when the Archbishop suggested that he might talk to the King, he was told that the King 'was very emphatic that on the subject of his relations with Mrs. Simpson he would listen to nobody but Mr. Baldwin [the Prime Minister], who had a right to speak to him and advise him'.[79] As a result, the Archbishop of Canterbury did not play an influential role in the Abdication Crisis.

Church and State Diverge 45

The King would listen only to the Prime Minister, but Baldwin had no easy answers. The British people were largely unaware of the crisis because the British press had observed a 'gentlemen's agreement' and published no report of the romance until the first of December. Based on consultations with his colleagues and correspondence from abroad, where the American press had widely publicized the King's friendship with Mrs. Simpson, Baldwin had concluded that the Dominions and the British people would not respond favorably to a marriage between their sovereign and a divorcée. As Chips Cannon wrote in his diary, 'The country, or much of it, would not accept Queen Wallis, with two live husbands scattered about'.[80] When Baldwin had first discussed the subject of Mrs. Simpson with the King in October of 1936, the Prime Minister had said with regard to divorce:

> You may think me Victorian, Sir. You may think my views out of date, but I believe I know how to interpret the minds of my own people; and I say that although it is true that standards are lower since the war it only leads people to expect a higher standard from their King.[81]

A possibility that the Government considered was a morganatic marriage. In such an arrangement Mrs. Simpson could marry the King, but she would not become Queen. She would remain a private citizen, and any children born to the couple would not be in the line of succession. On 2 December, the Cabinet rejected the proposal of a morganatic marriage.[82] The King then had to choose between the throne and Mrs. Simpson; he chose the latter.

Edward VIII signed the Instrument of Abdication on 10 December. After the King left the country, Archbishop Lang criticized that choice in an address broadcast on 13 December:

> From God he had received a high and sacred trust. Yet by his own will he has abdicated—he has surrendered the trust. With characteristic frankness he has told us his motive. It was a craving for private happiness. Strange and sad it must be that for such a motive, however strongly it pressed upon his heart, he should have disappointed hopes so high and abandoned a trust so great. Even more strange and sad it is that he should have sought his happiness in a manner inconsistent with the Christian principles of marriage, and within a social circle whose standards and ways of life are alien to all the best instincts and traditions of his people. Let those who belong to this circle know that to-day they stand rebuked by the judgment of the nation which had loved King Edward.[83]

The condemnation of not only the King, for not fulfilling his obligations to his subjects, but also his 'social circle', for leading him away from his duties, immediately evoked criticism, especially from those observers who saw Lang as a self-righteous judge blind to any considerations other than his definition of 'Christian principles of marriage'. Bishop Henson wrote in his diary

46   *Church and State Diverge*

that the Archbishop's address had a 'mixed reception'. Some admired it, but Henson agreed with those who saw the words as 'ill-timed, ungenerous, and unworthy'. He wrote, 'There was . . . a severity of censure in respect to the late monarch which savoured of "hitting a man when he is down"'.[84] That metaphor appeared in the following lines of verse:

> My Lord Archbishop, what a scold you are!
> And when your man is down, how bold you are!
> Of Christian charity how scant you are!
> And, auld Lang swine, how full of cant you are![85]

Lang later wrote that he had expected a 'torrent of abuse', but he noted that there were also many 'letters of gratitude'.[86] The response that he noted among all the others came from Prime Minister Baldwin, who wrote in 'gratitude and admiration' that the Archbishop had said just what was needed in the broadcast. He referred to Lang as 'the voice of Christian England'.[87]

That voice soon had to answer another question: Could the Church of England bless the marriage of the former King and Mrs. Simpson? During the months following the Abdication, the former Edward VIII, who had the new title of Duke of Windsor, stayed at the Baron Eugene de Rothschild's house near Vienna, while Mrs. Simpson remained in Cannes with friends. The distance separating them was intended to prevent gossip that could have interfered with the Simpson divorce. On 3 May 1937 the *decree nisi* in *Simpson* v. *Simpson* was made absolute. Legally, the Duke and Mrs. Simpson could be married, and the Duke hoped that a member of the clergy could perform the ceremony. Walter Monckton, who had been a close adviser to Edward VIII throughout the Abdication Crisis, told Alan Don, chaplain to Archbishop Lang, that the Duke would like for Canon Leonard Martin Andrews, who had served as chaplain to the King, to officiate. Canon Andrews was evidently willing to perform the ceremony, but he stipulated that there must be no objection from either King George VI or Archbishop Lang. Don responded to Monckton that Archbishop Lang would feel bound by the Convocation resolutions that deprecated the use of the marriage service for divorced persons and that Canon Andrews should be told of that decision.[88] Canon Andrews had to refuse to perform the ceremony because, in his words, 'it would be letting the church down, and as long as I hold office in the church I must keep the rules, however cruel they may seem'.[89]

Not only the Archbishop but also the new King opposed the use of a religious ceremony. George VI really had no choice. As Supreme Governor of the Church of England, he could not support a service that the Church would not accept. He wrote to the Duke of Windsor,

> I can't treat this as just a private family matter, however much I want to. I am afraid it will not be possible for Harry and George [the Dukes of

Gloucester and Kent, brothers of the King and the Duke of Windsor] or any of the family to come out to your wedding.[90]

The King told Monckton that no member of the Royal Family would attend the ceremony, and that no royal chaplain could officiate.[91] In the end, the Reverend Robert Anderson Jardine, Vicar of St. Paul's in Darlington, offered to officiate. He did so on his own initiative. After reading in a newspaper that the Duke of Windsor had been denied a religious blessing on his marriage, Jardine contacted one of the Duke's friends and offered to perform the ceremony. The Duke gratefully accepted.[92]

The Church of England did not support Jardine's participation. Ironically, Jardine's bishop was Hensley Henson of Durham, who had supported divorce reform. Henson, however, did not approve of Jardine's decision to perform the ceremony and issued the following statement:

> The Rev. R.A. Jardine has no authority to officiate outside his parish & diocese. If the Duke's marriage were to take place within the diocese of Durham, the Bishop could inhibit him, but the Bishop has no jurisdiction outside that diocese and must presume that Mr. Jardine has obtained permission from the Anglican Bishop who has authority over English clergymen on the continent of Europe.[93]

The Bishop who did have jurisdiction in northern and central Europe was the Bishop of Fulham, who sent a telegram to Jardine denouncing that clergyman for performing a marriage ceremony in France without the Bishop's consent.[94] Legally the Duke of Windsor was to be married to Mrs. Simpson by a French mayor. Neither Bishop Henson nor the Bishop of Fulham could stop Jardine from blessing a couple who had already been married in France.[95] Archbishop Lang wrote Henson that he was 'indignant' that one of the Bishop of Durham's clergy should have offered to officiate at the Duke of Windsor's wedding, but Lang admitted that the Church of England could not stop Jardine. Henson wrote in his diary, 'Probably his Grace's hierarchical *amour propre* is offended by this fresh evidence of the practical paralysis of discipline within the Church of England. He is humiliated in face of the Papists!'[96]

As he noted, the Archbishop of Canterbury could do nothing to stop the reading of the Prayer Book service. On 3 June 1937 the Mayor of Monts performed the civil ceremony in the Château de Candé near Tours, and afterwards the Reverend Jardine read the religious service. An oak chest covered with a tablecloth provided by the bride served as an altar. When Jardine refused to have a crucifix on the chest, a plain cross was quickly found.[97] A touching detail was reported by Lady Alexandra Metcalfe, who was present and whose husband, known as 'Fruity', served as the Duke's best man: 'Throughout the ceremony Fruity held for him [the Duke] the prayer book Queen Mary gave him when he was 10 with "To darling David from his

48 *Church and State Diverge*

loving Mother" written in it'. Lady Alexandra continued with a moving description of the wedding:

> It could be nothing but pitiable & tragic to see a King of England of only 6 months ago, an idolized King, married under those circumstances, & yet pathetic as it was, his manner was so simple and dignified & he was so sure of himself in his happiness that it gave something to the sad little service which it is hard to describe. He had tears running down his face when he came into the salon after the ceremony.[98]

On this poignant note, the former King Edward VIII and his new wife began their married life.

Many observers felt that the bishops of the Church of England had been harsh in refusing to allow a religious ceremony for the Windsors' wedding. Don, the chaplain to Archbishop Lang, wrote to one critic in defense of the Church's decision that it was based on a matter of principle and not on any animosity toward the former King. According to Don, if the Church had made an exception in the case of the Windsors, the 'enemies' of the Church would have lost no time in denouncing the Church for inconsistency and 'toadying to Royalty'.[99] In 1937, then, the Church of England's position was clear: No divorced person should be remarried in a religious ceremony. Not even a former King of England, never married himself, could marry a divorced woman according to the marriage service in the Prayer Book.

The Abdication Crisis appeared to strengthen the Church of England's position on divorce. According to the *Guardian*, events surrounding the King's departure demonstrated that 'there is latent in England a surprisingly deep respect for fundamental Christian morality'.[100] The widespread criticism of the Archbishop of Canterbury's speech seemed to be directed more against Lang personally than against the institution of the Church. One critic compared the Archbishop's leadership unfavorably to that of his predecessor: 'The broadcast was worse than a blunder. It was an offence against the merciful and compassionate spirit of the Christian religion. . . . Randall Davidson would have been more cautious and more prescient'.[101] While critics may have disparaged Archbishop Lang's leadership in the crisis, the Established Church did appear to offer a sense of conviction and stability in the midst of uncertainty. New proposals for divorce reform would soon challenge that conviction.

A.P. Herbert and the Matrimonial Causes Act of 1937

By 1937, a quarter of a century after the Majority Report of the Royal Commission had recommended that the grounds for divorce be extended, Parliament had still not acted on that recommendation; adultery remained the only ground for divorce. In the face of an unyielding statute, couples who wanted to end a marriage frequently resorted to perjury in order to achieve

Church and State Diverge 49

their goal. The problem of collusive divorces challenged both Church and State to reconsider policies and laws regarding divorce. Solicitors, barristers, and judges of the Divorce Court were particularly concerned about the problems of collusion and perjury because those offences represented a disrespect for the law that undermined the integrity of their tribunal. Sir Boyd Merriman, who became President of the Probate, Divorce, and Admiralty Division of the High Court in 1933, was dismayed not just because some spouses were guilty of collusion but rather because the collusive suit apparently had become the standard procedure for obtaining a divorce.[102] The Joint Committees of the Convocations of Canterbury and York had questioned witnesses about collusive divorces and deplored the practice in their 1935 report, but they did not recommend extension of the grounds for divorce as a solution to the problem. Even though both Church and State recognized the serious difficulties with the existing divorce laws, there was no general agreement about reform. Consequently, A.P. Herbert faced a complicated battle when he adopted the cause of divorce reform as an Independent Member of Parliament.

Alan Patrick Herbert, later Sir Alan Herbert, took 'a very good First' in Jurisprudence at Oxford in 1914, and he seemed destined for the Inns of Court. When he was called to the Bar by the Inner Temple after the First World War, however, he decided against a legal career. Instead Herbert became a professional humorist who wrote light verse, novels, comic lyrics for musical plays, and columns for *Punch*. His knowledge of the law, combined with his sense of humor, inspired Herbert to examine certain absurdities of the English legal system. His wit made him an effective critic. Herbert's *Misleading Cases* was quoted in the Royal Courts of Justice, the House of Lords, and the United States Supreme Court.[103]

In 1935, Herbert decided to run for one of the Oxford University seats in Parliament. Herbert described Oxford as 'that citadel of the Church of England', and his supporters estimated that the clergy constituted as much as thirty percent of the Oxford electorate, yet the candidate did not hesitate to advocate divorce reform. He later wrote, 'As for divorce and the Church I had formed . . . the opinion that the majority of churchmen were ready and even eager for a reasonable reform'.[104] Herbert's success at the polls appeared to validate his assessment. Despite his lack of party support and his controversial advocacy of divorce reform, he defeated both a Conservative and a Socialist to become the Junior Burgess for Oxford.

Herbert entitled his proposed legislation a 'Marriage Bill' because he claimed that its purpose was to strengthen marriage. He stated that argument in the preamble to the Bill, describing the purposes of the legislation as 'the true support of marriage, the protection of children, the removal of hardship, the reduction of illicit unions and unseemly litigation, the relief of conscience among the clergy, and the restoration of due respect for the law'.[105] Knowing that the Church would want specific reassurances of the protection of their rights, especially if the grounds for divorce were

50 Church and State Diverge

extended, Herbert and his supporters decided to include the following provision in the Bill:

> No clergyman of the Church of England shall be compelled to solemnize the marriage of any person whose former marriage has been dissolved on any ground and whose former husband or wife is still living or to permit any other minister of the Church of England to perform such a marriage service in his church or chapel.[106]

This provision granted the clergy greater independence than the 1857 Act in that a clergyman could refuse both to solemnize the marriage of a divorced person and to refuse the use of his church for such a ceremony.

Despite provisions that responded to the concerns of both Church and State, the Government would not sponsor Herbert's proposed legislation. Traditionally British governments had been reluctant to sponsor divorce legislation because the controversial reforms evoked strong opposition and not always equally significant support. In November of 1936, the Government was especially antipathetic to the subject of divorce because of the King's desire to marry Mrs. Simpson. Herbert had no choice but to navigate the Bill through Parliament personally. Rupert De la Bère, an Independent Member, had obtained the second place for the hearing of private Members' bills; he introduced the Marriage Bill in the House of Commons on 6 November 1936.

In a meeting on 18 November, two days before the debate on the Second Reading, the Cabinet discussed the proposal. While the Attorney General, Sir Donald Somervell, and the Home Secretary, Sir John Simon, favored the Bill, the Lord Chancellor, Hailsham, opposed the measure. The division within the Cabinet, as well as the Abdication Crisis, inhibited the Government's support of the legislation. The group agreed that Cabinet Ministers would not vote on the Bill and that the Attorney General would be the Government spokesman in the debate. The Cabinet instructed Somervell to adopt a neutral attitude toward the proposal but to inform the House that, if Members granted the Bill a Second Reading, a Law Officer would assist the Committee in its deliberations.[107]

By the time that Herbert's Bill emerged from Committee, there was much in it to commend the proposals to the Church of England. The additional protection for the consciences of the clergy with regard to the remarriage of divorced persons certainly met with clerical approval. Also, Section 1 of Herbert's Bill provided that a court would not grant a divorce within the first five years of a marriage. That provision reinforced the idea that a couple should take the marriage bond seriously since their union would last for at least five years, if not 'until death do them part'. Sir Claud Schuster, the Permanent Secretary in the Lord Chancellor's Office, told the Lord Chancellor that Archbishop Lang viewed the provision as an important concession.[108] Herbert had vowed to restore respect for the law, and his Bill included sections designed to achieve that goal. Section 4 of the 1937 Act required the court to determine whether or not the petitioner's suit involved connivance, condonation, or collusion with the respondent. If the petitioner could not satisfy the court with regard to these matters, the petition could be dismissed.[109] Herbert's proposed legislation took divorce very seriously indeed.

Accordingly, the Archbishop of Canterbury could not completely condemn the Bill. When the President of the Mothers' Union asked for guidance from the Archbishop on whether or not her organization should oppose the Bill, the response was ambiguous. While Lang would not say that he favored the proposals, he could not condemn the Bill in its entirety.[110] Similarly, when the Bishop of Guildford, John Victor Macmillan, wrote to the Archbishop on 27 November 1936, asking for advice on how to respond to the Marriage Bill, the reply called attention to the Joint Committees' 1935 Report, which had recognized that 'some amendment of the State law relating to grounds of divorce is demanded by the circumstances of the day'. The Joint Committees were of the opinion 'that the Church should be ready to give consideration to proposals for such amendment, provided that any proposed amendment does not tend to make marriage a temporary alliance or to undermine the foundations of family life'.[111] On this basis, Lang recommended that each bishop, in accordance with the general principles stated in the 1935 Report, should have the freedom to judge the proposed additional grounds for divorce in Herbert's Bill individually on the merits.[112] Recognizing the necessity of reform, the Archbishop of Canterbury did not take a firm stand on Herbert's Bill.

The differences of opinion among the bishops were evident in the debates when the Bill finally reached the House of Lords. When Lord Eltisley moved the Second Reading on 24 June 1937, the Archbishop of Canterbury was the first speaker from the Bench of Bishops. At the beginning of his comments, he described the difficulty that he confronted. On the one hand, the current divorce laws were unsatisfactory in that they encouraged abuses and disrespect for the law. Lang told the Lords that 'adultery is being treated with a levity which is really shocking to any sort of moral sense', and he cited 'hotel bill cases' to prove the point.[113] Herbert's Bill addressed these problems and also provided 'welcome relief to the conscience of the clergy'. For these reasons Lang could not vote against the Second Reading. On the other hand, he could not vote *for* the Second Reading because he believed that remarriage after divorce 'is inconsistent with the principles laid down by Christ'. In the end he abstained because he was caught between 'two positive duties, the one to be ready to make the law of the State better in its operation, and the other to do nothing which would weaken the witness to the high standards of the Christian marriage on which the welfare of the community so greatly depends'.[114]

Although he would not participate in the vote, Lang certainly contributed to the debate. In his remarks he indicated an important implication of the

52   *Church and State Diverge*

rejection of the Matthaean Exception by Biblical scholars. He agreed with scholars who argued that Jesus had not established adultery as an exception to the prohibition against divorce. In the past, Biblical criticism that had challenged the authenticity of the Matthaean Exception had appeared to reinforce the principle of the indissolubility of marriage. Lang, however, pointed to another interpretation: adultery might not be the only acceptable ground for divorce. The Archbishop went so far as to say, 'If there be any grounds of divorce which are permissible, it is difficult not to place wilful desertion in the same position as adultery'. Thus, Lang was willing to consider the extension of the grounds for divorce in the laws of the State. As for the Church of England, however, he repeated the Convocations' recent affirmation of the definition of marriage as 'a lifelong and indissoluble union for better or for worse of one man with one woman'.[115]

Archbishop Lang was not the only speaker to describe the tension between the necessity of divorce reform and the Christian definition of marriage. Archbishop Temple told the Lords, 'While I believe it is desirable that this Bill should pass into law, I do not think it is appropriate that an occupant of the Bishops' Bench should vote for it'.[116] The only bishop to disagree with the opinion that the House should pass the Bill was Furse of St. Albans. He told the Lords, 'Marriage we believe is not primarily for self gratification or merely to produce the happiness of one man or one woman. It is a vocation for service'. With regard to arguments based on 'hard cases', Furse declared:

> What your Lordships ought to administer today to this country is a moral tonic, so that all of us may face with greater courage and persistence the difficulties and hardships which are inevitable and, I believe, essential in the production of the finest human character.[117]

The perception that marriage involved inevitable suffering that the laws of England should do nothing to relieve placed Furse among the most conservative opponents of divorce reform.[118]

Henson of Durham followed Furse in the debate. He began by accusing the Bishop of St. Albans of not having read the Bill, and he proceeded to declare, 'I think that this Bill, if it were passed into law, so far from bringing the law of England into conflict with the law of Christ, would bring the law of England into deeper and truer harmony with that law'.[119] Henson made several strong arguments in favor of Herbert's proposals. He referred to the evidence collected by the Royal Commission as demonstrating the necessity of reform. The hard cases revealed in that Report represented grievances to be redressed and not suffering to be endured. Henson criticized Archbishop Lang's reliance on Biblical criticism and argued that 'the Church of Christ has never allowed itself to draw a distinction in religious authority between one canonical Gospel and another'. Rather than comparing the injunction in Mark to the exception in Matthew, Henson stated, 'I prefer to stand on the general position of the Church, and to say that our Lord's teaching, as we

Church and State Diverge 53

have it transmitted to us in the four canonical Gospels, teaches with every adequate reason that the marriage union is dissoluble'. Referring to another teaching of Jesus—'The Sabbath was made for man and not man for the Sabbath'—Henson said, 'The marriage union is made for man, not man for the marriage union'.[120] On this basis Henson would vote for the Bill. Herbert, who listened to the speech in the Lords, later wrote: 'In all that year of talk this was the speech that I most enjoyed. What art! What ease! What dignified mischief! What scholarly sincerity! I wish that Dr. Henson was a Member of the House of Commons'.[121] As Owen Chadwick has noted, especially since the Archbishops of Canterbury and York were both remaining neutral, Herbert was fortunate indeed that the Bishop of Durham would argue so persuasively that the Bill was a Christian bill.[122]

The Bishop of St. Edmundsbury and Ipswich, Walter Godfrey Whittingham, joined Henson in supporting the Bill. He had met with Herbert before Christmas to discuss the proposals. Herbert described him as 'a wise, human, and venerable man, and a most able Parliamentarian', who 'listened gravely' to the appeal of the Bill's sponsor. Herbert told the bishop, 'we deserve your help, for we respectfully say that we are pulling the Church's chestnuts out of the fire'.[123] Seven months later Bishop Whittingham told the House of Lords, 'I do not believe this is a State Bill divorced from Christian feeling. I believe it represents the truest Christian feeling of this country'. He added:

> It is often said that persons ought to be prepared to submit to sacrifice and accept a hard lot, feeling that it is for the good of the community that they should do so . . . but you cannot get this Christian spirit if you compel somebody . . . to consent to what involves a great sacrifice on his part and which he regards as radically unjust and unkind. The heart must go with it . . . I think we are mistaken when we insist upon the letter of the bond, disregarding the spirit that lies behind it.[124]

In the final vote on the Third Reading in the Lords, Bishops Whittingham and Henson voted for the Bill. Furse of St. Albans was the only bishop to align himself with the Non-Contents. No other bishop voted, and the final count was 79 to 28 in favor of the Bill. The House of Commons had agreed to a Third Reading by a vote of 190 to 37, and the Bill received the Royal Assent on 30 July 1937. Eighty years after the 1857 Act had established adultery as the only ground for divorce, Parliament accepted desertion for three years, cruelty, and incurable insanity as additional causes to end a marriage.

In the past, Cosmo Gordon Lang had opposed extension of the grounds for divorce. He had signed the Royal Commission's Minority Report in 1912, and in 1920 he had argued against Lord Buckmaster's Bill. His opposition to that Bill was based, however, not on religious authority but rather on 'the ground of public welfare'. In 1937 Archbishop Lang could no longer vote against divorce reform because he had come to believe that abuses of

54 *Church and State Diverge*

the existing laws were *harmful* to public welfare. He later wrote, 'Rightly or wrongly, I came to the conclusion that it was no longer possible to impose the full Christian standard by law on a largely non-Christian population'.[125] The attempt to do so had consequences that undermined the integrity of the judicial system.

Lang's perceived role in the Abdication Crisis also weakened the Archbishop's ability to organize strong resistance to the extension of the grounds for divorce. His speech following Edward VIII's departure had been so widely criticized that, as one commentator described it:

> The millions who listened to the broadcast were perplexed, perturbed, and wounded by its disregard of the English tradition for fair play and sportsmanship. They felt that the head of the Church of England had used his position ungenerously and unmercifully. . . . The nation silently and unanimously resented and repudiated Dr. Lang's lack of Christian charity and forbearance.[126]

Certainly the English people did not 'unanimously' repudiate the Archbishop of Canterbury, but they viewed Lang as unsympathetic to the former King. Bishop Henson quoted a 'New York Correspondent' as writing, 'A very distinguished editor of great influence has just said to me that in his view there has been much more of the spirit of Christianity in Edward's restraint and courtesy than in the pronouncements of the Archbishop of Canterbury'.[127] The refusal to allow the Duke of Windsor to be married in a Church of England ceremony tended to confirm the view that the Archbishop was uncharitable. Privately Lang had written in his diary, 'My heart aches for the Duke of Windsor, remembering his childhood, his boyhood, the rich promise of his services as Prince of Wales . . . I cannot bear to think of the kind of life into which he has passed'.[128] Yet publicly he had denounced the King in terms that left the Archbishop of Canterbury open to charges that he was vindictive and unforgiving.

In their speeches during the debates on Herbert's Bill, the Archbishops of Canterbury and York had both said that they favored reform of the State's divorce laws, yet as official representatives of the Church of England they could not vote for the legislation. In effect they recognized the necessity of separate laws for Church and State. In 1937, Parliament passed a statute that clearly deviated from the Church's definition of marriage. The Church of England then had to confront the task of restating its policies with regard to divorce and remarriage in light of the new legislation. Since the 1937 Act extended the grounds for divorce, that task assumed a new urgency because an inevitably larger group of divorced Anglicans would seek remarriage in church.

While the State had followed a path of reform, the Church chose a more restrictive course of action. In June 1938, both Convocations passed resolutions stating that marriage was 'indissoluble save by death'; that remarriage after divorce 'always involves a departure from the true principle of marriage as declared by our Lord'; that the Church should not permit the use of the Prayer Book Marriage Service for a divorced person whose former spouse was still living; and that the Church of England should be free to enforce its own discipline with regard to marriage. At the Autumn session in 1937, the Church Assembly had passed a motion approving the Convocations' 'considered judgment' that the Prayer Book Service should not be used for the remarriage of divorced persons whose former spouse was still living.[129] As divorce became more widely available through the extension of grounds, the bishops, clergy, and laity of the Church of England denied the use of the Church's rites for the remarriage of divorced persons.

In 1937, then, the Church diverged from the State by rejecting a wider acceptance of divorce. The debates on the 1937 Act had compelled the Archbishop of Canterbury to acknowledge that secular divorce laws, which affected society as a whole, could not be based strictly on Christian principles. Although the resolution of the Abdication Crisis had been consistent with the Church's position on divorce, the 1937 Act indicated that the Church of England could no longer serve as the principal guiding force in the formulation of divorce laws.[130] Having acknowledged that the Church could not determine divorce laws for all of society, the Church established a strict rule for its own members by declaring marriage indissoluble. The Church then faced the difficulties of enforcing that definition.

Notes

1. J. Roebuck, *The Making of Modern English Society from 1850* (New York: Charles Scribner's Sons, 1973), p. 100.
2. G. Rowntree and N. Carrier, 'The Resort to Divorce in England and Wales, 1858–1957', *Population Studies*, Vol. 11 (March 1958):201.
3. E. Norman, *Church and Society in England 1770–1970* (Oxford: Clarendon Press, 1976), pp. 267–268, quoting *Church Times*, 'The Abolition of Marriage' (10 August 1917) and 'The English Church Union and the new Divorce Proposals' (30 November 1917).
4. Enclosure in letter from Hugh Cecil to Archbishop Randall Davidson, dated 20 August 1917. Davidson Papers, Vol. 417, f 100. Lambeth Palace Library.
5. G. Bell, *Randall Davidson, Archbishop of Canterbury* (Oxford University Press, 1952), p. 991.
6. [1917] AC 406 at 407–409.
7. *Ibid.* at 464. Sumner described Lord Eldon's observation that 'the law does not give protection to those who contradict the Scriptures' as 'a dictum which, in its full width, imperils copyright in most books on geology' (461–462).
8. W. Goodhart, 'Buckmaster, Stanley Owen, first Viscount Buckmaster (1861–1934)', *Oxford Dictionary of National Biography*, Oxford University Press, 2004 [http://www.oxforddnb.com/view/article/32159].
9. S. Cretney, *Family Law in the Twentieth Century* (Oxford: Oxford University Press, 2003), p. 217, quoting *The Times*, 22 October 1922.
10. *Parliamentary Debates* (Lords), 5th series, 39 (10 March 1920):342.
11. *Ibid.*, 369.
12. *Ibid.*, 372, 376.

56   Church and State Diverge

13. J. Campbell, 'Smith, Frederick Edwin, first earl of Birkenhead (1872–1930)', *Oxford Dictionary of National Biography*, Oxford University Press, 2004; online edn, Sept 2015 [http://www.oxforddnb.com/view/article/36137].

14. *Parliamentary Debates* (Lords), 39 (24 March 1920):669. Reportedly, Birkenhead thought that his speech on the 1920 Buckmaster Divorce Bill was 'one of the greatest—perhaps the greatest—of his life'. Cretney, *Family Law in the Twentieth Century*, p. 780.

15. *Parliamentary Debates*, 39:679–691. With regard to Davidson's speech, his biographer George Bell wrote that 'he was not at his best' (Bell, p. 995).

16. *Parliamentary Debates*, 39:714.

17. *Ibid.*, 39 (20 April 1920):835.

18. Bell, quoting letter from Bishop Gore to the Archbishop of Canterbury, dated 25 April 1920, p. 997.

19. *Parliamentary Debates* (Lords), 40 (4 May 1920):104.

20. *Ibid.*, 40:117, 124.

21. *Ibid.*, 40:127–128.

22. *Ibid.*, 40 (11 May 1920):236 and 248.

23. *Ibid.*, 40:245.

24. *Ibid.*, 40 (22 June 1920):730.

25. *Parliamentary Debates* (Commons), 5th series, 127 (14 April 1920):1758.

26. Frederick Guest wrote to the Prime Minister, Lloyd George, that no one was expecting the motion to be defeated by such a large majority. 'Notes on the business of the House since its reassembling, 15 April 1920', Papers of Lloyd George (F/22/1/28), House of Lords Library, London.

27. Birkenhead, *Evening Standard* (12 May 1925). *Law Notes* 39 (May 1920):115.

28. A. Rendall, 'Divorce Law Reform', *The Times* (22 April 1920):12; G. Lane Fox, 'Divorce Law Reform', *The Times* (23 April 1920):12.

29. *The Evening Standard* (12 May 1925).

30. Birkenhead, *Contemporary Personalities* (London: Cassell and Co. Ltd., 1924), p. 160.

31. *Parliamentary Debates* (Lords), 44 (12 April 1921):887, 893.

32. Lord Gorell wrote to Archbishop Lang that Buckmaster later said that he thought that he should not have insisted on inserting the additional grounds for divorce. Lang Papers, Vol. 133, f 201. Lambeth Palace Library.

33. *Minutes of Evidence*, 1:151:3,464. When T. P. Griffithes, a solicitor, quoted Dr. Johnson before the Royal Commission in 1910, Lord Gorell asked if the quotation from Boswell's *Life of Johnson* should be considered outdated. Griffithes replied, 'It is a little old, but I submit it is equally good sense today'. *Ibid.*, 1:151:3,463.

34. *Ibid.*, 3:94:35,665.

35. Nancy Cott has used the term 'passionless' to represent 'the view that women lacked sexual aggressiveness, that their sexual appetites contributed a very minor part (if any at all) to their motivations, that lustfulness was simply uncharacteristic'. Cott argues that this view was 'a central tenet of Victorian sexual ideology'. N. Cott, 'Passionlessness: An Interpretation of Victorian Sexual Ideology, 1790–1850', *Signs*, Vol. 4 (Winter 1978):219–236.

36. *Parliamentary Debates* (Commons), 147 (13 August 1857):1542.

37. *Minutes of Evidence*, 2:410:22,583.

38. A. Holmes, *Hard Cases and Bad Laws: Divorce Reform in England, 1909–1937* (Ph.D. diss., Vanderbilt University, 1986), 114–115.

39. *Royal Commission on Divorce and Matrimonial Causes: Report* (1912), p. 88.

40. *Ibid.*, p. 191.

41. *Conference of Bishops of the Anglican Communion, Holden at Lambeth Palace, July 5 to August 7, 1920: Encyclical Letter from the Bishops, with the Resolutions and Reports* (London: SPCK, 1920), p. 114.

Church and State Diverge   57

42. *Parliamentary Debates* (Commons), 160 (2 March 1923):2355.
43. *Ibid.* (Lords), 54 (26 June 1923):596.
44. R. Lloyd, *The Church of England: 1900–1965* (London: SCM Press, 1966), p. 71.
45. Norman, p. 273.
46. K. Thompson, *Bureaucracy and Church Reform: The Organizational Response of the Church of England to Social Change 1800–1965* (Oxford: The Clarendon Press, 1970), pp. 175, 182.
47. Bell, pp. 1327–1328, 1339–1340.
48. *Ibid.*, pp. 1342, 1344, 1346–1347, 1351.
49. Norman, p. 342.
50. M. Grimley, *Citizenship, Community, and the Church of England: Liberal Anglican Theories of the State between the Wars* (Oxford: Clarendon Press, 2004), p. 166.
51. Bell, pp. 1361, 1365.
52. Lambeth Conference (1920), *Encyclical Letter from the Bishops, with the Resolutions and Reports*, p. 111.
53. *Ibid.*, pp. 109–111.
54. Lambeth Conference (1930), *Encyclical Letter from the Bishops with Resolutions and Reports* (London: SPCK, 1930), pp. 22, 42.
55. Holmes, *Hard Cases and Bad Laws: Divorce Reform in England, 1909–1937*, pp. 15–18.
56. 'Collusion in Divorce', *The Solicitors' Journal*, Vol. 74 (10 May 1930):291. One respondent went so far as to be photographed in bed with a woman who was not his wife. Such careful planning surely undermined the credibility of the evidence. 'A Novelty in Divorce Evidence', *The Solicitors' Journal*, Vol. 72 (14 January 1928):23.
57. Cretney, *Family Law in the Twentieth Century*, p. 811.
58. Convocation of Canterbury, Sitting together of Joint Committees on Marriage, Evidence of Sir John James Withers, MP, Solicitor, on 14 June 1932, p. 11. Lambeth Palace Library.
59. Other sources reveal collusive practices. Colonel J.C. Wedgwood, MP for Newcastle-under-Lyme, provided evidence of a 'hotel divorce' in 'Col. Wedgwood on His Divorce', *The Times* (30 June 1919):9. In her autobiography, Elsa Lanchester wrote that husbands would pay her £100 or more to 'spend one pure night in a hotel'. *Elsa Lanchester Herself* (New York: St. Martin's Press, 1983), p. 58.
60. A. Winnett, *Divorce and Remarriage in Anglicanism* (London: Macmillan & Co Ltd, 1958), p. 213.
61. Convocations of Canterbury and York, Joint Committees on Marriage, Evidence of the Right Hon. Lord Buckmaster, 8 July 1932, pp. 12–14. Lambeth Palace Library.
62. Bell, p. 999.
63. Convocation of Canterbury Joint Committee on Marriage, 'Four Questions on Marriage and Divorce: Summary of Answers'. Bell Papers, Vol. 147, ff 110, 114.
64. Convocations of Canterbury and York, *The Church and Marriage, Being the Report of the Joint Committees of the Convocations of Canterbury and York* (London: SPCK, 1935), p. 30.
65. *Ibid.*, pp. 23, 31.
66. *Ibid.*, p. 28; Appendix VI, Part B, p. 91.
67. *Ibid.*, pp. 34, 37.
68. Winnett, *Divorce and Remarriage in Anglicanism*, p. 216.
69. K. Kirk, *Marriage and Divorce* (London: Centenary Press, 1933), pp. 95–97
70. *Ibid.*, p. 117.
71. *Ibid.*, pp. 130, 137, 146–147.

58   *Church and State Diverge*

72. Winnett, *Divorce and Remarriage in Anglicanism*, p. 222.
73. If not otherwise noted, the account here is derived from P. Ziegler, *King Edward VIII: A Biography* (New York: Alfred A. Knopf, 1991); F. Donaldson, *Edward VIII: A Biography of the Duke of Windsor* (Philadelphia and New York: J. B. Lippincott Company, 1974); and S. Williams, *The People's King, the True Story of the Abdication* (New York: Palgrave Macmillan, 2003).
74. Donaldson, p. 246.
75. S. Cretney, 'The King and the King's Proctor: The Abdication Crisis and the Divorce Laws 1936–1937', *Law Quarterly Review* (October 2000):585.
76. J. Lockhart, *Cosmo Gordon Lang* (London: Hodder and Stoughton, 1949), pp. 397–398.
77. Diaries, Entry for 15 November 1936, Henson Papers, Vol. 68, f 95, Durham Cathedral Library.
78. Lockhart, p. 395.
79. *Ibid.*, p. 399. Lang later wrote, 'I am disposed to think that I might have *written* to Edward VIII if only to liberate my conscience. Yet almost certainly this would have invoked, even if any reply had been given, the sort of slight which *I* personally might have understood but to which the Archbishop of Canterbury ought not to be exposed'. Lang, 'Edward VIII. "The King's Matter"', Lang Papers, Vol. 318, f 110.
80. Donaldson, p. 259.
81. *Ibid.*, p. 240.
82. *Ibid.*, pp. 274–275, 284.
83. Lockhart, p. 405.
84. Henson Diaries, Entry for Friday, 18 December 1936, Vol. 68, f 167.
85. Lockhart, p. 406, note 1. The last three words, of course, are a play on 'Cantuar', the Latin title that the Archbishop of Canterbury used as a substitute for the surname.
86. Lang, 'Edward VIII. "The King's Matter"', Lang Papers, Vol. 318, f 115.
87. Letter from Stanley Baldwin to the Archbishop of Canterbury, dated 14 December 1936. Lang Papers, Vol. 192, f 379. Lang noted the praise in his account of the Abdication Crisis. Lang Papers, Vol. 318, ff 115–116.
88. O. Chadwick, *Hensley Henson: A Study in the Friction between Church and State* (Oxford: Clarendon Press, 1983), p. 230.
89. Ziegler, p. 314.
90. *Ibid.*, p. 307.
91. S. Bradford, *The Reluctant King: The Life and Reign of George VI 1895–1952* (New York: St. Martin's Press, 1989), p. 241.
92. Chadwick, p. 232.
93. Henson Diaries, Entry for Wednesday, 2 June 1937. Vol. 69, ff 251–252. Henson wrote in his diary, 'The local papers give great prominence to the unspeakable Jardine, whom they describe as a notable clergyman, renowned for his preaching & beloved by the people!!! When in . . . truth, the man is in bad repute, up to the ears in debt & loathed by his clerical brethren'. *Ibid.*
94. Enclosure in a letter from the Bishop of Fulham to the Archbishop of Canterbury, dated 2 June 1937. Lang Papers, Vol. 156, f 238.
95. Chadwick, p. 233.
96. Henson Diaries, Entry for 3 June 1937, Vol. 69, ff 253–254.
97. Chadwick, p. 232.
98. Donaldson, p. 347.
99. Letter from the Rev. A. C. Don, dated 15 June 1937. Lang Papers, Vol. 156, f 244.
100. Grimley, p. 189, quoting *Guardian* (8 January 1937):25.
101. J. Douglas, 'Plain Words to the Archbishop', untitled newspaper, undated. Lang Papers, Vol. 148, f 408.

Church and State Diverge 59

102. Sir Boyd Merriman to Sir Claud Schuster, 16 November 1936, Public Record Office, LC02, 1195, 3012/48.
103. R. Pound, *A. P. Herbert: A Biography* (London: Michael Joseph, 1976), pp. 35, 65–66, 127.
104. A. Herbert, *The Ayes Have It* (New York: Doubleday, Doran & Company, 1938), pp. 5, 11, 13.
105. *Ibid.*, p. 229.
106. *Ibid.*, pp. 65, 223.
107. Public Record Office, Lord Chancellor's Papers, LC02/1195, Cabinet 66 (36).
108. Cretney, *Family Law in the Twentieth Century*, p. 245.
109. Stephen Cretney reports that the legal profession had difficulty with this provision since it required the petitioner to prove a negative. *Ibid.*, p. 244, n. 291.
110. Letter from Mrs. Theodore Woods to Archbishop Lang, dated 21 November 1936, and Letter from Alan Don, Lang's chaplain and secretary, to Mrs. Woods, dated 23 January 1937. Lang Papers, Vol. 152, ff 290, 303.
111. Convocations of Canterbury and York, *The Church and Marriage*, p. 32.
112. Letter from Alan Don, Lang's chaplain and secretary, to the Bishop of Guildford, dated 1 December 1936. Lang Papers, Vol. 152, ff 292–293.
113. *Parliamentary Debates* (Lords), 5th series, 105 (24 June 1937):745.
114. *Ibid.*, 744, 751.
115. *Ibid.*, 747, 750.
116. *Ibid.*, 782.
117. *Ibid.*, 763, 765.
118. Henson later wrote of the debate in his diary that the Bishop of St. Albans 'was at his very worst: noisy, vulgar, familiar, buffoonish. The peers could not but laugh at an exhibition which was really pitiable'. Henson Diaries, Entry for Thursday, 24 June 1937, Vol. 69, f 298.
119. *Parliamentary Debates* (Lords) (24 June 1937):769.
120. *Ibid.*, 769–771, 774. Herbert later wrote a novel entitled *Made for Man* (London: Methuen, 1958).
121. *The Ayes Have It*, p. 173.
122. Chadwick, p. 224.
123. *The Ayes Have It*, pp. 121–122.
124. *Parliamentary Debates* (Lords) (19 July 1937):584.
125. Lockhart, p. 235.
126. J. Douglas, 'Plain Words to the Archbishop'. Lang Papers, Vol. 148, f 408.
127. Henson Diaries, Entry for 31 December 1936, Vol. 68, f 195.
128. Lockhart, p. 406.
129. Winnett, *Divorce and Remarriage in Anglicanism*, pp. 226–227.
130. G. Machin, 'Marriage and the Churches in the 1930s: Royal Abdication and Divorce Reform, 1936–7', *Journal of Ecclesiastical History*, Vol. 42 (January 1991):81.

3 Till Death them do Part
The Church and Divorce, 1945–1960

Is Marriage Indissoluble? The Church's Response in the 1940s

The Church of England confronted wartime challenges under new leadership after the resignation of Archbishop Lang on 21 January 1942. The obvious successor to Lang was William Temple, who became the new Archbishop of Canterbury after thirteen years as Archbishop of York. In the past Temple had adhered to the Church's definition of marriage as a lifelong union. He advocated strict standards for the Church in that he opposed the blessing of a remarriage after divorce. By the time that he became the Archbishop of Canterbury, Temple was alarmed by the increase in the number of divorces. According to his biographer, F.A. Iremonger, the Archbishop came to believe that the problem at the heart of the growth in divorce was 'the fulfillment of personal desire at the will of each individual, which he regarded as "disastrous for public policy"'.[1] The familiar argument that divorce was harmful to the community appeared even more serious in wartime. In an address to the Church of England Men's Society in July 1943, Temple emphasized the significance of sexual relationships:

> To use that function of our nature as an opportunity of passing amusement always involves treating another person as a plaything or a toy. That is destructive of the freedom we are fighting to maintain, for the heart of that freedom is the dignity of personality.[2]

From this perspective casual sexual relationships and marital infidelity appeared almost unpatriotic.

Archbishop Temple's untimely death at the age of 63 on 26 October 1944 removed a particularly articulate and widely respected opponent of divorce reform from the debate. On 2 January 1945, the Government nominated Geoffrey Fisher, Bishop of London, as the new Archbishop. An obituary notice after Fisher's death described his strength by comparing him to Temple: 'Fisher, without possessing Temple's particular gifts, was able to supply what his predecessor lacked. The hand of providence can be seen in giving the Church an administrator when the work of the prophet was done'.[3]

Fisher's gifts as an administrator would be tested as he became a central figure in the postwar debate over divorce reform.

During the Second World War, the number of divorce petitions had increased to the point that Lord Chancellor Jowitt told the Cabinet on 3 September 1945 that the courts could barely cope with the cases. In response, on 26 June 1946, the Government appointed a Committee on Procedure in Matrimonial Causes under the Chairmanship of Mr. Justice (later Lord) Denning to consider reforms that would expedite divorce suits and reduce costs.[4] In the House of Lords, on 28 November 1946, Archbishop Fisher responded to the goal of expediting divorce proceedings. Arguing that every divorce is 'a point of disease in the body politic', he noted the incongruity of the Denning Committee's assignment with regard to divorce: 'Here is a social disease, which the State recognizes as a social disease. The guardians of the public welfare know that they must deplore it; at the same time they are put into a position in which they must assist to spread it more quickly'. Although he 'deplored' the increase in the number of divorce petitions, Fisher acknowledged the responsibility of the state to make established legal procedures available to all citizens: 'If the community desires the divorce laws to be as they are, then the legal provisions must be accessible to all, and administered with efficiency and with reasonable rapidity'. Yet he also warned, 'You cannot cheapen divorce in terms of time and money without at the same time cheapening marriage in its spiritual significance'.[5] If divorce became more readily available, Fisher feared that couples would not take their marriage vows as seriously as they had when the union was more clearly defined as a lifelong legal contract.

Fisher regarded the establishment of 'machinery' for reconciliation as the 'most important duty' of the Denning Committee.[6] He had served as President of the Marriage Guidance Council, which had been formed as a voluntary organization registered as a charity in 1938. Since the Council was not specifically Christian, Fisher had experience working with professional specialists in medical, social, and legal fields to devise appropriate means of saving marriages. He felt strongly that the State, and not just the Church, should provide the means for encouraging reconciliation before a couple resorted to divorce. In the summer of 1946 he gave evidence to that effect before the Denning Committee, arguing that the State should play an active role in helping to preserve marriages because divorce threatened social stability.[7] While recognizing the value of attempts to achieve reconciliation, the Denning Committee also realized that the English people would be suspicious of 'official supervision or interference in the private affairs of individuals'.[8] Archbishop Fisher agreed and favored public subsidies to voluntary organizations, rather than the establishment of government agencies, as a means of saving marriages. He told the House of Lords that 'the work can be done only by voluntary societies. It is essentially personal and pastoral; it is essentially spiritual and it delves deeply into personal lives'.[9]

62 The Church and Divorce, 1945–1960

In 1947, the same year that the Denning Committee reported, Robert Mortimer, the Regius Professor of Moral and Pastoral Theology at Oxford, published a revision of T.A. Lacey's influential *Marriage in Church and State*. When the book first appeared in 1912, Lacey had written of divorce: 'I believe that in point of fact there can be no such thing; marriage is a natural relation which can no more be dissolved by law than the relation of brother and sister'.[10] Mortimer agreed that marriage is 'indissoluble by natural law'. Indeed, in rewriting the section of Lacey's book dealing with the teaching about divorce in the Gospels, he referred to the statements of Jesus as 'clear, emphatic, and uncompromising'. Whereas Lacey had devoted attention to the Matthaean Exception, Mortimer, influenced by New Testament criticism, wrote, 'We may therefore dismiss this exceptive clause—save for fornication—as being meaningless'.[11] For Christians, in Mortimer's view, the marriage bond could not be dissolved. Both Mortimer and Kenneth Kirk, in a new edition of *Marriage and Divorce* (first published in 1933 and revised in 1948), confirmed the indissolubility of marriage.[12]

Yet, by the late 1940s, the term 'indissolubility' itself appeared to be ambiguous. The Lambeth Conference of 1948 appointed a Committee to study 'The Church's Discipline in Marriage'. In an appendix on 'Indissolubility', the Committee described two views of the term's meaning:

> On the one hand there is the view that there is an essential element in the marriage relationship between husband and wife, which by its very nature persists till death, whatever the circumstances, and which no power on earth can terminate. According to such, divorce is not simply sinful; it is impossible. . . . The other view . . . regards the indissolubility of marriage, not so much as a fact, as an obligation which for Christians has an absolute character. It follows that, by the sin of one or both partners, the personal relationship in marriage can, in fact, be so completely destroyed as to be equivalent to the dissolution of the marriage bond by death. . . . The possibility of divorce, although always to be deplored as defeating God's absolute intention for marriage, cannot always be ruled out.[13]

According to the Committee's definition, marriage was both 'a holy estate, instituted by God and . . . involving the union for life of one man and one woman to the exclusion of all others' and a contract, 'created by the free, competent, and open consent of the parties who contract it', and 'not terminable by either party: it establishes a permanent relationship'.[14] Although the Committee stated that the contract was 'not terminable by either party', they did not state that the union was indissoluble.

Disagreements over the interpretations of 'indissolubility' also prompted the Convocations to revise the proposed Canons that had been drafted by the Archbishop's Commission on Canon Law, whose Report had been published in 1947. The proposed Canon XXXVI, entitled 'Of Holy Matrimony', had read: 'The Church of England affirms, as Our Lord's principle

The Church and Divorce, 1945–1960 63

and standard of Marriage, a life-long and indissoluble union'. The Convocation of Canterbury changed the definition to read: 'The Church of England affirms, according to our Lord's teaching, that marriage is a union permanent in its nature and lifelong', while the York Convocation's revision read: 'The Church of England affirms as Our Lord's principle and standard of marriage a lifelong permanent union'.[15] Marriage was defined as a lifelong union, but not one that was impossible to dissolve.

A. R. Winnett, whose influential *Divorce and Remarriage in Anglicanism* was published in 1958, described the decisions of the Convocations and the Lambeth Conference of 1948 not to use the word 'indissoluble' as possibly indicating 'a doubt whether the notion of a *vinculum* has validity apart from the personal relationship of the parties in marriage'. The concept of a *vinculum*, a metaphysical bond that humans could not break, had long been at the heart of the argument that marriage was indissoluble. According to Winnett, pastoral experience in counseling those whose marriages had broken down had led many of the clergy to question the traditional understanding of indissolubility.[16] Frequently, it was difficult to discern a *vinculum* in the 'hard cases'. The recent increases in divorce rates appeared to undermine the concept of the indissolubility of marriage, and the Church found it increasingly difficult to maintain that principle.

The Lambeth Conference of 1948 constituted the first meeting of that assembly of Anglican bishops since 1930. Depression and war had transformed society during the past eighteen years, and the Committee assigned to study the Church's marriage discipline had to take those changes into consideration. The Committee Report stated, 'The truth is that public opinion in favour of permanence in marriage has gravely declined, and divorce is ceasing to carry a public stigma'.[17] Since the bishops on the Committee believed that the 'two strongest controls over conduct are religion and public opinion', they recommended maintaining the Church's definition of marriage as a lifelong union, declaring, in a phrase that would be repeated often, 'We cannot condone what our Lord condemns'.[18] While 'public opinion' might accept divorce, the Church would not.

Although the Church officially maintained the definition of marriage as a lifelong union, the clergy had a responsibility to offer pastoral care to those individuals who had remarried after divorce. The bishops stated in the Committee Report:

> On the one hand, therefore, discipline must not be so rigorous as to exclude from the Church's pastoral care those who have re-married after divorce. On the other hand it must not be so lax as to affront the consciences of Church people, or encourage the idea that divorce does not matter.[19]

On that basis the Committee considered two questions of discipline: remarriage in church after divorce and admission to Holy Communion for those

64 *The Church and Divorce, 1945–1960*

who had remarried after divorce. The bishops stated, 'While recognizing a difference of theological opinion, we are yet agreed on the matter of Marriage Discipline'.[20] In Resolution 94 they affirmed that a divorced person whose former partner was still living could not be married according to the rites of the Church. According to Resolution 96, the case of any divorced person who had remarried and who wished to be admitted to Holy Communion should be referred to the bishop.[21] Despite dramatic social changes and theological disagreements over indissolubility, the bishops decided to maintain strict standards.

Royal Commission on Marriage and Divorce, 1951–1956

While the Church reviewed its marriage doctrine and discipline, the State confronted both an increase in the number of divorce petitions and dissatisfaction with existing laws. Since separation by mutual consent was not a ground for divorce, individuals who were legally married but who had been separated for many years frequently established stable, but illicit, unions with other partners. The birth of illegitimate children to those couples was viewed as a serious social problem. One possible solution was to make separation for seven years or more a ground for divorce.

That reform was presented to Parliament in a Matrimonial Causes Bill introduced by Eirene White, a newly elected Labour MP, in 1951. The proposed legislation would have added a new ground for divorce in that either spouse of a couple who had lived apart for seven years, with no reasonable hope of reconciliation, could file for divorce without having to prove a matrimonial offence.[22] White's Bill raised concerns in the Church of England. If both parties agreed to end the marriage, then the dissolution was divorce by consent, a possibility that threatened the Church's definition of marriage as a lifelong union because either party could end it. Another concern was a figure who continued to haunt divorce reformers—the innocent wife abandoned by her husband after many years of marriage and divorced against her will. Addressing that possibility, White's Bill included a provision that would enable the court to refuse a decree if a petitioning husband could not demonstrate that he had made provisions for the financial maintenance of his family.[23] Although the Matrimonial Causes Bill was given a Second Reading by a vote of 131 to 60 on 9 March 1951, White agreed to withdraw it after the Government promised to appoint a Royal Commission to review divorce reform.[24] For the second time in fifty years, the debate moved from Parliament to a Royal Commission.

A comparison of the Archbishops' attempts to influence the selection of Royal Commissioners in 1909 and in 1951 indicates a significant shift in the relationship between Church and State in England. In 1951 the Archbishops of Canterbury and York hoped to participate in the selection of the Commissioners as had Archbishops Davidson and Lang in 1909. On 12 March 1951, the Archbishop of York, Cyril Garbett, wrote to Archbishop Fisher.

The Church and Divorce, 1945–1960   65

Garbett opposed the appointment of a Royal Commission because it would probably serve to encourage the extension of the grounds for divorce. On the other hand, since White's Matrimonial Causes Bill (what Garbett called 'this wretched Bill') had received a Second Reading, the Archbishop of York realized that a Commission could also serve the Church's purpose by delaying the passage of legislation. In advising Archbishop Fisher against attempting to play an active role in the appointment of a Commission, Garbett revealed significant Parliamentary concern about the role of bishops in the political process. Garbett wrote that 'a number of the members of the House of Commons are at the moment apparently very sensitive about "episcopal interference", and quite an absurd cry might be raised about archepiscopal interference'.[25]

Concerns about the appearance of 'archepiscopal interference', however, did not stop the Archbishops from attempting to exert their influence in the appointment of a Royal Commission in 1951. Just as Archbishop Davidson had met with Prime Minister Asquith and the Lord Chancellor to attempt to persuade them to appoint representatives of the Church to the Royal Commission in 1909, so did Archbishop Fisher communicate with Lord Chancellor Jowitt in 1951. The Prime Minister's Office announced the decision to appoint a Royal Commission on 14 March 1951, and five days later the Archbishop of Canterbury wrote to the Lord Chancellor. Fisher said that, while he had agreed with Jowitt's dislike of the idea of a Royal Commission on marriage in the past, he thought that the appointment of such a Commission was now inevitable. He approved of the Government's decision to establish a Commission because he recognized the value in a thorough investigation of the issues. Jowitt replied that he hoped to be able to meet privately with Fisher to seek the Archbishop's advice. The Lord Chancellor also suggested that Fisher should begin to think of individuals that he might want to recommend as members of the Royal Commission.[26] Having indicated that he wanted to consult the Archbishop of Canterbury regarding the Royal Commission, the Lord Chancellor was compelled to retract that suggestion two months later, after his colleagues discouraged him from meeting with Fisher.[27] In 1909 Archbishop Davidson had been in direct contact with both the Prime Minister and the Lord Chancellor about the appointment of the Royal Commission; in 1951 the Cabinet discouraged the Lord Chancellor from even speaking to the Archbishop of Canterbury. Clearly the leaders of the Church of England would not be able to play a significant role in the selection of the Royal Commissioners in 1951.

In a memorandum to the Cabinet, Lord Chancellor Jowitt addressed the question of whether or not bishops and other representatives of the churches should be invited to serve on the Royal Commission. One problem with including such representatives was that churches other than the Church of England would require representation, and the size of the Commission would have to be increased dramatically. Beyond that logistical consideration was the understanding that representatives from Christian churches would be committed to a particular point of view with regard to divorce.

66   The Church and Divorce, 1945–1960

Those who thought that representatives of the churches should be appointed argued that the public would expect that view to be respected, especially since there was not a clear distinction between the Christian and the secular view of marriage in 1951. Others argued that representatives of an institution that had publicly declared that marriage was indissoluble would not be open-minded. With regard to the question of objectivity, the Lord Chancellor cited the Report of a Departmental Committee on the Procedure of Royal Commissions, which had stated in 1910 that 'those selected as Commissioners should, as far as possible, be persons who have not committed themselves so deeply on any side of the questions involved . . . as to render the probability of an impartial inquiry . . . practically impossible'.[28] Ultimately the Government decided to appoint impartial individuals. Whereas the Archbishop of York and two other Commissioners with close ties to the Church of England had served on the Royal Commission of 1909, no recognized representative of the Church of England served on the Royal Commission appointed in 1951.[29]

The determination to avoid those who held strong views was evident in the selection of a Chair. When the Lord Chancellor asked Lord Eustace Percy if he would serve in that position, Percy agreed to let his name go forward, but he wanted to let the Prime Minister and the Lord Chancellor know that he strictly adhered to the principle of the indissolubility of marriage on the basis of his religious beliefs. Percy opposed the suggestion that secular marriage laws in England should be considered apart from religious principles. If the Royal Commission were required to consider reforms on that basis—specifically the extension of the grounds for divorce—then he was not qualified to serve as Chairman.[30] Since Percy was clearly not impartial, the Cabinet decided not to appoint him as Chair and instead offered the position to Fergus Morton, whom Stephen Cretney has described as 'an eminent Chancery Judge . . . known to the Lord Chancellor's Department for his "safe" handling in the previous year of the *Committee on the Law of Intestate Succession*'.[31] Morton was certainly not the reformer that Lord Gorell had been, nor were the other members of the Royal Commission as clearly aligned on the issues as the Commissioners of 1909 had been.

The Archbishops were disappointed that there was no clerical representative since, as the Archbishop of York wrote to Archbishop Fisher, a Commissioner would have more opportunities to present arguments based on the Church's position from within rather than outside of the Royal Commission. In his presidential address to the Convocation of York, Garbett publicly expressed regret that the Commission did not include an official representative of the Church of England because the 'Church still took the largest number of marriages in this country, and many of its bishops and clergy had an intimate knowledge of the problems which would be discussed'.[32]

Nevertheless, the Archbishops were able to put their views strongly before the Royal Commission through the testimony of a prominent witness—the

The Church and Divorce, 1945–1960   67

Archbishop of Canterbury himself. In preparing his testimony, Archbishop Fisher decided not to emphasize Christian doctrine but rather to base his arguments on 'national well-being'.[33] In the memorandum that he submitted to the Royal Commission for consideration before he testified, Fisher stressed the importance of basing recommendations regarding divorce reform on a 'general principle'. He argued that if the only principle applied to the consideration of divorce reform was to be simply that of 'relieving hardships and injustices', then the Commissioners would be attempting to cure symptoms 'without diagnosing the causes [of] . . . the underlying disease'. Fisher suggested that a general principle could be found in the Book of Common Prayer, where marriage was defined as 'a union permanent in its nature and life-long'.[34] Fisher acknowledged that, since the Royal Commission was considering reform of laws that affected the entire population and not just Christians, it 'could not base its recommendations solely on the grounds of Christian doctrine'. The Archbishop believed, however, that adherence to the Christian standard would benefit all citizens and, therefore, 'whether explicitly on Christian grounds or simply on grounds of national well-being, the principle should be to adhere as far as possible to the Christian standard'.[35]

The reliance on arguments based on social utility distinguished Fisher's testimony in 1952 from clerical testimony in 1910. Whereas the earlier witnesses had concerned themselves with the validity of the Matthaean Exception and other Scriptural references to divorce, Fisher said that the general principle that he proposed could stand apart from Christian grounds and rest solely on the ground of 'national well-being'. Fisher stated, 'It is therefore not relevant to argue before the Commission the meaning of particular texts and other points of scholarship'.[36] The contrast with testimony in 1910 is striking. The earlier Royal Commission had heard witnesses such as Charles Gore, Hensley Henson, William Sanday, Ralph Inge, and Hastings Rashdall, whose views on the indissolubility of marriage varied widely. The conflict of opinion led the Commissioners to conclude that they could not base their recommendations on religious considerations. In 1952 the Archbishop of Canterbury based his testimony on the good of the community as a whole. He thereby avoided the disagreements over Scriptural passages that had weakened the arguments of clerical witnesses in 1910.

With regard to Eirene White's proposal to extend the grounds for divorce to include separation of seven years, Archbishop Fisher expressed concern for women who could be divorced against their will. He stated that the change 'rests upon no principle other than the convenience of the offending party. It goes beyond the evils of divorce by consent, and introduces compulsory divorce against the legally innocent party'. Bishop Wand told the Royal Commission of a more serious objection on the part of the Church to White's proposal. If individuals married with the understanding that the contract could be dissolved after a seven-year separation, then 'marriage could no longer be regarded as a life-long union'. The Church would find it

68   *The Church and Divorce, 1945–1960*

difficult to recognize a State marriage that could be ended on such grounds.[37] The Church wanted to maintain its recognition of civil marriages.

In his memorandum, Archbishop Fisher also emphasized the importance of protecting the interests of children: 'It should be recognized that the loss to children and to the social order may outweigh the benefit (so far as it is a benefit) brought to married persons whose hardships are relieved by divorce'.[38] The Mothers' Union, whose very name indicated an interest in children, also took up the cause before the Royal Commission. Of particular concern was the problem of children in unhappy homes. When asked if divorce might lead to a healthier environment for such children, Rosamond Fisher, President of the Mothers' Union and wife of the Archbishop of Canterbury, replied, 'We are led to believe that almost any home is better than none'. Evidently Mrs. Fisher also believed that, after a divorce, one home was better than two; she recommended denying one parent access to the children. When she was asked, 'You really are suggesting that, even where both parents think it is sensible to divide the children, during the school holidays, for instance, this should be stopped by the court?' Mrs. Fisher replied:

> I do feel that to deny access to the one parent may impose most severe hardships on the parent, and possibly for a time on the children, but in the end, if they could be brought up by one of the parents it would probably make for greater stability in their lives.[39]

Mrs. Fisher believed that many parents were putting their own happiness ahead of the welfare of their children, and she wanted the divorce courts to put the interests of the children first.

The Modern Churchmen's Union was another organization identified with the Church of England whose representatives appeared as witnesses before the Royal Commission. In a Memorandum submitted in advance, they identified the organization as 'a society of clergy and laymen, founded in 1898 for the advancement of liberal religious thought'. Although the Memorandum stated that the Union was 'as anxious as anyone else to uphold the Christian ideal of marriage', the members also believed 'that this ideal is best maintained not by the rigorist view that marriage is incapable of dissolution but by the recognition that in certain cases divorce is necessary and permissible as being the lesser of two evils'. The Memorandum added: 'We know that this view has the support of a large number of clergy and, we believe, of the majority of the laity of the Church of England'. To support that claim, in an Appendix to the Memorandum, the Union presented evidence from the Diocese of London regarding remarriage after divorce. A questionnaire sent to incumbents in 1947 had posed the question:

> Do you consider that the Church ought invariably to refuse to solemnize the marriages of divorced persons, or are there, in your opinion, cases

The Church and Divorce, 1945–1960   69

in which this question should be decided by a Church Court constituted for the purpose?

Of the responses, 290 favored 'invariable' refusal to solemnize remarriage in church, while 218 did not.[40] Those figures revealed the existence of substantial disagreement among the clergy over the question of remarriage in church after divorce.

The Union's Memorandum emphasized the right of the incumbent to make the decision about whether or not a divorced person could be remarried in church. The Matrimonial Causes Act of 1937 had granted the clergy freedom of choice with regard to remarriage, but the Church had instructed the clergy to refuse to solemnize the marriage of a divorced person in church. The Modern Churchmen's Union claimed that the Church was denying 'the legal right of the clergy to exercise their own discretion in the conducting of such marriages'.[41] Based on the 1947 survey, the Union had concluded that many among the clergy favored allowing remarriage in church. Yet the Church, through official statements and bishops' instructions, strongly discouraged the clergy from exercising their legal right to conduct such services.

The Royal Commission had been appointed to consider reforms to the secular laws and not to comment on the marriage discipline of the Church of England. Indeed, when the Chair began questioning the representatives of the Modern Churchmen's Union, he said that the questions of the remarriage and admission to Communion of divorced persons were 'outside our terms of reference'.[42] On the question of extending the grounds for divorce, which *was* an issue to be considered by the Commission, Dr. W.R. Matthews, the Dean of St. Paul's who testified on behalf of the Modern Churchmen's Union, said that the group did not want to extend the grounds and were 'quite definitely opposed to . . . what might be described as divorce by consent'. According to the Union's Memorandum, the termination of a marriage only because 'the parties have become dissatisfied with the state of [the] marriage or with each other' would not only be 'contrary to Christian principles' but also 'against public policy'. Although Dr. Matthews testified that the Modern Churchmen's Union thought that the Church of England's policy on the admission of remarried divorced persons to Communion was 'unduly rigorous', the group did agree with Archbishop Fisher that basing secular marriage laws on Christian principles would benefit the community as a whole.[43] On that point these witnesses associated with the Church of England were united.

On 20 July 1953, after the Commissioners had stopped receiving evidence and were reviewing various recommendations, Lord Morton wrote to the Archbishop of Canterbury to suggest a dramatic plan: 'All couples marrying in England after a specified date shall have the choice between marriage in a Christian Church, which will be dissoluble only by death, and marriage in a Registry Office, to which the ordinary Divorce Laws will apply'.[44] Morton

70 *The Church and Divorce, 1945–1960*

had not recommended the plan to his colleagues on the Royal Commission when he wrote to Archbishop Fisher, who raised strong arguments against the proposal. In a letter to Morton dated 22 July 1953, Fisher wrote:

> I do not think any organized Church would tolerate Parliamentary action to lay down what discipline they must observe in the matter of marriages. . . . I think there would be very strong Parliamentary objection to passing Statute Laws which deprive certain citizens of the right to avail themselves of the statutory provisions for divorce.[45]

In a memorandum on a subsequent conversation with Lord Morton, Fisher reiterated that neither the Church nor Parliament would agree to deny Christians 'a civil liberty granted to other citizens'. As an alternative to Morton's plan, the idea occurred to Fisher that every person to be married could make the choice:

> Either he could be married, whether in Church or in the Registry does not matter, either he could be married by a formula which included the words 'till death us do part' [or not]. Those who married with that formula or its equivalent would not subsequently have any right of approach to the Divorce Courts.

Fisher told Morton that, if he wanted to raise the standards of marriage, he should offer the possibility of 'a marriage with no possibility of appeal to a Divorce Court' to all citizens.[46]

Neither Morton's nor Fisher's proposal could seriously be considered as possible reforms because there were too many objections, but the private exchange between the two men reveals several important points. Morton, who was selected as an 'impartial' Chair of the Royal Commission, was clearly committed to limiting the number of divorces. Allowing the Church to enforce the definition of marriage as a lifelong union evidently seemed to him to be an answer to the dilemma of restricting divorce while still offering relief to the hard cases. While his plan may have appeared to be a reasonable compromise to Morton, Archbishop Fisher's response demonstrated his dislike of a proposal that would have distinguished civil marriages from marriages in church. In his memorandum on Morton's plan, Fisher also revealed disagreement within the Church of England on the question of divorce:

> Such a proposal would split the Church of England from top to bottom. There are many Clergy and a great number of laity in the Church of England who would maintain that sometimes divorce is the right course, or at least the best course, and that sometimes those who have been divorced are right to marry again.[47]

Fisher had attempted to present a 'united front' to the Royal Commission, but clearly there were significant divisions within the Church.

The Church and Divorce, 1945–1960   71

In their Report, published in March of 1956, the Morton Commissioners sought to present a unanimity that did not exist. They stated, 'We are, with one exception [Lord Walker], all agreed that the present law based on the doctrine of the matrimonial offence should be retained', yet they revealed substantial differences of opinion in their arguments. Nine of eighteen Commissioners opposed introducing 'the doctrine of breakdown of marriage' (as opposed to the commission of a matrimonial offence), while nine other Commissioners favored granting a divorce after a seven-year separation, which they deemed evidence that the marriage had broken down. Five of the latter nine would require the agreement of both spouses, while four agreed that the objection of one of the spouses should not be an absolute bar to divorce.[48] The recommendations were far from unanimous.

One Commissioner, the Scottish judge Lord Walker, opposed the retention of the matrimonial offence as the basis of the divorce laws. Lord Walker was not a liberal reformer who favored divorce by consent; rather, he believed that the matrimonial offence had sometimes become 'a technical cause of action without a real cause for complaint', resulting in the dissolution of some marriages that might otherwise be maintained. Since existing laws enabled a husband and wife to agree to divorce and then to end their marriage by presenting a false suit to the court, Lord Walker thought that divorce by consent was already effectively available. He favored abandoning the matrimonial offence and replacing that principle with 'a provision that marriage should be indissoluble unless, having lived apart for not less than three years, either party shews that the marriage has broken down'.[49]

The divisions within the Morton Commission on the fundamental question of the matrimonial offence made it difficult for the Government to introduce legislation extending the grounds for divorce. Lord Mancroft, the Under-Secretary of State for the Home Department, had actively promoted the appointment of the Royal Commission in 1951. Regretfully, he told the House of Lords in the debate on 24 October 1956, that, in light of the equal division among the Commissioners, 'I am afraid that I must tell the House that Her Majesty's Government can hold out no present hope of being able to introduce legislation dealing with this'. He added, 'If the Royal Commission had demonstrated an unquestionable demand for major reform along one particular line or another, then the situation might well have been different'.[50] Lord Chancellor Kilmuir agreed with Mancroft's assessment. The divisions among the Commissioners meant that 'no-one could possibly expect a Government to announce legislation on this subject'.[51] The Report did not inspire reform.

Bishops in the House of Lords appeared relieved by the Report. Robert Mortimer, who had expressed the view that marriage is indissoluble in his revision of Lacey's *Marriage in Church and State* in 1947, had been appointed Bishop of Exeter in 1949. In that role, he told the House of Lords in 1956 that he welcomed the Royal Commission Report because 'the Church has been saved a very great embarrassment by the fact that the Commission have not been able to recommend divorce by consent or any alteration of the existing doctrine that divorce is for matrimonial offence'.

72 The Church and Divorce, 1945–1960

Mortimer then explained why a divorce based on a matrimonial offence was acceptable to the Church:

> One party to a marriage is released from the duty of discharging the obligations of that marriage . . . because, on account of the conduct, past, present or continuing, of the other partner, the discharge of those obligations has become intolerable or incompatible with personal safety, physical or mental. That being the condition, a higher authority relieves the party from the duty of discharging all or part of the obligations of the marriage.

If the State accepted divorce by consent in place of the matrimonial offence, the divorce decree, 'so far from being the action of a higher authority, would be merely an act of notarial registration'. The Church would be 'embarrassed' because, in such a system, the clergy would not know if a couple intended to establish a lifelong union or to contract a marriage 'terminable at will by either or both of them'. Accordingly, the Church was 'profoundly grateful to the Commission for having reported as they have'.[52] Surely Mortimer was also grateful that he did not have to reconcile his description of a 'higher authority' relieving a spouse from the duty of maintaining a marriage with his earlier stated view that marriage is indissoluble.

The participation of representatives of the Church of England in the official consideration of divorce reform between 1951 and 1956 differed significantly from the roles they played between 1909 and 1912. In 1909 Archbishop Randall Davidson was determined for the Church to be influential in any official consideration of the State's laws of marriage and divorce. The Government appointed three representatives of the Church to serve on the Royal Commission in 1909, and that Commission scrupulously considered different viewpoints within the Church. Ultimately the Commissioners decided in 1912 that they could not base their recommendations on a consideration of Christian principles, both because Christians disagreed over those principles and because Parliament must legislate for all citizens and not just Christians. By the time that the Government appointed another Royal Commission in 1951, it was clear that the Church no longer played a decisive role in the formulation of the State's laws of marriage and divorce. Both the lack of representatives from the Church on the Morton Commission of 1951 and its minimal attention to Church doctrine illustrated the shift. The Morton Commission did receive evidence and hear testimony from three groups associated with the Church of England, but they did not review the detailed testimony on theological and doctrinal issues that had required so much time and study on the part of the Gorell Commission. In their Report, the Morton Commissioners stated that they could not base their recommendations on Christian principles because the State 'has to legislate for all its citizens, whatever their religious beliefs may be',[53] a conclusion remarkably similar to that of the Gorell Commission.

The Church and Divorce, 1945–1960 73

The 1956 Report was not as persuasive as the 1912 recommendations because the Morton Commissioners were unable to reach the consensus about proposed reforms that the Gorell Commission had achieved. In 1912 the Royal Commission issued a strong Majority Report recommending the extension of the grounds for divorce, but the Church's representatives were able to write an influential Minority Report that impeded implementation of the Majority's recommendations. The Morton Commissioners were unable to issue Majority and Minority reports because they were equally divided into two groups of nine. That division made it impossible for them to issue conclusive recommendations.

Since the Morton Commissioners could not recommend significant changes to the divorce laws, disappointed reformers were bitterly critical of the Report.[54] Among the most scathing comments were those of the social scientist O.R. McGregor in *Divorce in England: A Centenary Study*, published in 1957. Citing the lack of statistical data and other evidence from the social sciences, McGregor described the Morton Commission Report as 'one of the most impressive collections of unsupported cliché ever subsidized by the taxpayer'. As an example of the problem, McGregor referred to the crucial question of whether it was more damaging to a child to live in an unhappy home or to endure separation from a parent through divorce. Both the National Association for Mental Health and the British Medical Association had emphasized to the Commission the absence of the scientific evidence necessary to address the question, and yet the Mothers' Union had stated in their evidence, 'We are led to believe that almost any home is better than none'. The absence of a professional social scientist on the Commission further contributed to the lack of attention to evidence from that area. In McGregor's words:

> No Commissioner possessed expert knowledge of the considerable body of modern sociological research on such topics, or was equipped with an understanding of the techniques and potentialities of social investigation developed during the last twenty years. Lacking such essential assistance, the Morton Commission joined the Jumblies and went to sea in a sieve.[55]

McGregor's praise of the Gorell Commission sharpened his criticism of the Morton Commission. He described the 1912 Report as 'a model of relevance, clarity and the thorough analysis of evidence', adding that the Gorell Commission 'defined the questions at issue, sifted and secured evidence relevant to them, clarified opposing points of view, and made straightforward recommendations'. Their Report, McGregor wrote, was characterized by 'intellectual distinction'.[56] In a different vein, he claimed that the 1956 Report

> contributes nothing to our knowledge, and fails even to clarify and define opposing viewpoints or to facilitate public discussion. . . . It is a matter of opinion whether the Morton Commission is intellectually the

74   *The Church and Divorce, 1945–1960*

worst Royal Commission of the twentieth century, but there can be no dispute that its Report is the most unreadable and confused.[57]

McGregor's attack may have been exaggerated, but it was effective. Stephen Cretney has written that 'McGregor's book has been influential in creating an enduring and strongly unfavourable perception of the Morton Commission'.[58]

In more recent years criticism of the 1956 Report has reinforced McGregor's assessment of the Royal Commission's narrow perspective. Carol Smart has linked the Morton Commission to the Church of England in looking to the past for guidelines in regulating marriage.[59] Both the Royal Commission and the Church viewed the new emphasis on personal fulfillment in relationships, in place of the traditional emphasis on the duties of marriage, as a dangerous symbol of the moral decline of the country. According to the Morton Commissioners, the remedy for the problem was 'fostering in the individual the will to do his duty by the community'.[60] From that perspective individuals should maintain their marriages whether those unions were happy or not. While the Royal Commission officially encouraged self-sacrifice as a means of coping with the social changes that challenged the strict view of marriage that they sought to maintain, the nine Commissioners who had favored recognition of the breakdown of marriage had argued:

> We see no benefit to society, to the individual or to the State in maintaining marriages in name which are no longer, and on all foreseeable estimates will never be, marriages in fact and which secure few or none of the purposes for which marriage was designed.[61]

All of the Royal Commissioners could not endorse that position in 1956, but less than a decade later a group appointed by the Archbishop of Canterbury would reach the same conclusion when they stated, 'If a marriage is broken and dead from the sociological point of view, it is not upholding the sanctity of marriage to say that it still exists'.[62] That argument was not completely persuasive in 1956, and the Morton Commission was unable to issue effective recommendations. The failure to achieve reform in the late 1950s meant that unhappy couples would continue to attempt to deceive the courts in order to end their marriages. The perception remained, according to Smart, that secular laws were 'thoroughly hypocritical' and that the position of the Church was 'harsh and unyielding'.[63] The Church of England may have welcomed the 1956 Report as a victory in the continuing struggle, but many observers saw it as an uninformed step backward.

Princess Margaret and Group Captain Peter Townsend

While the Royal Commission was deliberating, the Church confronted another crisis within the Royal Family over the remarriage of divorced persons. Group Captain Peter Townsend, a decorated Battle of Britain pilot,

The Church and Divorce, 1945–1960 75

became equerry to King George VI in 1944. Townsend had married Rosemary Pawle in 1941, and they had two sons. First the war and then Townsend's service to the King kept the couple separated for long periods. The marriage foundered, and Townsend was granted a divorce in 1952 on the ground of his wife's adultery.[64]

Princess Margaret, the younger daughter of George VI, had first met Townsend when he became her father's equerry. The two became better acquainted in 1947, when Townsend accompanied the Royal Family on a tour of South Africa. On the death of George VI in 1952, Townsend became comptroller to the Queen Mother and was appointed an equerry to the new Queen, Elizabeth II. Townsend and Princess Margaret grew closer, and in April of 1953, he proposed. When the couple told the Queen, she was sympathetic, as was the Queen Mother, but both women inevitably compared the situation to the Abdication Crisis. Although Princess Margaret was not a reigning monarch, she was third in the line of succession. Under the Royal Marriages Act of 1772, she was required to have the Queen's consent to her marriage. However sympathetic the Queen may have been to her sister, she was the Supreme Governor of the Church of England and could not consent to a marriage between the Princess and a divorced man. After she turned 25, however, the Princess could marry without the permission of the Queen, although she would still need the consent of Parliament. Princess Margaret agreed to her sister's request to wait for a year. During that time her relationship with Peter Townsend became known to the world at Elizabeth II's Coronation on 2 June 1953. While waiting for her carriage after following her mother's procession out of Westminster Abbey, Princess Margaret saw Peter Townsend and, in what was seen as 'a gesture of extreme tenderness and intimacy', brushed a piece of fluff from his uniform. Within two weeks the press was publishing speculative comments, and the Queen and her Government confronted a difficult decision.[65]

When Prime Minister Churchill first heard the news, he exclaimed, 'What a delightful match! A lovely young royal lady married to a gallant young airman, safe from the perils and horrors of war!' His wife intervened to remind him of the difficulties. When he consulted his Cabinet, Churchill found that almost all of them advised against the marriage of Princess Margaret to Peter Townsend. In an audience with the Queen on 16 June, the Prime Minister told her that both the British Cabinet and the Commonwealth Prime Ministers opposed the marriage. He agreed with her other advisers that Peter Townsend should be sent away. When the Group Captain was given a choice of Brussels, Johannesburg, or Singapore as his next posting, he chose Brussels, a location that would place him closer to both the Princess and his two young sons. The Queen Mother and Princess Margaret left for an official trip to Rhodesia on 30 June, and Townsend was sent to Brussels on 15 July, before the two returned.[66] The Princess and the Group Captain still hoped to marry.

Archbishop Fisher became involved in a bit of a contretemps with the press over the controversy in April of 1955, while he was in Africa to inaugurate

76 The Church and Divorce, 1945–1960

the Central African province of the Church. *The Times* correspondent in Cape Town reported that the Archbishop had 'discounted recent speculation about Princess Margaret's marriage plans'. From Grahamstown the next day, the same correspondent wrote:

> Dr. Fisher denied here to-day that he used the words 'There is no truth in the rumour' when asked at Cape Town yesterday whether Princess Margaret and Group Captain Peter Townsend were to marry. He said he had replied 'No comment' to a question about the rumour. He had said the rumour was a stunt, 'and a most offensive one at that,' by a few English newspapers.[67]

After he returned to England, the Archbishop was questioned again about the statements that he had made in Africa. According to *The Times*, 'He said emphatically that he had made no comment in replying to questions concerning Princess Margaret'.[68] Despite his denial, the perception persisted that the Archbishop had stated that there was no truth to the rumour that Princess Margaret and Peter Townsend were to be married. In his autobiography, Townsend wrote of the reports on the Archbishop's statements in Africa that 'he was denying a fact to which the Queen, Head of the Church, was privy and upon which she had sought his advice. It was a sorry thing to see this good man joining the ranks of those who knew the facts, but manipulated them in public as they saw fit'.[69] In the confusion over his statements in Africa, Archbishop Fisher did not appear as an effective leader of the Church of England.

On 21 August 1955, Princess Margaret celebrated her twenty-fifth birthday. She was reunited with Group Captain Townsend in London on 13 October 1955, and reporters pursued the couple relentlessly.[70] Despite the popular enthusiasm for the young couple's romance, commentators both in England and in the Commonwealth raised concerns about a possible marriage. As reported in *The Times*, an article in the *Sydney Morning Herald* said that 'if Princess Margaret married Group Captain Townsend they should retire into "decent dignified obscurity"'. The article criticized the British Government and the Royal Family for their silence on the matter, stating that 'all those who cared for the dignity of the British Crown must hope that the British Parliament would now insist that the matter should be removed from the "flood of irresponsible rumour in which it has floundered for three years"'.[71] Actually it was difficult for Anthony Eden, who had become Prime Minister in April of 1955, to take a strong stand against the marriage. Eden had divorced his first wife in 1950, and he had married Clarissa Spencer-Churchill, the niece of the then Prime Minister, in 1952.[72] Eden was not in a position to take the kind of high-minded attitude to divorce that Prime Minister Baldwin had taken in 1936. It would have been awkward for Eden, the first divorced person to become Prime Minister, to lecture Princess Margaret on the impropriety of a marriage between the Queen's sister and a divorced man.

The Church and Divorce, 1945–1960 77

An influential editorial in *The Times* on 26 October expressed sentiments similar to those of Prime Minister Baldwin two decades earlier. According to *The Times*, the Queen had become a symbol 'in whom her people see their better selves ideally reflected', and her family played a role in that reflection. Princess Margaret was contemplating a union 'which vast numbers of her sister's people, all sincerely anxious for her lifelong happiness, cannot in conscience regard as a marriage'. Since 'the Royal Family is above all things the symbol and guarantee of the unity of the British peoples', the Princess should consider the effect of her marriage on the nation as a whole. Whatever decision the Princess's conscience guided her to make, 'her fellow-subjects will wish her every possible happiness—not forgetting that happiness in the full sense is a spiritual state, and that its most precious element may be the sense of duty done'.[73] The call to self-sacrifice was based not on adherence to the Church's standards but on duty to one's country.

Princess Margaret confronted a difficult decision. If she married Peter Townsend, she would be compelled to renounce her rights to the throne, and the couple could not be married in church. The Princess had to look only to her uncle, the Duke of Windsor, to envision the kind of life that awaited her if she married a divorced man. By 24 October Townsend and Princess Margaret had decided that they would not marry.[74] Having made the decision, the Princess went to Lambeth Palace to see Archbishop Fisher on 27 October; she stayed for nearly an hour. Finally Princess Margaret issued a statement, which was published in *The Times* on 1 November 1955:

> I would like it to be known that I have decided not to marry Group Captain Peter Townsend. I have been aware that, subject to my renouncing my rights of succession, it might have been possible for me to contract a civil marriage. But, mindful of the Church's teaching that Christian marriage is indissoluble, and conscious of my duty to the Commonwealth, I have resolved to put these considerations before any others.
>
> I have reached this decision entirely alone, and in doing so I have been strengthened by the unfailing support and devotion of Group Captain Townsend. I am deeply grateful for the concern of all those who have constantly prayed for my happiness.[75]

The couple had parted the evening before the day that the statement was published. Townsend left England and traveled widely. In 1959 he married again and had three children.[76] In 1960 Princess Margaret married Antony Armstrong-Jones, later the Earl of Snowdon, and had two children. The Snowdons divorced in 1978. To frequent reports of the Princess's unhappy personal life, the stock answer became, 'They should have let her marry Townsend'.[77]

The day after Princess Margaret had issued her formal statement, Richard Dimbleby of the BBC interviewed Archbishop Fisher at Lambeth Palace. The interview had been arranged long before the Princess had made her decision,

78   *The Church and Divorce, 1945–1960*

but naturally Dimbleby asked Fisher about her statement. The Archbishop told him that 'there had been no Church pressure on Princess Margaret in reaching her decision not to marry Group Captain Townsend'.[78] What apparently infuriated the public was that Fisher also said that 'he did not care "two hoots" what people might be saying and that much of it represented a "popular wave of stupid emotionalism"'.[79] After the interview, according to Fisher's diary, the 'vile elements of the press' made the Church and the Archbishop the 'scapegoat' for ending the romantic hopes that the Princess could marry the Group Captain.[80] The fact that the Princess had visited the Archbishop on 27 October, a few days before she issued her statement, fueled the perception that Fisher had pressured her not to marry Townsend. Under the headline 'A RISING TIDE OF ANGER (CRISIS HAS COME TO THE SERENE CLOISTERS OF THE CHURCH OF ENGLAND)', an article in the *Daily Mirror* on 5 November stated that 'a wave of anger mounts against the Primate, bringing with it a tide of doubt about the teachings of the Church on divorce'.[81] As the Abdication Crisis had brought unfavorable publicity to Archbishop Lang, the decision of Princess Margaret led to expressions of hostility against Archbishop Fisher and the Church's divorce policies.

Not everyone shared that negative view of the Archbishop; indeed some observers praised him. Fisher wrote in his diary, about the BBC interview, 'I have heard from countless quarters that it made a very real salutary and helpful impression amongst all sorts of people'.[82] A tally of correspondence sent to Lambeth Palace regarding Princess Margaret confirmed the division of public opinion:

> 178 people wrote expressing opinion against the marriage.
> 207 people wrote expressing themselves in favour of the marriage.
> 26 people wrote merely asking for clarification of the Church's attitude
> to divorce and remarriage.[83]

The numbers reveal how controversial the question of remarriage after divorce remained.

Three years after Princess Margaret had decided not to marry Peter Townsend, Randolph Churchill responded to press reports about the Princess in order to defend Archbishop Fisher. In a letter to *The Spectator* on 23 May 1958, Churchill wrote:

> A number of newspapers have sought to suggest that Her Royal Highness was thwarted from marrying the man she wished by the Archbishop of Canterbury. . . . A similar *canard* was spread about the abdication of King Edward VIII, and the public was invited to believe that the King was chased from his throne by a conspiracy organized by Archbishop Lang.

According to Churchill, Princess Margaret had decided not to marry Townsend before she visited the Archbishop on October 27. Fisher, however, supposing that she was seeking his advice, 'had all his books of reference spread around him carefully marked, and cross-referenced. When Princess Margaret entered, she said, and the words are worthy of Queen Elizabeth I, "Archbishop, you may put your books away; I have made up my mind already"'.[84] While Archbishop Fisher appreciated the attempt to support him, he was puzzled by the phrase 'his books of reference spread around him'. He wrote to Randolph Churchill that, on the occasion of Princess Margaret's visit, 'the books in my study were all in their usual places'. Churchill responded with an apology but was concerned that an attempt to correct the public record about the books would detract from the more important point—that the Archbishop had not pressured the Princess. Churchill believed that the rumour that Fisher had intervened to prevent the Princess from marrying Townsend 'has done incalculable harm to the Church of England'.[85]

Princess Margaret evidently had made the decision not to marry Peter Townsend without direct pressure from Archbishop Fisher. In her own account of their meeting, the Princess recalled that when the Archbishop went to a bookcase for a reference book, she said, 'Put it back. I have come to give you information, not to ask for it'.[86] In her formal statement she said that she had made the decision 'entirely alone', but that she was 'mindful of the Church's teaching that Christian marriage is indissoluble'. The image that endured was that of a beautiful young princess kept from the man she loved by an inflexible Church. It was an image and a story that evoked much criticism both of Archbishop Fisher and of the Church's policies regarding remarriage after divorce.

The Archbishop of Canterbury and Sir Alan Herbert

As the possible marriage of Princess Margaret to Group Captain Townsend became a topic of public discussion, individuals throughout the country raised questions about the Church's teachings on divorce. In response Archbishop Fisher wrote *Problems of Marriage and Divorce*. In defining marriage he stated that 'the Church requires for a true marriage the intention of lifelong union as expressed in the marriage service'. As a source of this definition, Fisher described the environment in which Jesus had lived. Instead of Scriptural passages, he cited social conditions in the Mediterranean world during the first century. Jews, Romans, and Greeks allowed both divorce, sometimes for trivial reasons, and remarriage. In the teaching that marriage was a lifelong union, then, early Christians 'routed the whole practice of the contemporary world' and 'revolutionized marriage'. The Church 'created a new belief in monogamous lifelong marriage as a duty to God, and imposed it upon its members and in the end on the civilized world'. According to Fisher, 'the impetus for such an assault and victory must have come from our Lord. It could not have happened otherwise'. The Church had no choice but 'to preserve this victory of Christ'.[87]

80   *The Church and Divorce, 1945–1960*

Jesus had set the standard of lifelong marriage for his followers, but he had not provided instructions for responding to marriages that failed. Archbishop Fisher wrote that the existence of sin meant that not everyone would be able to maintain the standards established by Jesus; some marriages did fail. The Church had to deal with those failures by establishing its own marriage discipline. Since Jesus had not referred to 'the use of the marriage service' or 'admission to communion', Fisher believed 'that here as elsewhere he would leave the Church free, in reliance upon his Holy Spirit, to find its way according to his will'.[88] Although Fisher wrote that there is 'only one standard of marriage, that of our Lord', the Archbishop did not 'shelter behind a rigorist attitude which says that our Lord forbade divorce and that is the end of the matter'. Indeed he wrote:

> Let me say quite frankly that in some cases where a first marriage has ended in tragedy, a second marriage has, by every test of the presence of the Holy Spirit that we are able to recognize, been abundantly blessed. For this very reason I do not find myself able to *forbid* good people who come to me for advice to embark on a second marriage. . . . I tell them that it is their duty as conscientiously as they can to decide before God what they should do. If they remarry, they will never again be able to bear a full and clear witness to our Lord's declaration of what marriage is: but the decision is on their conscience and they must decide whether this lasting spiritual loss is in their judgement outweighed by a call of God to seek spiritual gain in a second marriage.[89]

To his recognition that couples could sometimes be blessed in a second marriage, Archbishop Fisher then added, 'But that does not mean that the Church should marry them'.[90] In 1955, as Princess Margaret made the difficult decision not to marry Peter Townsend, Archbishop Fisher confirmed the strict standard that the Church of England had established twenty years earlier.

According to the Archbishop, there could be no exceptions to the rule against remarriage in church after divorce. Fisher acknowledged that the Church had made exceptions in the past, but he said that they could no longer do so for a number of reasons. Since 1857, Fisher wrote, the increase in the number of divorces had pushed the Church in the direction of a strict marriage discipline because the 'Church realized that the mounting tide of divorces was threatening to overthrow the whole Christian conception of marriage. It was no longer a question of deciding about "exceptions" to our Lord's standard but of preserving that standard itself for the nation'.[91] Fisher also wanted to protect the clergy, who, he said, 'would find themselves in an impossible position' if they were permitted the freedom to make the decision in each case on its merits. They would find it difficult to determine the accuracy of the stories that were presented to them because 'they would lack the means of securing reliable evidence'.[92]

Archbishop Fisher did address the pain of those parishioners who could not be married in church. If any couple felt that denial of remarriage in church was a 'cross of suffering', then 'they should bear it for the Church, so that it may not, in its official acts of marrying, compromise the standard entrusted to it by our Lord'. The call to self-sacrifice was somewhat mitigated by the possibility of admission to Holy Communion. Pastoral ministry could guide divorced persons from the frustration caused by the denial of a church marriage to the joy of reunion with the community through admission to Communion. Fisher wrote, 'I am satisfied that when parish priest and bishop concur, it is entirely right that the bishop should admit to communion in these cases'. He argued that the bishop's approval was necessary both to protect priests from the complaints of their parishioners and to maintain a consistent standard in the decisions.[93] The Church of England's policies regarding divorced persons, as described by the Archbishop of Canterbury in 1955, were no remarriage in church but readmission to communion with the approval of both priest and bishop.

During this period, A.P. Herbert, who had become Sir Alan Herbert in 1945, remained a prominent critic of the Church's policies. As the sponsor of the Matrimonial Causes Act of 1937, Herbert had agreed to the provision in the legislation that had granted the clergy the right to refuse to solemnize the marriage of a divorced person. In his speech on the Second Reading, Herbert had said, 'I think in these matters the Church ought to be master in its own household'.[94] Subsequently, in resolutions passed by Convocation in 1938 and by the Lambeth Conference in 1948, the Church had stated that a divorced person whose former spouse was still living could not be married according to the rites of the Church. While the 1937 Act had stated that a clergyman could not be *compelled* to solemnize such a marriage, the statute did not deprive him of the right to marry the couple. The Church appeared to deny the clergy a right granted by Parliament.

In 1954 Herbert expressed his frustration over this matter in *The Right to Marry*. The Church of England did not have the legal authority to forbid the clergy to exercise a right granted to them by statute law, yet bishops continued to issue such instructions. According to a member of the clergy who wrote to Herbert:

> It is quite true that Bishops cannot impose any legal penalties on a clergyman who marries a divorced person in his church while the former partner is still alive. . . . But Bishops have methods of expressing disapproval in many ways. They can refuse to visit a Parish for Confirmations or other occasions; they can cut off diocesan grants; they can deny all preferment (and this would weigh heavily with younger men). Unless therefore a clergyman is independent financially as well as morally he would find himself very awkwardly placed in face of his Bishop's disapproval.[95]

82 *The Church and Divorce, 1945–1960*

Herbert had thought that the Church would allow the clergy discretion in the decision, and he was aggrieved by what he saw as the Church's betrayal of the agreement reached in 1937. In his view, as reflected in the title of his book, the Church had deprived both the divorced person and the clergy of the right to marry, a right that Parliament had granted to both.

Herbert recommended changing the restrictions on the clergy and revising the marriage vows. No clergyman should be compelled to marry a divorced person to another spouse, and a clergyman who did perform such a ceremony should suffer no penalty. Herbert also proposed a return to the provision of the 1857 Act that required a clergyman who refused to marry a divorced person to permit the use of his church for another member of the clergy who was willing to perform the ceremony.[96] Another possible change suggested by Herbert was a revision of the marriage vows. In the marriage service in the Book of Common Prayer, when a woman was asked, 'Wilt thou have this Man to thy wedded husband . . . ? Wilt thou obey him, and serve him, love, honour, and keep him in sickness and in health; and, forsaking all other, keep thee only unto him, so long as ye both shall live?' she was to answer, 'I will', and the man then also promised to be faithful to the woman 'so long as ye both shall live'. Herbert argued that these vows could become impossible for one of the spouses to keep. What if either husband or wife deserted the other? How could the faithful spouse keep the other 'in sickness and in health' under those circumstances? In the marriage vows each party was asked to respond, not only for himself or herself but also for the other, with the absolute 'I will' to the vow 'so long as ye both shall live'. Herbert questioned how the Church could require an innocent spouse to maintain those lifelong vows after 'the contract has not merely been broken and repudiated, but terminated by the State'.[97]

The Service of Baptism in the Book of Common Prayer appeared to Herbert to offer an alternative response in the marriage vows. In the Service of Baptism, to the question, 'Wilt thou then obediently keep God's holy will and commandments, and walk in the same *all the days of thy life?*' the answer was, '*I will endeavor so to do, God being my helper*'.[98] To Herbert this response was 'modest, reverent, and right', and in the marriage vows would release the spouses, one of whom might be the innocent party in a divorce suit, from 'promising the impossible, to be responsible not only for himself, but for the wickedness of the guilty or the cruelty of Fate'.[99]

Herbert expressed his views on the Church of England's marriage discipline more colorfully in a novel entitled *Made for Man*, published in 1958. Hensley Henson had inspired the title in his speech on Herbert's Marriage Bill in 1937, when, as Bishop of Durham, he had told the House of Lords: 'We should say "The marriage union is made for man, not man for the marriage union"'. Herbert's novel describes two couples who are refused a marriage service in church. Herbert clearly links one couple to Princess Margaret and Group Captain Townsend. The prospective groom is Daniel Drew,

The Church and Divorce, 1945–1960 83

a Lieutenant Commander in the Royal Navy, who had been the innocent petitioner in his divorce from an actress, Dame Marion Marne. He wants to marry the Duchess of Clowes, a Duchess in her own right and godchild of the Archbishop of Canterbury.[100] Despite the close family relationship with the Archbishop, that prelate cannot agree to marry the couple in church. Herbert observes, 'Here was this sweet and lovely girl, an idol of the people, wanting to marry a handsome naval officer—and she couldn't'. The 'pubs' see it as a case of 'Romance against the Church'. Reinforcing the comparison with Princess Margaret, Herbert includes the statement, 'On Friday morning the Duchess of Clowes visited Lambeth Palace. Everybody said "No comment"'.[101]

The other couple is Lady Primrose, the daughter of the Admiral of the Fleet the Earl of Caraway and Stoke, and Cyril Sale, an author whose wife has deserted him, moved to America, and married an airman. Sale has divorced his wife, and, although Primrose is a devout communicant, the Rector of her parish church has refused to marry the couple. Her father recruits Sir Ewan Harker, a fictionalized Sir Alan Herbert, to advise the family. Herbert used the character of Harker to present the view that the Church had departed from the intentions of Parliament with regard to the policies regarding the remarriage of divorced persons. At one point in the novel Harker issues a statement to the press:

> In 1937 there was a misunderstanding. The House of Commons intended one thing, the Bishops intended another, and, as the clause was not clear enough, the Bishops have had their way. In my book *The Right To Marry* I gave the draft of a Bill to make the law clear and to enforce the intention of the House of Commons.[102]

Herbert has Harker present the draft of another Bill that will correct the 'misunderstanding'. The fictional Bill, entitled 'Matrimonial Causes (Duties of the Clergy)', states that 'it is the lawful right of every citizen whose marriage is dissolved by death or due process of law to marry a second time, and . . . it is the right of every parishioner to take part in the services provided by the Church of England as by law established'. The provisions of the Bill would have enabled the clergy to perform a marriage service for the guilty party in a divorce suit without fear of ecclesiastical discipline. Additionally no clergyman could refuse admission to Holy Communion to a person who had remarried after divorce.[103]

It must have been satisfying to Herbert to publicize through his novel a Bill that would have resolved his frustrations with the Church's policies. Ultimately the two couples in *Made For Man* are able to marry, but only after the Archbishop and the Rector have been led to believe that the former wives of Daniel Drew and Cyril Sale are dead. The apparent dramatic suicide of Dame Marion Marne emphasized what Herbert saw as the absurdity of the Church's policies. Dame Marion had to kill herself before her former

84   *The Church and Divorce, 1945–1960*

husband could marry the Duchess of Clowes in church. Herbert's fictional account of tragedy linked to the denial of remarriage after divorce challenged the Church to review its strict discipline.

Rigor Maintained: An Act of Convocation, 1957

Archbishop Fisher had stated the Church's prohibition of remarriage in church after divorce clearly in *Problems of Marriage and Divorce*, but the Church needed a strong official statement in order to be able to enforce the interdict. Although both Convocations in 1938 and the Lambeth Conference in 1948 had passed resolutions confirming the definition of marriage as a lifelong union and prohibiting the remarriage of a divorced person in church, those official statements did not have the force of law. Canon law represented another possible means of strengthening the prohibition of remarriage in church. The Archbishops' Commission appointed in 1947 to propose revisions of the canon law of the Church of England had drafted a clause that prohibited the marriage in church of any divorced person whose former spouse was still living, but the Canon Law Steering Committee ultimately recommended the omission of that clause from the proposed canons.[104] Including the clause in the canon law of the Church would require the approval of Parliament. Archbishop Fisher told the May 1956 session of Canterbury Convocation that 'there were clergymen who for reasons of conscience felt that the liberty allowed to them by the law at present should not be taken from them' and that 'the sympathy of Parliament would be with the aggrieved clergy'.[105] Rather than risk Parliament's rejection of a proposed change in the canon law of the Church of England, Fisher decided to proceed in another direction.

The Archbishop turned once again to Convocation as a body that could clarify and strengthen the Church's position. Chaired by the Bishop of London, Dr. Montgomery Campbell, a Convocation of Canterbury Joint Committee on the Pastoral Care of Those Who Have Re-married after Divorce issued a Report in July of 1956. The Committee's formal recommendation to Convocation was: 'No public service shall be held for those who have contracted a civil re-marriage after divorce'. On the question of the readmission to Holy Communion, the Committee recommended to Convocation that the bishop must make the decision in each case.[106] When the Joint Committee's Report was sent to the Convocation of Canterbury in the form of Resolutions, Canon A.P. Shepherd questioned the legality of Convocation Resolutions. In the debate in the Lower House, he argued that, according to the Act for the Submission of the Clergy, 'Convocation was explicitly forbidden to enact . . . any constitutions or ordinances, provincial or synodal, by whatsoever name or names they might be called, except in the form of a Canon'.[107] Even if the regulation were in the form of a Canon, Shepherd argued that it would be illegal because it involved denying parishioners access to Holy Communion, a right granted to them by the laws of England.

The Church and Divorce, 1945–1960 85

Shepherd told the House that 'a Canon was illegal if it were contrary to the existing law'. According to Shepherd, then, the Resolutions were illegal both because of their form and their content. He also said that his concerns had been expressed in the 'daily Press' as 'an increasing feeling of unrest about Convocation legislation'.[108] Nevertheless, the Convocation of Canterbury continued to consider the Resolutions.

Disagreements over the issues addressed in the Resolutions were apparent not only in Convocation debates but also in surveys of the clergy. The Reverend H.J.C. Matthews reported in the debates in the Lower House that 406 clergymen in the diocese of Lichfield had responded to an enquiry that revealed deeply held opinions: '235 of the 406 clergymen who had replied were very strongly opposed to the Resolutions, 155 were in favour of them, and 16 were undecided'.[109] In the debate in the Lower House on 21 May 1957, Canon C.K. Sansbury reported that all the clergymen in the diocese of Canterbury had been asked to respond to the question, 'Do you agree that those who marry after divorce may in suitable circumstances be admitted to Holy Communion by discretion?' In response, 231 of the clergy had said 'Yes', and 6 had said 'No'. The clergy had then been asked, 'Who should have the discretion to admit such people to Communion, the bishop of the diocese or the parish priest?' The division had been greater in response to the second question: '125 said it should be the bishop and 74 said it should be the parish priest, and 31 said that the bishop and the parish priest should together make the decision'.[110] Despite the significant divisions on the issues, the Resolutions based on the Joint Committee's Report were passed in both the Upper and Lower Houses of the Convocation of Canterbury in May, 1957.

On 1 October 1957, the Archbishop of Canterbury, in Full Synod, declared the Resolutions passed in May to be an Act of Convocation. The provisions included the following:

> 1 (3) That . . . the Church should not allow the use of that [Marriage] Service in the case of anyone who has a former partner still living.
>
> 2(A) (a) When two persons have contracted a marriage in civil law during the lifetime of a former partner of either of them, and either or both desire to be baptized or confirmed or to partake of the Holy Communion, the incumbent or other priest . . . shall refer the case to the Bishop of the diocese.
>
> 2(B) No public Service shall be held for those who have contracted a civil marriage after divorce.[111]

In the President's Address to the Full Synod, Archbishop Fisher summarized the legal significance of this Act:

> The Church by its own spiritual authority forbids the re-marriage in church of divorced people who have a former partner still living, but

86 *The Church and Divorce, 1945–1960*

this has no statutory authority. The law of the land gives clergymen the right to refuse to take such marriages, but does not yet forbid clergymen to take them.

Although the Act had no statutory authority, 'it has that spiritual force which properly belongs to the Church's highest instrument of spiritual authority. Clergymen who disobey it do so at their own spiritual peril'.[112] Clergymen were not legally prohibited from marrying divorced persons in church, but the 1957 Act of Convocation strongly discouraged them from availing themselves of that liberty.

While the Convocation of Canterbury confirmed the strict standards of 1938 with regard to remarriage after divorce, the Church's Moral Welfare Council and its successor, the Board for Social Responsibility, were developing a new approach to other social questions related to the family. The pattern of reasoning is evident in *The Family in Contemporary Society*, a report produced by a group convened by the Moral Welfare Council at the request of the Archbishop of Canterbury. The group was asked to study both 'Problems of Population' and 'Effects of Rapid Social Change on Family Life'. With regard to the second topic, the group concluded that the Church must take social changes into consideration in formulating policies, and representatives of the Church should consult professionals in fields such as the social sciences and medicine in analyzing the implications of those social changes. As the group wrote in their report:

> The Church . . . is called again to study: not, we suggest, to study in the abstract, but to study its theology in relation to the things that are—the 'given' by revelation together with the 'given' by situation. In such study there is an essential element of exchange, of generative conversation between those with knowledge in different professions. We believe that a Church which hopes to make any impact in its local situation must set its theologians and its administrators to work with the men and women of integrity (be they Christians or not) engaged locally in academic study, field research, or administration or community service; in order, first to understand what the situation really is, and then to order Church life and activity within it accordingly.[113]

In testimony before the Royal Commission on divorce in 1910, Hastings Rashdall and Ralph Inge had both argued that contemporary social conditions, as well as Christian principles, must be taken into account in the formulation of secular divorce laws. The group that produced *The Family in Contemporary Society* in 1959 encouraged the Church to seek the advice of specialists in secular fields in order 'to understand what the situation really is'. That approach guided the Reverend Gordon Dunstan, who served as the secretary of the group, in developing a pattern of reasoning that would subsequently inform the debate over divorce within the Church of England.

The Church and Divorce, 1945–1960   87

The Family in Contemporary Society was influential in the decision of the 1958 Lambeth Conference to reverse the Church's position on contraception.[114] According to Resolution 115 of that Conference, 'the responsibility for deciding upon the number and frequency of children has been laid by God upon the consciences of parents everywhere'.[115] Parents and not the Church would decide about contraception. The Resolution was a milestone in that it marked 'the first time a Christian body of world-wide dimensions has made an authoritative public declaration against the Roman Catholic attitude on this subject'.[116] It is striking that the Church of England took a rigorist stand against divorce in 1957, and yet the Lambeth Conference approved 'family planning' the very next year. Of course, contraception was a much different issue from divorce reform. The decision was private rather than public, and technological and medical advances gave couples more choices than had been available in the past. The issues had changed dramatically within a relatively short period of time. With regard to divorce reform, on the other hand, the Church had been considering the questions at least since the Reformation in the sixteenth century. Tradition and Scriptural passages operated against divorce reform in a way that was impossible with contraception. Yet the new approach of considering social changes and consulting secular professionals provided a pattern that would be useful in the consideration of divorce reform during the 1960s.

Notes

1. F. Iremonger, *William Temple Archbishop of Canterbury* (London: Oxford University Press, 1948), p. 449.
2. *Ibid.*, p. 448.
3. P. Welsby, *A History of the Church of England, 1945–1980* (Oxford University Press, 1984), pp. 10–11, quoting *Church Times* (22 September 1972).
4. S. Cretney, *Law, Law Reform and the Family* (Oxford: Clarendon Press, 1998), pp. 137, 142.
5. *Parliamentary Debates* (Lords), 144 (28 November 1946):484–485.
6. *Ibid.*, 485.
7. *Final Report of the Committee on Procedure in Matrimonial Causes* (Cmd. 7024—February 1947) (London: HMSO; rpt. 1953), pp. 8–9; and E. Carpenter, *Archbishop Fisher: His Life and Times* (Canterbury Press, 1991), p. 382.
8. *Final Report of the Committee on Procedure in Matrimonial Causes*, pp. 8, 12.
9. *Parliamentary Debates* (Lords), 146 (27 March 1947):891.
10. T. Lacey, *Marriage in Church and State* (New York: Samuel R. Leland, 1912), p. x.
11. *Marriage in Church and State*, fully revised and supplemented by the Rev. R. C. Mortimer (London: SPCK, 1947; rpt. 1959), pp. 22–23.
12. A. Winnett, *Divorce and Remarriage in Anglicanism* (London: Macmillan, 1958), p. 241.
13. *The Lambeth Conference 1948: The Encyclical Letter from the Bishops; together with Resolutions and Reports* (London: SPCK, 1948), p. 104.
14. *Ibid.*, p. 98.
15. Winnett, *Divorce and Remarriage in Anglicanism*, pp. 233–234.
16. *Ibid.*, pp. 238–239.
17. *The Lambeth Conference 1948: The Encyclical Letter from the Bishops*, p. 97.

88 *The Church and Divorce, 1945–1960*

18. *Ibid.*, pp. 97–99.
19. *Ibid.*, p. 100.
20. *Ibid.*, p. 105.
21. Roger Coleman, ed., *Resolutions of the Twelve Lambeth Conferences 1867–1988* (Toronto, Canada: Anglican Book Centre, 1992), pp. 115–116.
22. B. Lee, *Divorce Law Reform in England* (London: Peter Owen, 1974), p. 26.
23. S. Cretney, *Family Law in the Twentieth Century* (Oxford University Press, 2003), p. 325.
24. *Ibid.*, pp. 327–328.
25. Letter from the Archbishop of York to the Archbishop of Canterbury, dated 12 March, 1951. Fisher Papers, Vol. 88 (1951), f 289. Lambeth Palace Library.
26. Letter from the Archbishop of Canterbury to the Lord Chancellor, dated 19 March 1951, and reply, dated 21 March 1951. Papers from Lord Chancellor's Office, 'Royal Commission on Divorce—Appointment of members and terms of reference,' Public Record Office, LCO2/6131.
27. Letter from Lord Chancellor to Archbishop of Canterbury, dated 28 May 1951. Fisher Papers, Vol. 88, f 307. Lambeth Palace Library.
28. Memorandum by the Lord Chancellor entitled 'CABINET—Royal Commission on Divorce'. [April, 1951]. PRO LCO2/6131.
29. One of the Commissioners was Robert Beloe, an educational reformer, who was appointed Lay Secretary to the Archbishop of Canterbury in 1959. In that position, as a representative of Archbishop Michael Ramsey, he played a significant role in the debates over divorce reform during the 1960s. Cretney, *Family Law in the Twentieth Century*, p. 779.
30. Letter from Eustace Percy [Rector of King's College, Newcastle upon Tyne] to the Lord Chancellor, dated 5 April 1951. PRO LCO2/6131.
31. Cretney, *Family Law in the Twentieth Century*, p. 329.
32. Letter from the Archbishop of York to the Archbishop of Canterbury, dated 15 May 1951. Fisher Papers, Vol. 88, f 304. Lambeth Palace Library. 'Royal Commission on Marriage: Dr. Garbett on Omission of Churchmen', *The Times* (19 September 1951):2.
33. Letter from The Archbishop of Canterbury to the Bishop of London, dated 26 March 1952. Fisher papers, Vol. 105, f 41. Lambeth Palace Library. Bishop Wand of London appeared with Archbishop Fisher before the Royal Commission.
34. *Minutes of Evidence Taken before the Royal Commission on Marriage and Divorce* (London: Her Majesty's Stationery Office, 1952), p. 137. Archbishop Fisher testified on 28 May 1952.
35. *Ibid.*, p. 138.
36. *Ibid.*, p. 160.
37. *Ibid.*, pp. 141, 150.
38. *Ibid.*, p. 142.
39. *Ibid.*, pp. 83, 87.
40. *Ibid.*, pp. 507, 509.
41. *Ibid.*, p. 508.
42. *Ibid.*, p. 509.
43. *Ibid.*
44. Letter from Lord Morton, Chair of the Royal Commission on Marriage and Divorce, to the Archbishop of Canterbury, dated 20 July 1953. Fisher Papers, Vol. 128 (1953), f 218. Lambeth Palace Library.
45. Letter from Archbishop of Canterbury to Lord Morton, dated 22 July 1953. Fisher Papers, Vol. 128 (1953), f 223. Lambeth Palace Library.
46. Memorandum entitled 'COMMISSION ON MARRIAGE AND DIVORCE—Conversation with Lord Morton of Henryton on Tuesday, July 28th, 1953'. Fisher Papers, Vol. 128 (1953), ff 228, 231–233.

The Church and Divorce, 1945–1960   89

47. *Ibid.*, ff 226–227.
48. *Royal Commission on Marriage and Divorce: Report 1951–1955* (London: HMSO, 1956), pp. 13–14, 25.
49. *Ibid.*, 'Statement of His Views by Lord Walker', pp. 340–341. Cretney, *Family Law in the Twentieth Century*, p. 337.
50. Cretney, *Family Law in the Twentieth Century*, p. 798; *Parliamentary Debates* (Lords) (24 October 1956):994, 997.
51. *Parliamentary Debates* (Lords) (24 October 1956):1058.
52. *Ibid.*, 1036–1037. Bishop Mortimer and the Archbishop of York, Michael Ramsey, were the only two prelates to address the Lords in the debate on the Royal Commission Report in 1956. Both of these men, Mortimer as Bishop of Exeter and Ramsey as Archbishop of Canterbury, would play central roles in the debates over divorce reform during the 1960s.
53. *Royal Commission Report* (1956):7–8.
54. Cretney, *Family Law in the Twentieth Century*, p. 340.
55. O. McGregor, *Divorce in England: A Centenary Study* (London: Heinemann, 1957), pp. 163, 176, 181.
56. *Ibid.*, p. 26.
57. *Ibid.*, p. 193.
58. Cretney, *Family Law in the Twentieth Century*, p. 341.
59. C. Smart, 'Divorce in England 1950–2000: A Moral Tale?' in *Cross Currents: Family Law and Policy in the United States and England*, eds. S. Katz, J. Eekelaar, and M. MacLean (Oxford University Press, 2000), pp. 363–385.
60. *Royal Commission Report* (1956):9–10.
61. *Ibid.*, 25.
62. *Archbishop's Group on Reform of Divorce Laws*, MSS3460, Minutes of Second Meeting on 28 July 1964. Lambeth Palace Library.
63. Smart, p. 370.
64. T. Aronson, *Princess Margaret: A Biography* (London: Michael O'Mara Books Limited, 1997), pp. 89–90; and R. Lacey, *Majesty: Elizabeth II and the House of Windsor* (London: Harcourt Brace Jovanovich, 1977), p. 176. According to Aronson, 'Group Captain Townsend was granted a divorce on the grounds of his wife's "misconduct" with John de Laszlo, son of the celebrated society portrait painter, Philip de Laszlo. Townsend, the innocent party in the dissolution, was given custody of their two sons. Two months later, the former Mrs Townsend married her lover' (p. 125).
65. Aronson, pp. 126–128, 130 and S. Bradford, 'Margaret Rose, Princess, Countess of Snowdon (1930–2002)', *Oxford Dictionary of National Biography*, Oxford University Press, Jan 2006; online edn, Sept 2013 [http://www.oxforddnb.com/view/article/76713].
66. Aronson, pp. 131–132.
67. 'Dr. Fisher on Rumours about Princess', *The Times* (21 April 1955):18.
68. 'Dr. Fisher and the Press: Reply to Africa Tour Questions', *The Times* (24 May 1955):7.
69. P. Townsend, *Time and Chance: An Autobiography* (London: Methuen, 1978), p. 219.
70. Aronson, pp. 140–141.
71. 'Princess Margaret: An Australian Press Opinion', *The Times* (27 October 1955):8.
72. R. James, *Anthony Eden* (New York: McGraw-Hill, 1986), p. 356. According to James, 'Churchill, who had sadly seen the marriages of two of his children end and whose own marriage had had its stormy moments, much disliked divorce but had come to accept it'. Accordingly, he sympathized with Eden about the divorce (p. 356).
73. 'Princess Margaret', *The Times* (26 October 1955):9.

90 *The Church and Divorce, 1945–1960*

74. Aronson, pp. 143–144.
75. 'Princess Margaret at Lambeth Palace', *The Times* (28 October 1955):8 and 'Statement by Princess', *The Times* (1 November 1955):8.
76. M. De-la-Noy, 'Townsend, Peter Woolridge (1914–1995)', *Oxford Dictionary of National Biography*, Oxford University Press, 2004; online edn, May 2008 [http://www.oxforddnb.com/view/article/59143].
77. Aronson, p. 147.
78. 'No Pressure on Princess', *The Times* (3 November 1955):10.
79. E. Carpenter, *Archbishop Fisher: His Life and Times* (Norwich: Canterbury Press, 1991), p. 289.
80. Excerpts from Archbishop Fisher's Diary preceding November 19, 1955'. Fisher Papers, Vol. 160, ff 252–253. Lambeth Palace Library.
81. W. Purcell, *Fisher of Lambeth: A Portrait from Life* (London: Hodder and Stoughton, 1969), p. 246.
82. Archbishop Fisher's Diary. Fisher Papers, Vol. 160, f 252. Lambeth Palace Library.
83. Fisher Papers, Vol. 160, f 254. Lambeth Palace Library.
84. Purcell, pp. 247–248.
85. Letter from the Archbishop of Canterbury to Randolph Churchill, dated 10 June 1958, and response, dated 22 June 1958. Fisher Papers, Vol. 201, ff 204–205. Lambeth Palace Library.
86. Aronson, p. 145.
87. Archbishop [Fisher] of Canterbury, *Problems of Marriage and Divorce* (London: SPCK, 1955), pp. 6, 9.
88. *Ibid.*, p. 10.
89. *Ibid.*, pp. 13, 20, 23–24.
90. *Ibid.*, p. 24.
91. *Ibid.*, p. 18.
92. *Ibid.*, p. 22.
93. *Ibid.*, pp. 24–27.
94. A. Herbert, *The Right to Marry* (London: Methuen, 1954), p. 17.
95. *Ibid.*, p. 38.
96. *Ibid.*, p. 54.
97. *Ibid.*, pp. v, 58.
98. *Ibid.*, p. 70. The italics are Herbert's.
99. *Ibid.*, pp. 70–71.
100. In a bit of unintentional foreshadowing, Herbert gave the Duchess the name Diana. The 'Fleet Street familiarity for Diana' was 'Di', and the proposed marriage was referred to as the 'Dan and Di affair'. A. Herbert, *Made for Man* (London: Methuen & Co Ltd., 1958), pp. 16, 23. Forty years later another Diana, the Princess of Wales who was called 'Di' by the popular press, would be at the center of a divorce scandal.
101. *Made for Man*, pp. 18, 27, 46.
102. *Ibid.*, p. 190.
103. *Ibid.*, pp. 179–180.
104. Winnett, *Divorce and Remarriage in Anglicanism*, p. 246.
105. *Ibid.*, pp. 246–247.
106. *Report of the Joint Committee on the Pastoral Care of Those Who Have Re-Married after Divorce* [No. 689] Convocation of Canterbury (1956):7–8.
107. *Chronicle of Convocation*, Lower House (22 May 1957):111.
108. *Ibid.*, 111–112.
109. *Ibid.* (22 May 1957):126.
110. *Ibid.* (21 May 1957):64.
111. *Chronicle of Convocation*, Session XIX (1 October 1957): iii–iv.

112. *Ibid.*, 210.
113. *The Family in Contemporary Society: The Report of a Group Convened at the Behest of the Archbishop of Canterbury* (London: SPCK, 1959), p. 23.
114. J. Lewis and P. Wallis, 'Fault, Breakdown, and the Church of England's Involvement in the 1969 Divorce Reform', *Twentieth Century British History*, Vol. 11, No. 3 (2000):316.
115. *Resolutions of the Twelve Lambeth Conferences 1867–1988*, p. 147.
116. Lewis and Wallis, p. 316.

4   *Putting Asunder*
The Church and Divorce
Reform in the 1960s

Archbishop Michael Ramsey and *Honest to God*: The New Morality

Emerging from a period of relative social stability, the Church of England faced challenges on many fronts during the 1960s. Theologically, the decade was a time of uncertainty, as familiar doctrines and teachings came into question. Socially and politically, the State confronted the issues of abortion, homosexuality, contraception, pornography, and capital punishment, as well as divorce. The Archbishop of Canterbury who guided the Church through these turbulent years was Michael Ramsey. A respected theologian, he had served as Bishop of Durham and Archbishop of York before becoming Archbishop of Canterbury. Ramsey believed that Establishment had the effect of 'enfolding the Church in the whole life of the community'.[1] Accordingly, in confronting the dramatic social changes of the 1960s, Ramsey proved to be an activist Archbishop who was determined that the Church of England would not be ignored in the legal responses to those changes. In particular, he played an influential role in the debates on divorce.

Ramsey's participation in the Parliamentary debates on one issue—the decriminalization of homosexual acts—serves to illustrate his approach to reform. The Wolfenden Report, which recommended that private homosexual acts between consenting adults should no longer be considered a criminal offence, was issued in 1957, when Ramsey was Archbishop of York. He supported the Report's recommendations. By 1965, when the House of Lords considered a Bill based on those recommendations, Ramsey was Archbishop of Canterbury. Surely it took courage to take a strong stand on such a divisive issue, but Ramsey did not shrink from the debate. Although the Bill ultimately passed, the Archbishop became the subject of very unpleasant criticism. Ramsey later felt that he had made a mistake in demonstrating how much he knew about the physical aspects of homosexual sex. He supported the Bill and had read about the subject in order to be properly informed. Many thought, however, that it was unseemly for an Archbishop to indicate specific knowledge of the subject. According to Ramsey's biographer Owen Chadwick, 'One peer attacked him for contributing to pornography

Divorce Reform in the 1960s 93

by means of Hansard', while a female correspondent referred to 'the sanction given to sodomy by the Archbishop of Canterbury'.[2] Despite such criticism, Ramsey felt that the Church had contributed to making the law more humane and just. Although he believed that 'homosexual behaviour is wrong and sinful', he did not think that restrictive laws served to overcome the problem.[3] He would take a similar stand on divorce.

The early months of 1963 witnessed several serious challenges to the traditions and teachings of the Church of England regarding marriage. The widespread use of contraceptives appeared to encourage sexual activity outside of marriage, which the Church had historically condemned. On 17 February, Archbishop Ramsey declared, 'Sexual morality is in a mess'.[4] In an article in *The Times*, he attempted to clarify the Church's standards. Ramsey argued that marriage was much more than a sexual union. Monogamy, in his view, represented a combination of sexual desire (Eros), comradeship (Philia), and divine love (Agape). By giving sex a dominant role in the relationship, men and women misinterpreted the true meaning of marriage. Although he urged compassion rather than harshness for those who were divorced, he maintained that the Church's insistence on monogamy was in harmony with the natural relationship between a man and a woman.[5]

A month after Ramsey had issued this statement, on 19 March, the publication of *Honest to God* by Bishop John Robinson of Woolwich dramatically challenged the Church of England on a number of issues. Robinson was a bit notorious because he had appeared in court in 1960 to defend the publication of D.H. Lawrence's *Lady Chatterley's Lover*. In his written evidence he had said, 'Lawrence did not share the Christian valuation of sex, but he was always straining to portray it as something sacred, in a real sense as an act of holy communion'.[6] That opinion was well publicized. Thus, when *The Observer* published a summary of *Honest to God* on 17 March 1963, two days before publication, under the headline 'Our Image of God Must Go', the combination of Robinson's reputation and the evocative characterization resulted in record sales for the book.[7]

In *Honest to God*, Robinson encouraged Christians to move beyond mythological understandings of God as 'up there' or 'out there' to a deeper perception of God as 'the ultimate depth of all our being, the creative ground and meaning of all our existence'.[8] Those familiar with the works of the theologians that Robinson cited—Paul Tillich, Rudolf Bultmann, and Dietrich Bonhoeffer—did not think that the ideas expressed in *Honest to God* were completely new.[9] Yet there was outrage among those who saw the book as heresy. The *Church Times* commented, 'It is not every day that a bishop goes on public record as apparently denying almost every Christian doctrine of the Church in which he holds office'.[10] In a more colorful denunciation, one woman said of Robinson, 'If the Archbishop of Canterbury doesn't unfrock him, I and the women of England will'.[11]

The furor over the theological points in *Honest to God* overshadowed the ideas that Robinson expressed in the chapter entitled 'The New Morality'.

94 *Divorce Reform in the 1960s*

These ideas were much more significant to the debate over divorce reform. Robinson challenged the concept of the metaphysical indissolubility of marriage, comparing it to the pre-modern, mythological view of God that the modern age had discarded. Stating that 'people no longer accept the authority of Jesus even as a great moral teacher', he argued that the teachings of Jesus should not be interpreted legalistically. The moral guide should be the individual situation and not the view that God has established 'laws which never shall be broken'. Believing that nothing, including premarital sex and divorce, is intrinsically 'wrong or sinful', Robinson concluded that 'the only intrinsic evil is lack of love'.[12] Archbishop Ramsey responded to that point in an interview with *The Economist* in 1964:

> I think that the idea that law has no place in Christian morality is very misleading indeed. Love is the greatest virtue and the motive of morality, love of God and love to man, but the life of love is a love that obeys divine laws and precepts and loves to do so. This dichotomy between law and love is very misleading indeed.[13]

According to Ramsey, then, love does not supersede the law; rather the two are complementary.

In March of 1963, at the same time that Robinson published *Honest to God*, Douglas Rhymes, a canon in Southwark Cathedral, preached a series of sermons that provided the basis for a book entitled *No New Morality*, published in 1964. Rhymes, like Robinson, argued against legalism in establishing a moral code. He believed that traditional morality, based on authoritarian laws, was being rejected, and he saw this development, not as a complete dismissal of moral standards, but rather as a rejection of authority. For Rhymes, 'The great difference is between convention, which is born of the law, and compassion, which is born of the love of Christ'.[14] Once again the dichotomy was between law and love.

Against the background of the new morality, sexual scandals in the Government also appeared to undermine traditional moral standards. According to Bernard Levin:

> In the late spring of 1963 men and women all over Britain were telling . . . such stories as that nine High Court judges had been engaging in sexual orgies, that a member of the Cabinet had served dinner at a private party while naked except for a mask, a small lace apron and a card round his neck reading, 'If my services don't please you, whip me', that another member of the Cabinet had been discovered by police beneath a bush in Richmond Park where he and a prostitute had been engaging in oral-genital activities and that the police had hushed the matter up, that the Prime Minister, Harold Macmillan, had known about some, or all, of these matters but had taken no action.[15]

While these stories represented unsubstantiated rumors, the scandal involving John Profumo forced Macmillan's Government to confront questions of sexual behavior among high level politicians more directly. Profumo, who was the Secretary of State for War, had an affair with Christine Keeler, who also had a sexual relationship with the Russian naval attaché in London. Initially Profumo had denied the affair with Keeler. When he was forced to admit that he had lied privately to his colleagues in the Cabinet and publicly to Parliament, the outcry was so great that Profumo was forced to resign on 4 June 1963.[16] Profumo's disgrace appeared to have serious implications for both Church and State. The *British Weekly* stated portentously that the scandal 'encouraged the belief abroad that Britain is finished, not only as a military power but as a moral power', while the *Church Times* said:

> Christians cannot regard moral decadence and corruption in public life as matters of no public concern. Rottenness in high places, lying, sexual licence and the widespread social acceptance of adultery cut at the roots of the nation's life, because they are contrary to the law of God.[17]

From this perspective, the debate on divorce reform in the spring of 1963 occurred against a background of scandal that challenged both the political authority of the State and the moral authority of the Church of England.

The Church and the Abse Bill

More than ten years after Eirene White had introduced her 1951 Bill making a seven-year separation a ground for divorce, and five years after the Morton Commission had reported in 1956, the grounds for divorce had not been extended beyond those listed in the 1937 Act. Then, on 8 February 1963, Leo Abse, a Welsh MP, introduced a Bill that would have made separation for seven years a ground for divorce. Abse, a solicitor with a large divorce practice, was a rather colorful figure and an influential social reformer. While his attire tended to 'floral shirts, rat-catcher trousers and chunky seal rings', he has been described as 'a brilliantly skilled master of parliamentary procedures [who] probably had a greater influence on the development of law relating to family matters than any other MP in the twentieth century'.[18] In a persuasive speech promoting the 1963 Bill, Abse emphasized the provisions that would have encouraged reconciliation rather than the extension of grounds.

While Archbishop Ramsey saw the value in encouraging reconciliation, he objected to Abse's Bill as a whole, especially to the provision that would have extended the grounds for divorce to include separation for seven years. He considered that clause to represent divorce by consent. Ramsey was also concerned about innocent spouses, especially wives, who could be divorced against their wishes after a seven-year separation.[19] The issue of consent is

96   *Divorce Reform in the 1960s*

key to both of Archbishop Ramsey's concerns. What was known as 'divorce by consent', when both parties agreed to a divorce, was troublesome to the Church because it negated the definition of marriage as a lifelong union. How could a couple recite the vow 'till death us do part', knowing that they could end the marriage after a seven-year separation? Legally, if marriage could be ended by the consent of the spouses, then the union represented a private contract terminable at the will of the parties. For those who believed that marriage served the interests of the community, the State should necessarily be involved in ending a union. The desires of the couple were not the only consideration. Under the provisions of Abse's Bill, both divorce *by* consent and the divorce of an innocent spouse *without* that person's consent were possible. These alternatives were not acceptable to the Church.

Ramsey's opposition to Abse's Bill inspired a remarkable campaign against the legislation. Orchestrated from Lambeth Palace largely by Robert Beloe, the Archbishop's Lay Secretary who had been a member of the Morton Commission, the campaign employed a variety of tactics both inside and outside Parliament. Beloe encouraged bishops to attend debates in the House of Lords to support the Church's opposition to the Bill. He also met with representatives of the Mothers' Union, advising them that letters from individual constituents impressed MPs more than letters from diocesan Presidents of the organization. He encouraged them to urge their members to write such letters without reference to the Mothers' Union. Inside Parliament, Beloe worked with William van Straubenzee, a Conservative MP and an active member of the Church of England, and Eric Fletcher, a front bench representative of the Labour Party, to organize the opposition.[20] Abse later wrote that 'a secret all-Party cabal of church and chapel members had been formed to kill the Bill'.[21]

While Beloe directed a campaign behind the scenes against Abse's Bill, it soon became clear that an official statement on divorce from the Church of England would be helpful to those who opposed the extension of grounds. In the debate on Abse's Bill on 8 February, Sir Peter Agnew had said that the Church was 'not taking a strong line, or indeed any line, upon the Bill'.[22] Conservative MPs began to ask for a statement of the Archbishop's position. Thinking that a joint statement would be more effective than a statement from the Church of England alone, Ramsey began discussions with representatives from the Free Churches and the Roman Catholic Church. On 3 April 1963, the Church Information Office released a statement signed by the Archbishops of Canterbury and York and the Archbishop of Wales, the Archbishop of Birmingham on behalf of the Roman Catholic Church, and the Moderator and the General Secretary of the Free Church Federal Council. While approving the 'proposals designed to promote reconciliation', the statement condemned the clause in Abse's Bill that would have allowed divorce after a seven-year separation. The statement read in part:

> In the fulfillment of our duty to uphold the Christian meaning of marriage we are concerned for the welfare of the State and the people. At

Divorce Reform in the 1960s 97

present both a church marriage and even a register office marriage are at one in affirming that the two partners enter upon a lifelong covenant. We think that there would be an increasing tendency to enter upon this covenant less seriously if the law allowed it to be ended on the principle of the partners' own desire to end it.[23]

When a representative of the *Times* informed Abse that 'this was the first occasion in the ecclesiastical history of Britain that, on a matter of doctrine, all the churches had combined', and asked for a comment, Abse later wrote that he replied that he was not surprised: 'It had taken a Jew to found the Christian churches and evidently took another one to unite them'.[24]

Three days after the churches had issued their joint statement, Sir Jocelyn Simon, the President of the Probate, Divorce, and Admiralty Division of the High Court, in a speech in Exeter, identified divorce after a separation with divorce by consent. Simon stated, 'Divorce by the free consent of the parties meant that society was disclaiming concern in the endurance and stability of marriage'. He also emphasized the unfortunate position in which many middle-aged wives might find themselves:

Is it consonant with our idea of justice that a husband who has enjoyed the services of his wife during her springtime and summer should be able to cast her away in the autumn and claim that the marriage has irretrievably broken down because he has certainly no intention of returning to a woman who has lost all attraction for him?[25]

Archbishop Ramsey had also expressed concern about the abandonment of older married women. John Heenan, the Roman Catholic Archbishop of Liverpool, made the point in dramatic terms: 'The unscrupulous man would use a whole series of young women to satisfy his pleasure, and when he tired of them would take a few years' rest before starting another adventure'. Abse responded that 'however vivid such fantasies might be to the Archbishop, they told us more about the emotional problems of the professional celibate and his morality than they did about reality'. As evident from this statement, Abse had decided 'to go down with guns blazing'.[26]

Opposed publicly and strongly by representatives of both Church and State, Abse finally agreed to a compromise that preserved the reconciliation sections of the Bill. Jeremy Bray, a Labour MP, proposed to Abse that the Bill could be passed without the seven-year separation clause. Abse said, 'I could do a deal with Jeremy Bray: some of his colleagues spoke to me as if they had a private line to God but he clearly limited his claim to a line to the Archbishop of Canterbury, and that was a far more important telephone number for me'.[27] When the Bill reached the Report stage on 3 May, Abse withdrew the clause with great reluctance. He told the House of Commons: 'It has been indicated to me by those Members of the House who fully share the views expressed in the statement issued by the Church leaders that, if I

98 *Divorce Reform in the 1960s*

pursue this Clause, using the procedural devices properly open to them, this Bill will be talked out'.[28] Rather than lose the entire Bill, he surrendered the seven-year separation clause, and the Bill was passed.

Beloe's campaign had been successful in forcing Abse to withdraw the seven-year separation clause in the House of Commons. The Archbishop of Canterbury and his supporters now prepared to carry the battle into the House of Lords, which was scheduled to consider the Bill as a Committee of the Whole House on 21 June. Ramsey recognized the importance of demonstrating that it was not the Church of England alone that opposed extending the grounds for divorce to include a seven-year separation. In March he had written to the Archbishop of York that, if the clause reached the House of Lords and was then rejected, 'perhaps by the votes of the bishops', then a 'bishops v. the people situation' might be created.[29] Beloe, who once again was active in coordinating the opposition, agreed. While he hoped that the presence of the bishops would be significant, 'though not excessive', Beloe wrote to Ramsey that the Archbishop of Canterbury should not 'appear as the whipper up of opposition'.[30] Privately, Ramsey and Beloe recruited both bishops and lay peers to speak against what they termed 'Mr. Abse's Clause' in the House of Lords.

In Ramsey's speech on the Bill, he sought to defend the Church against charges that churchmen were attempting to impose their beliefs on all citizens. He said that his views on the separation clause were based not only on his religious beliefs but rather on 'what is likely to be good and right for the country as a whole'. The crux of the clause, for Ramsey, was the issue of consent. To enable one spouse, after a separation of seven years, to divorce the other without his or her consent would be unjust to the spouse who did not agree to the divorce. If, on the other hand, both parties consented to the divorce, Ramsey also saw dangerous results:

> If it is a matter of consent it alters by reflex implication, the meaning of the marriage covenant. It makes the words 'till death us do part' mean in effect 'until we ourselves decide that we are tired of one another and agree to end it'.[31]

The Archbishop believed that marriage was a lifelong covenant, and spouses should not be able to *choose* to end it.

While Ramsey described the difficulties with divorce by consent in terms of Christian doctrine and belief, he discussed the possibility of divorce without consent in light of 'sociological considerations'. Here he identified the two social problems that were frequently cited by both sides in debates over divorce reform—illegitimacy and abandonment. Those who favored a seven-year separation as a ground for divorce pointed to individuals who had abandoned their marriages, for whatever reason, and formed new 'illicit' relationships. The children produced through those unions would be illegitimate. If the parent could divorce his or her spouse and marry the new

Divorce Reform in the 1960s   99

partner, then the children could be legitimatized. Ramsey and other opponents of the separation clause looked not to the illegitimate children of the second union but rather to the abandoned spouse and children of the original marriage. He asked, 'Is it right to try to legitimise children by divorcing someone else?' and argued, 'Do not try to meet the hardship of some in such a way as to weaken the security of the many'.[32] On both doctrinal and social grounds, then, Ramsey opposed extending the grounds for divorce to include a seven-year separation.

The Archbishop did recognize, however, the difficulties with the current divorce laws. He denounced the necessity of fabricating a matrimonial offence in some cases in order to obtain a divorce. Yet he also believed that there was no honorable or blameless way to end a marriage. What he sought, he said, was

> a principle at law of breakdown of marriage which was free from any trace of the idea of consent, which conserved the point that offences and not only wishes are the basis of the breakdown, and which was protected by a far more thorough insistence on reconciliation procedure first.[33]

In order to establish such a principle, Ramsey told the House of Lords that he was asking some of his fellow churchmen to look at the questions and produce suggestions that would address the issues that he had raised. Abse felt that the Archbishop's public announcement of his intention to appoint a group to study divorce reform was intended to defeat Abse's Bill in the House of Lords,[34] just as earlier announcements that Governments intended to appoint Royal Commissions had delayed reform. Ramsey's goal of defeating the separation clause was accomplished. The vote against the proposal to extend the grounds for divorce to include a seven-year separation was 52 to 31 in the House of Lords.[35] The provisions in the Bill that were viewed as encouraging reconciliation were preserved in the Matrimonial Causes Act of 1963, but the debate about the necessity of proving offences moved outside of Parliament, as Archbishop Ramsey began to recruit the group that would produce *Putting Asunder*.

The Archbishop's Group: Membership and Goals

When he told the House of Lords that he intended to ask a group to study questions relating to divorce, Ramsey had said, 'It is very difficult to see what can be done, but I am concerned that we should try'.[36] He had expressed that sentiment in a letter to the Archbishop of York on 6 June, when, referring to the appointment of the group, he said that 'it is very doubtful whether they will be able to produce anything constructive'.[37] Obviously, Ramsey's attitude toward the group's work was pessimistic. Although he certainly recognized the hardships caused by the current divorce laws, he wanted courts

100   *Divorce Reform in the 1960s*

to be able to end marriages on the principle of breakdown, 'free from any trace of the idea of consent'. From the beginning it was difficult to see what reforms he could support.

Ramsey had said that he planned to assemble a group of his 'fellow churchmen', and Anglican theologians were prominent among the members of the Group. Robert Mortimer, Bishop of Exeter, served as Chair. His background in canon law, moral theology, and divorce studies made Bishop Mortimer an obvious choice. In 1947, as Regius Professor of Moral and Pastoral Theology at Oxford, he had served on the Archbishops' Commission on Canon Law and published both his best-known work, *The Elements of Moral Theology*, and a revision of T.A. Lacey's influential *Marriage in Church and State*. In recognition of his legal acumen, in 1948, Mortimer was appointed Chancellor of the Diocese of Blackburn, a position usually filled by either a barrister or a solicitor.[38] Mortimer was respected for his fine legal mind, his scholarly study of marriage, and for his abilities as, to use the words of Ramsey's biographer Owen Chadwick, 'the learned moral theologian among the bishops'.[39]

Mortimer had made his views on divorce clear in his published works. In his revision of Lacey's book, he had written that marriage is 'indissoluble by natural law' and had dismissed the Matthaean Exception as 'meaningless'. Mortimer was writing a decade after Herbert's Act had extended the grounds for divorce, and he was therefore compelled to write a new chapter on the relationship between Church and State. While he stated, 'The Church holds that divorce and remarriage is contrary to the natural order, against the revealed will of God and socially disastrous', he understood the necessity of recognizing the State's authority to grant divorces. In commenting on the differences between Church and State regarding marriage, Mortimer wrote:

> There is divergence, but no irreconcilability of conflict. The State appears to evince no desire to force its own law on the Church. . . . In the grave question of divorce, she [the Church] admits the duty and necessity of the State to legislate for all citizens, and not for Christians only. She will not deny the authority of the State to allow divorce for 'the hardness of men's hearts,' even though she deplores the unwisdom of the action. But she will not, and cannot, allow her own members to disobey the Gospel.[40]

While maintaining the Church's teachings on the indissolubility of marriage, the Bishop who became the Chair of the Archbishop's Group appointed in 1964 recognized that the State's laws could not adhere to that standard.

Another clerical representative was Gordon Dunstan, whose research had been so valuable to the group that wrote *The Family in Contemporary Society*. A respected theologian who also studied social questions, Dunstan had been recognized for his efforts to find a balance between Church doctrine and contemporary conditions.[41] As Dunstan began to study questions

Divorce Reform in the 1960s 101

regarding divorce, it was clear to him that theologians could not evaluate reforms without considering the legal and social implications of the issues. Nor should lawyers and sociologists ignore the theological questions. As he wrote to Professor R.M. Titmuss at the London School of Economics in 1961:

> It seems to me silly that those with a sociological interest in the problem should work for years and produce proposals for reform which are then looked at by the Church, and probably opposed on entirely other grounds, namely the principles of moral theology and canon law. . . . It would be so much better if, (to state the ideal), sociologists and moralists could present the next proposal for reform together.[42]

Dunstan recognized that looking at the questions from only one perspective could not produce effective reforms.

Dunstan's writings on divorce reflect his attention to different viewpoints. In *The Family is Not Broken*, published in 1962, he quoted statistics to demonstrate that divorce rates had actually fallen after 1947 and that the marriage rate was increasing. He criticized those alarmists who cited an increasing divorce rate as evidence of the deterioration of the family and instead concluded that the evidence revealed 'a strong will and desire to make marriage and family life succeed'.[43] Dunstan's purpose in writing *The Family is Not Broken* was to study relevant evidence and then to describe the current state of the family. He had not intended to address the question of how the Church should respond to the issues that he raised, but, at the request of friends who had read the early chapters, he did include a chapter entitled 'Prescription'. Here he emphasized the theological principle of acceptance for those who have not been able to conform to the Church's standards with regard to marriage. He felt that denunciation and condemnation would evoke negative responses; the Church's purpose should be reconciliation. Using an evocative image, Dunstan wrote, 'The Church will not win the rebellious adolescent by becoming a nagging mother'.[44]

Dunstan continued to consider the legal and social, as well as the theological, aspects of divorce when he began to meet with a group of lawyers, theologians, and sociologists who discussed their overlapping concerns regarding reforms.[45] At a meeting of the group at the Institute for Advanced Legal Studies on 17 January 1962, Dunstan read a paper entitled 'Morality and the Matrimonial Law'. With regard to the position of Church and State on divorce, Dunstan stated that 'the State has taken power legally to dissolve a bond which strict theology says is indissoluble'. While he recognized the necessity of granting divorces because of the 'social disruption arising from the disorder of fundamental relationships', he wanted the State to emphasize the integrity of marriage. Dunstan said that the question to be asked regarding divorce reform was: 'What principle on which to found a law of dissolution of marriage most effectively witnesses to the principle that

102 *Divorce Reform in the 1960s*

marriages ought not to be (or, indeed, cannot be) dissolved?'[46] The State had to grant divorces, but the law should indicate that marriages ought not to be dissolved. Dunstan said that he could only ask the question about a principle on which to base divorce laws; he could not answer it. That task would be left to the Archbishop's Group.

Helen Oppenheimer was yet another member of the Group who viewed the questions from a philosophical and theological perspective. She described herself as 'by training a philosopher' and added, 'It is philosophical theology which is my main interest, and from this I arrived at the subject of Christian ethics'.[47] In *Law and Love*, published in 1962, Oppenheimer noted that one of Christ's references to divorce is located in the Sermon on the Mount, where the precepts are no longer based on the definitions in the old law. Oppenheimer wrote: 'Just as human love asks more of us than can "reasonably" be expected, so does the teaching of Christ. It cannot therefore be enforced as law, or injustice will be the only result'. In Oppenheimer's words, 'There is no *Christian* answer to the question, "In what circumstances may I divorce my wife?" any more than there is to the question, "How little need I give to the poor?" or "How often must I forgive my brother?"'[48] According to Oppenheimer, then, a strict interpretation of Biblical texts could not be the basis for secular divorce laws.

G. B. Bentley, Canon of Windsor, who was also invited to serve as a moral theologian on the Archbishop's Group, wrote the Foreword to Oppenheimer's book. He agreed with the assertion that Jesus's words regarding divorce should be viewed in the context of the Sermon on the Mount. Bentley said that 'the Church does not think it appropriate to make disciplinary laws about the other offences against family love—angry words, lustful thoughts . . . why then should it do so in the case of divorce and remarriage?' Yet he believed that the question was not limited to moral considerations because, in Bentley's view, a metaphysical bond existed between husband and wife.[49] From that perspective, marriage was indissoluble; Bentley would be resistant to the extension of the grounds for divorce.

Professor Norman Anderson, the Director of Advanced Legal Studies at the University of London, had been recommended by Dunstan to serve on the Group as a representative of the legal profession. Anderson, an evangelical Christian, had arranged the seminars of lawyers, sociologists, and theologians to whom Dunstan had read his paper on 'Morality and the Matrimonial Law'.[50] Dunstan also recommended Lord Devlin, a Law Lord who had analyzed the relationship between law and morality. Other members of the Group representing the legal profession were Quentin T. Edwards and Viscount Colville of Culross, who were both barristers, and Joan Rubinstein, a solicitor with a large divorce practice.[51]

The Archbishop's advisers wanted to include sociologists as members of the Group. O. R. McGregor had noted that not one professional social scientist had served on the Morton Commission, which had, as a result, failed to consider the social consequences of divorce. In attempting to address that criticism by inviting sociologists to serve on the Group, the Archbishop's advisers encountered the complication of religious considerations. For example, in a meeting with the Home Secretary and other officials, Beloe was told that Professor Titmuss could be a valuable member of the Group because he was a recognized expert in sociology. They thought, however, that he was an agnostic. Ultimately, Ramsey decided not to invite Titmuss to serve because the Archbishop wanted everyone in the Group to be a 'committed Christian'. Beloe suggested Professor Donald MacRae, a sociologist at the London School of Economics, who was identified as a Presbyterian.[52] MacRae became a member of the Group, but the hope that they could include sociological evidence in their recommendations ended when MacRae was unable to submit his findings in time for the Group to review, approve, and include the data in the formal report. On more than one occasion MacRae offered to resign,[53] but Bishop Mortimer and other members insisted that he remain because they wanted to submit evidence on the social consequences of divorce. MacRae's tardiness thwarted that hope.[54]

The Archbishop's Group defined their purpose in the first pages of their Report, entitled *Putting Asunder: A Divorce Law for Contemporary Society*:

> How the doctrine of Christ concerning marriage should be interpreted and applied within the Christian Church is one question: what the Church ought to say and do about secular laws of marriage and divorce is another question altogether. . . . Our own terms of reference make it abundantly clear that our business is with the second question only.[55]

Before reviewing possible reforms, the Group was careful to distinguish between Christian doctrines and secular laws. The traditional Christian definition of the marriage bond was the *vinculum matrimonii*, 'the non-empirical unity believed to arise from God's joining the spouses together in one flesh, which is beyond human power to dissolve'.[56] Secular divorce laws did not affect that union; a divorce granted by the State could only terminate the legal rights and duties of marriage. The Group noted that, as long as adultery was the only ground for divorce, the Church of England had been able to recognize the dissolution of a marriage because the laws had a Biblical foundation. Once Parliament had extended the grounds beyond those sanctioned in the New Testament, however, the Church could not fully accept secular divorce laws.[57]

Since Church and State had different views of divorce, an obvious question appeared to be: What business does a group appointed by the Archbishop of Canterbury have in recommending changes in secular divorce laws? After defining their terms of reference, the Group proceeded to justify the Church of England's active role in the process. They referred to the words of Jesus, when he told his followers, 'For your hardness of heart Moses allowed you to divorce your wives', interpreting the phrase 'hardness of heart' to include those who did not accept the teachings of Jesus about marriage and divorce.

104   *Divorce Reform in the 1960s*

In a non-Christian society, divorce was necessary. The Church could not practicably maintain marriage as a lifelong union in such a community, but Christians could participate in framing divorce laws that they felt would contribute to the good of the nation as a whole. Their recommendations would not be based on Christian doctrine but rather on principles that the wider community would accept as socially beneficial.[58] In a significant statement that demonstrated that their purpose was not to maintain the Church's definition of marriage, the Group wrote: 'If a marriage is broken and dead from the sociological point of view, it is not upholding the sanctity of marriage to say that it still exists'.[59] This statement indicated that the Group would view questions regarding secular divorce laws apart from traditional Church teachings.

A major reason for the Church of England to be involved in discussions of divorce reform was the fact that it was an Established Church. If the State passed divorce laws that appeared to change the nature of the marriage contract, so that a man and a woman did not enter that contract as a lifelong covenant, then the Church would not be able to recognize the validity of marriages contracted in a registry office. The Chairman of the Archbishop's Group, Bishop Mortimer, indicated that one of the group's goals should be to avoid the introduction of a system of two types of marriages, one civil and the other religious.[60] Although Church and State viewed divorce and the right of remarriage differently, the Established Church must still necessarily be concerned with secular matrimonial laws and reforms.

The Report of the Archbishop's Group

From the outset, the Group recognized fundamental problems with the principle of the matrimonial offence. The commission of an offence that might bring one marriage to an end might be forgiven in the case of another. In other words, the offence was not what ended the marriage. The Group did not recommend divorce by consent as an alternative to the matrimonial offence because they believed that the community had an interest in each marriage. The union should not be 'treated as a private contract of partnership, terminable at the joint will of the parties themselves without any effective intervention by the community'.[61] By the time of their third meeting on 5 November 1964, the Group had 'seemed to reach a consensus of opinion that there was a strong prima facie case for the substitution of breakdown of marriage instead of the matrimonial offence as the ground for divorce'.[62]

In defining the breakdown of marriage, the Group emphasized the possibility of reconciliation:

> The fundamental principle is that the court should consider the present state of the marriage, and where there is no reasonable probability of such a reconciliation as would enable the parties to live together for their mutual support and comfort, the marriage can be considered to have failed.[63]

Whereas previously the procedure in a divorce case had been accusatorial, now the procedure would be inquisitorial. The Group compared a divorce case based on the principle of breakdown to a coroner's inquest in that the court would be required to inquire into the causes of the failure of the marriage and then declare it 'dead'. Offences that had previously been grounds for divorce would now constitute evidence of breakdown. The Group felt that this approach provided a more realistic view of the marital relationship. The significance of an act of adultery would be determined by its effect on the marriage; it would no longer serve as a single reason for dissolving a marriage.[64]

The Group argued strongly against the idea of simply adding breakdown to the list of recognized grounds for divorce. They felt that the two principles were mutually incompatible. In divorce laws based on an offence, an innocent spouse sued a guilty spouse for divorce. To enable a guilty spouse to divorce an innocent spouse on the basis of the breakdown of the marriage was clearly inconsistent with the adversarial nature of suits based on matrimonial offences. Additionally, the Group feared that simply adding breakdown as an additional ground would make divorce easier. If a couple could not successfully prove that one of them had committed an offence, they could always resort to the principle of breakdown as, perhaps, more easily established.[65]

Although they favored basing a divorce on the breakdown of the marriage, the Group recognized significant problems associated with that principle. R. J. A. Temple, Q. C., told them, 'I do not think that breakdown of marriage is a triable issue'. Justice Ormrod agreed, stating that, especially in a case where the couple had not separated, 'I fail to see how any tribunal can decide whether or not the marriage has broken down . . . because the court would have to decide what the parties might do in the future'.[66] In their Report, the Group responded to this objection by noting that judges currently had to determine 'reasonable probability of a reconciliation between the parties' in cases where the couple had been married less than three years.[67] In their deliberations, the Group had also referred to the Morton's Commission's use of the term 'reasonable man' in defining a broken marriage: 'Would the reasonable man expect the parties to come together again?' In using such a standard to determine the breakdown of a marriage, the Group recognized that each case would have to be judged on the particular circumstances of the marital relationship; there could not be an objective test for breakdown.[68]

A major objection to the breakdown principle was the evident unfairness of enabling a petitioner to divorce an innocent spouse against his/her will. It seemed unjust to enable a 'guilty' petitioner to divorce an 'innocent' spouse. The Group responded to this concern in *Putting Asunder* by insisting that 'we should learn to think in terms, not of "innocent" and "guilty" parties, but of the condition of the matrimonial relationship'. A petitioner in a divorce case was asking the court to evaluate the state of the marriage, not to determine guilt or innocence. After assessing the evidence, if the court

106 *Divorce Reform in the 1960s*

declared a legal end to the marriage, the Group said that 'it would not be giving a decree "in favour" of the petitioner or endorsing his or her conduct, but simply giving effect to a finding of fact'.[69]

Closely related to concerns about the ability of one spouse to divorce the other against his/her will was the perception that society was obligated to protect wives and mothers. Lady Summerskill had raised the issue in the debates in the House of Lords on both 22 May and 21 June 1963. Envisioning an innocent, abandoned wife divorced against her will, she called the proposed legislation 'a husband's bill'. She told the House of Lords that men and women had completely different attitudes toward marriage. According to Lady Summerskill, a mother would maintain a marriage at all costs in order to protect her children. Parliament had a responsibility to help women threatened with divorce to keep their families together because, Lady Summerskill said emphatically, 'something which is opposed to the interests of the mothers is opposed to the interests of the State'.[70]

In *Putting Asunder*, the Archbishop's Group referred to Lady Summerskill's arguments. In addressing the difficulties of the abandoned wife who did not want a divorce, they made a distinction between maintaining the legal bonds of marriage and protecting the security of the family. They argued that only a healthy marriage could guarantee the 'stability' of a home. Refusing to dissolve an 'empty' legal tie, when the spouses no longer lived together, did not serve to stabilize a marriage that was already broken. With regard to a wife who wanted to maintain her legal status as a married woman and therefore resisted a divorce, the Group had argued that, in ending an unhappy marriage, 'wounding cannot be avoided'.[71] Hard cases could not be used to justify maintaining broken marriages.

The Group discussed the idea that the doctrine of breakdown might actually be more consistent with the Church's teachings than the matrimonial offence had been. Divorce based on a matrimonial offence appeared to give 'artificial prominence to arbitrarily selected actions', while divorce based on the breakdown of the marriage represented 'the legal recognition of an unhappy failure'.[72] Although a couple entered marriage with the intention of maintaining a lifelong covenant, sometimes the relationship did disintegrate beyond the possibility of reconciliation. As the Group had noted, to maintain such a union did not uphold the sanctity of marriage. To withdraw legal recognition from a marriage that was irretrievably broken would be less objectionable to Christians than to dissolve a marriage on the basis of non-Biblical grounds determined by a secular legislature and court. From this perspective the doctrine of breakdown appeared to be more compatible with Christian teachings than divorce by consent.

Another problem noted by the Archbishop's Group concerned the fact that, if a husband and a wife could decide to end their marriage without a judicial decree, then marriage would be strictly a private contract. The court, representing the community's interest in maintaining the permanence of marriage, should have a decisive voice in any divorce.[73] Eulalie Spicer, a solicitor who had been in charge of the Law Society's Services Divorce Department and who had worked on the 1949 legal aid and advice scheme, clearly distinguished between the concepts of divorce by consent and the breakdown of marriage in her testimony before the Group: 'The parties may agree that their marriage has broken down, but the court will decide whether or not it actually has broken down'.[74] While it would seem that a couple should know whether or not their marriage could be maintained, opponents of divorce by consent insisted that a judge would have to be satisfied that the marriage had indeed irretrievably broken down. In their deliberations, the Group had noted that, in effect, divorce by consent already existed in that a couple who wanted to end their marriage could achieve that purpose by convincing a court, perhaps falsely, that one of them had committed a matrimonial offence. If a judge had to determine the actual breakdown of the marriage, and not just the commission of an offence, then the number of divorces based on consent could possibly be reduced.[75]

After careful consideration of the arguments, the Group recommended that English divorce laws should be based solely on the principle of the breakdown of marriage. They recognized that such a change would require courts to alter proceedings in a divorce case significantly. First, in their definition of the breakdown of a marriage, the Group had indicated that there must be no reasonable probability of reconciliation. An immediate task of the court, then, would be to determine whether attempts at reconciliation had been made. Although the Group did not think that the parties should be compelled to consult a marriage guidance counselor, they did insist that the court should be satisfied that the couple had at least pursued the possibility of reconciliation. The Group wanted to expand the court's role not only in inquiring into attempts at reconciliation but also in determining the custody and care of children and in assessing maintenance. In order to fulfill those obligations, clearly the staffs of both the courts and the reconciliation agencies would have to be expanded.[76]

The Group appointed by the Archbishop of Canterbury produced a remarkable Report in 1966. They studied divorce and made recommendations in an atmosphere of social turmoil—Leo Abse compared it to 'legislating on a moving staircase'.[77] Contemporary challenges to traditional Church teachings and doctrines also complicated their task. Yet they produced a well-reasoned, lucid Report that moved in a dramatically different direction from earlier legal and ecclesiastical recommendations. In concluding that broken marriages should be ended and that the matrimonial offence should be abandoned, the Group set the stage for the debate that would produce the 1969 Divorce Act.

The Response to *Putting Asunder*

Putting Asunder was published on 29 July 1966, and the responses were immediate and dramatic. On the date of publication an editorial in *The Times* stated, 'It is doubtful whether there has been published in recent times

108 *Divorce Reform in the 1960s*

a more persuasive, thoughtful, or constructive plea on behalf of the break-down of marriage doctrine, or a more effective condemnation of the present method of divorce'. In the same issue, however, a staff reporter noted the controversial nature of the Report and stated that it 'could well lead to allegations against the Church of England that it is setting double standards if not actually facing both ways'.[78] The Archbishop's Group had been careful to define its purpose in terms of reviewing the secular laws of divorce and not of interpreting Christian doctrines. Their recommendations, however, stood in such stark contrast to the Church's position on divorce that observers could not fail to comment on the difference. One referred to the Report as appearing 'to give man advice about that which man should not do'.[79]

Reformers were delighted that a group appointed by the Archbishop of Canterbury had so strongly denounced the existing system of divorce laws. O. R. McGregor, who had been critical of the Morton Commission's Report, wrote that, in urging the Church of England to reconsider the questions in new terms, the Archbishop's Group was helping to break the 'log jam' that had hindered reform in the past.[80] Leo Abse wrote, 'Never has there been published a more effective condemnation of the divorce doctrine of absolute matrimonial offences' and added that the 'candour with which the matrimonial offence was condemned meant that the theological apologia which for centuries had buttressed the doctrine was ended'. Despite this praise, Abse believed that the Group's proposals to replace the existing system were impractical.[81] He was not alone among the legal profession in criticizing the Group's recommendations. In a divorce case the court would have to determine that the marriage had actually broken down, that attempts at reconciliation had been made, that maintenance had been provided, and that the custody of the children had been properly determined. The inquiries necessary for a judge to make such decisions would require radical changes in procedure and a substantial increase in the personnel assisting the court. Many lawyers and judges thought that such changes were simply not feasible.

While they may have regarded the Group's proposals as unrealistic, certain prominent members of the legal profession welcomed suggestions for changes in the divorce laws. *Putting Asunder* was published in an atmosphere conducive to reform. In 1964 the Labour Government of Harold Wilson replaced the Conservative Government of Sir Alec Douglas-Home, and Gerald Gardiner became Lord Chancellor. Gardiner was committed to law reform, as demonstrated by the publication of the influential collection of essays entitled *Law Reform NOW*, which he had co-edited in 1963. Gardiner was a guiding force in the creation of the Law Commission, which was established by statute in 1965 with the purpose of reviewing laws and proposing reforms. On 15 June, a little more than a month after the 1965 Law Commissions Act had received the royal assent, the Law Commissioners issued the *First Programme*, in which they committed themselves to an examination of the laws of marriage and divorce.[82]

Sir Leslie Scarman, who had been a judge in the Probate Divorce and Admiralty Division of the High Court since 1961, was the first Chairman of the Law Commission. In his testimony before the Archbishop's Group on 19 February 1965, Scarman had made his views on divorce reform clear. He said that he did not favor making breakdown of marriage the only ground for divorce; he believed that the matrimonial offence should be retained. His concern was leaving too many decisions to the discretion of the judge. According to Scarman, breakdown of marriage could be made the single ground for divorce only if family courts, with a judge assisted by social workers hearing cases in private, could be established in place of the current judicial system. He told the Group, 'Speaking as an ordinary citizen, I would like to see breakdown of marriage as the exclusive and universal ground for divorce, but what one wishes and what one gets are two different things'.[83] The practicality of the lawyer would have to be reconciled with the idealism of the Group.

Scarman was not the only member of the Law Commission who favored divorce reform. Andrew Martin, Q.C., who held the Chair of International and Comparative Law at Southampton, had co-edited (with Gardiner) *Law Reform NOW*, which contained a chapter on family law that recommended significant reforms of the laws of marriage and divorce. The Commission also included Professor L.C.B. Gower, a solicitor who had handled divorce cases before his appointment to a chair in the University of London. His testimony before the Morton Commission in the 1950s had dramatically emphasized the hypocrisy and collusion that were widespread in the current administration of the divorce laws.[84]

Even before the publication of *Putting Asunder* in July of 1966, the Law Commissioners had indicated their interest in the work of the Archbishop's Group. On 7 March 1966, Scarman wrote to the Archbishop of Canterbury requesting to see, in confidence, the Group's Report when it was submitted. Scarman told Ramsey that, while family law reform was a major concern of the Law Commission, the Commissioners did not want to commit themselves to a particular view until they had read the Report of the Archbishop's Group.[85] At a meeting of the Archbishop's Group later in March, Bishop Mortimer reported that the Archbishop had agreed to Scarman's request that their Report be sent to the Law Commission 'in confidence in advance of publication'.[86] Surely the Commissioners recognized the advantage of conveying the impression that they were commenting on the Archbishop's Group's proposals rather than recommending reforms of their own. No longer would divorce reformers be challenging the Church of England. Instead, they would be commenting on recommendations that came directly from a Group appointed by the Archbishop of Canterbury. Proposals supported by both Church and State could expect a more positive response than earlier reforms introduced in Parliament.

Officially, Lord Chancellor Gardiner referred *Putting Asunder* to the Law Commission immediately after its publication on 29 July 1966.

110 *Divorce Reform in the 1960s*

The Law Commission presented its Report, *Reform of the Grounds of Divorce: The Field of Choice*, to the Lord Chancellor in October.[87] The Parliamentary debate on *Putting Asunder* was scheduled for November, and the Law Commissioners wanted their proposals considered in that debate. They refer to *Putting Asunder* in the very first sentence of their Report, stating that the Lord Chancellor had referred the document to them immediately after publication and asked for their advice. The title of their Report is taken from their understanding of their purpose in reviewing the laws of divorce: 'Perhaps the most useful service that we can perform at this stage is to mark out the boundaries of the field of choice'. In pursuing that goal, the Law Commissioners described the objectives of a 'good divorce law':

(i) To buttress, rather than to undermine, the stability of marriage; and
(ii) When, regrettably, a marriage has irretrievably broken down, to enable the empty legal shell to be destroyed with the maximum fairness, and the minimum bitterness, distress and humiliation.[88]

The debate continued to be couched in terms of maintaining the stability of the family while addressing individual cases of hardship.

As they outlined the boundaries of the field of choice, the Law Commissioners agreed with the Archbishop's Group that the matrimonial offence should no longer remain the basis for divorce. They divided the proposal to make the breakdown of marriage the sole ground for divorce into two subcategories: breakdown with inquest and breakdown without inquest.[89] The Law Commissioners disagreed with the Archbishop's Group's insistence that a judicial inquest was necessary to determine if a marriage had indeed broken down. Referring to the inquest as an 'inquisitorial investigation', the Commissioners questioned the desirability of exposing, in public, the complete history of a marriage that had failed. From a practical standpoint, the Law Commissioners noted that requiring an inquest would mean that cases would take longer and cost more. In short, the Law Commissioners welcomed the Archbishop's Group's rejection of the matrimonial offence principle, but believed that the insistence on an inquest was 'procedurally impracticable'.[90]

The Law Commissioners argued that it was unnecessary to institute an inquest to establish that the marriage had broken down because, they stated:

> The realities of the situation are that unless the marriage had broken down the parties would not be before the court. Conceivably, it may not have broken down irretrievably, but if cohabitation has ended and both parties are convinced that reconciliation is impossible the chances of saving it are remote. The parties are likely to be better judges of the viability of their own marriage than a court can hope to be, even with the most elaborate and searching inquest.[91]

Divorce Reform in the 1960s   111

That last statement brought _Field of Choice_ into direct conflict with _Putting Asunder_. The Archbishop's Group had wanted the court, rather than the husband and wife, to determine whether the marriage had broken down. To enable a couple to establish breakdown by simply agreeing that their marriage had broken down represented divorce by consent, a policy opposed by both the Archbishop of Canterbury and the Group that he had appointed. The Law Commissioners agreed in not recommending the adoption of such a policy, noting as 'particularly cogent' the argument that divorce by consent 'might enable marriages to be dissolved which had not broken down irretrievably'. The Commissioners also realized that both parties might not agree to a divorce, but that the economically stronger partner could force the weaker to accept it.[92] To emphasize the agreement of the Archbishop's Group and the Law Commissioners in opposing divorce by consent distracts attention from a fundamental difference between the two committees. They disagreed about the necessity of a judicial inquest to determine if a marriage had broken down. That disagreement would challenge Parliamentary reformers as they proceeded to consider revision of the divorce laws.

Acceptance of Breakdown: The House of Lords and The Church Assembly

On 23 November 1966, the Bishop of Exeter opened the debate in the House of Lords on _Putting Asunder_. In his speech, Bishop Mortimer reviewed the major points of agreement and disagreement between the Archbishop's Group and the Law Commissioners. He continued to reject divorce by consent, asking with sarcasm, 'What would the marriage vow really amount to—"Till death us do part, or we both decide to call it a day?"'[93] The main point of difference between _Putting Asunder_ and _The Field of Choice_ was the Archbishop's Group's insistence on a judicial inquest to determine the breakdown of a marriage. Bishop Mortimer disagreed with the Law Commissioners that the husband and wife would be the best judges of whether or not the marriage had ended. He responded to the rhetorical question, 'Who can better judge the condition of a marriage than the parties themselves?' by saying, 'The answer to that, of course, my Lords, as any marriage guidance counselor will tell you, is: almost anybody else'. He succinctly stated the position established in _Putting Asunder_: 'To protect the lifelong character of the marriage vows from being utterly destroyed by the feasibility of divorce, it is essential that the final decision be that of the community and not of the parties themselves'.[94] The Bishop noted the Law Commissioners' objections to the insistence on an inquest—that it would require more time and personnel—but he made it clear that the judicial inquiry was the crucial element in the Archbishop's Group's proposal of the breakdown principle as the sole ground for divorce.

Lord Chancellor Gardiner told the House of Lords that he had wondered if he should comment on the dispute between _Putting Asunder_ and _The Field_

112   *Divorce Reform in the 1960s*

of Choice as to the practicability of insisting on an inquest in each divorce case. He decided to do so, he said, because 'I am the person who knows better than anyone else in the country which is right about this, because I spend my life on questions of Judge power and availability of courts'.[95] The Lord Chancellor was in a somewhat awkward position. Clearly, he favored reform and yet, as 'the Minister who is responsible for this branch of our law', he had to tell the Lords that 'the Government's attitude to this debate is one of neutrality'. He was careful not to express a personal opinion about the various proposals for reform because he did not want the Lords to think that he was speaking for the Government.[96] The Lord Chancellor did, however, indicate that he felt that a thorough inquest in divorce cases was not practicable.

Baroness Summerskill criticized *Putting Asunder* on other grounds. Referring to divorce reformers as 'marriage-breakers', she told the Lords:

> The Archbishop's Group have produced a curious and disappointing document called *Putting Asunder*, in which they have failed to recognize that the stability of the family should have governed all their thinking. For this reason their proposals will baffle the churchgoer. . . . These proposals can be interpreted only as a rejection of a lifelong marriage contract and the substitution of trial marriage.[97]

Her concern for abandoned wives and children made it impossible for Lady Summerskill to consider a proposal that could enable a husband to divorce a wife against her will. Her speech evoked questions from the Bishop of Exeter and criticism from Lord Dilhorne, who denounced her 'most unwarranted and most unjustified attack upon the excellent Report'.[98]

Lady Summerskill's characterization of *Putting Asunder* as a 'disappointing document' appeared in stark contrast to the opinions of most of the other speakers. Some expressed concern that the Archbishop's Group's recommendations were impractical, but more praised than criticized the Group's efforts. The general mood favored divorce reform, and the breakdown principle recommended by the Archbishop's Group appeared to be an alternative preferable to the matrimonial offence as a basis for divorce. The main question that emerged, as Archbishop Ramsey said in the debate, was how to 'bridge the gap' between 'breakdown with inquest', as recommended by *Putting Asunder*, and 'breakdown without inquest', as described in *The Field of Choice*.[99] At the end of the evening both the Lord Chancellor and the Bishop of Exeter indicated that the gap was bridgeable. Bishop Mortimer, who had given the first speech of the debate, also gave the last. He concluded by saying that 'to-morrow morning I am going, with one other member of the Archbishop's Group, to have a friendly discussion with Mr. Justice Scarman and one other member of the Law Commission about this gap between divorce with inquest and divorce without inquest'.[100] The bridging of the gap had begun.

Divorce Reform in the 1960s   113

While representatives of the Archbishop's Group and the Law Commission discussed reconciling their differences, Archbishop Ramsey confronted the task of guiding the debate on marriage and divorce within the Church of England. He decided to delay the debate that had been scheduled in the Convocation of Canterbury for January 1967 until after the Church Assembly could discuss the issues at their meeting in February. Professor Norman Anderson, who had served on the Archbishop's Group, was a member of the Church Assembly and played an influential role in the debate on 16 February 1967. Anderson felt certain that Parliament would pass divorce reforms, and he wanted the Church directly involved in designing those laws. Accordingly, to the motion

> that this Assembly, recognizing the unsatisfactory state of the present law of divorce, views sympathetically any attempts to alter and improve it which will have the effect of increasing the stability of marriage,

Anderson proposed adding the more specific phrase, 'and welcomes the Report of the Group appointed by the Archbishop of Canterbury entitled *Putting Asunder* and believes that the fact that a marriage appears finally to have broken down should be the sole grounds of civil divorce'. The Assembly passed the motion, as amended.[101] By this vote the Church Assembly formally rejected the principle of the matrimonial offence and accepted breakdown as the only ground for divorce. An official body of the Church of England had recognized the need to abandon what had been a central feature of Anglican policies regarding divorce laws for over a century.

While the Assembly did affirm 'the Church's belief in the Christian principle of marriage as a life-long partnership of one man and one woman', they also passed the following motions:

> That this Assembly emphasizes the Church's compassionate concern for all those who have been divorced or who suffer in any way from the operation of the laws of marriage and divorce.
>
> That this Assembly requests Their Graces the Archbishops to instruct the Convocations of Canterbury and York to consider ways in which the Church can better exercise its pastoral ministry towards all such people, including those of them who remarry.[102]

The Assembly not only passed the resolution asking the Convocations to review the Church's pastoral ministry to divorced persons, they also accepted the more specific motion of Canon D.K. Dean of Southwark: 'That this Assembly requests the Convocations to give fresh consideration to the question of the marriage in Church of persons who have been divorced'.[103] This request made the Church Assembly meeting in February of 1967 especially noteworthy. The Assembly not only rejected the matrimonial offence in favor of the principle of breakdown, but, a decade after the Convocation

114 *Divorce Reform in the 1960s*

of Canterbury had passed an Act prohibiting divorced persons from remarrying according to the rites of the Church, the Church Assembly requested reconsideration of the issue.

Archbishop Ramsey and "Bridging the Gap"

In the debate in the House of Lords on 23 November 1966, Archbishop Ramsey provided ecclesiastical support for the rejection of the matrimonial offence as a basis for divorce. In a remarkable statement he said:

> There is, I believe, nothing sacrosanct about the principle of the matrimonial offence as a basis for the law of divorce. It is true that it is a principle which has an ecclesiastical origin, but a quite imprecise ecclesiastical origin. . . . The matrimonial offence came to be the principle for the divorce laws in modern States for historical reasons, but not, I believe, for any reasons of Divine necessity.[104]

After 1857, the Church of England had accepted divorces based on the ground of adultery largely because a Biblical passage had seemed to sanction that particular ground. In a rather dramatic departure from the traditional teachings of the Church, Archbishop Ramsey agreed with *Putting Asunder* in repudiating the principle of the matrimonial offence. The vote in the Church Assembly in February of 1967 reinforced the Archbishop's acceptance of the Group's recommendation on this crucial point.

In further defining his position, Ramsey repeated his opposition both to divorce by consent and divorce on the ground of separation. Quoting *Putting Asunder*, he said of divorce by consent, 'Since it gives the court as representing the country no effective part in a divorce, it virtually repudiates the community's interest in the stability of marriage', and he added, 'I believe that divorce by consent is contrary to the nature of the meaning of the marriage contract as a life-long union'. Ramsey continued to argue against separation as a ground for divorce when he told the Lords, 'I am convinced that if separation in itself is made a ground for divorce, first, there will be occasions when a marriage might have been saved although a divorce has to be given, and, secondly, there will be also occasions of great injustice'. Ramsey made it clear in his speech that he agreed with the Group that he had appointed in recommending breakdown with an inquest as the only ground for divorce. Clarifying the principle, he said that separation and consent 'may be partial evidences of breakdown, but neither consent alone nor separation alone give[s] the court the total answer which it ought to be given in the interests of the community'.[105] An inquest was necessary to determine breakdown.

Ramsey hoped that representatives of the Archbishop's Group and the Law Commission could 'bridge the gap' between breakdown with inquest and breakdown without inquest. The day after the debate in the Lords, on 24 November 1966, those representatives began that task. While the Law

Commissioners were willing to accept breakdown as the sole ground of divorce, they indicated to members of the Archbishop's Group that the insistence on a judicial inquest was impractical. In light of the fact that there were 150 divorce court judges, granting the wide judicial discretion that was a necessary feature of the inquest would lead to a great deal of uncertainty, which would complicate the work of solicitors in advising their clients.[106] Very early in their discussions, the Law Commissioners began to persuade the representatives of the Archbishop's Group to move away from the insistence on a judicial inquest.

The draft that Leslie Scarman sent to members of the Archbishop's Group on 15 December basically followed the outline of the proposed 'breakdown without inquest' as presented in *The Field of Choice*. A divorce would be granted on proof that the marriage had irretrievably broken down. Proof of breakdown would be evidence of any one of the following: adultery, intolerable behavior (substituted for the old matrimonial offence of cruelty), a two-year separation with the agreement of both parties, or a five-year separation.[107] The Group met on 19 January to consider the proposals. They did not think that a single act of adultery should be considered proof that a marriage had broken down; accordingly they recommended that the language should be changed to indicate that the situation must be intolerable.

The Group wanted any proposed Bill to state clearly that a matrimonial offence would serve only as evidence that the marriage had broken down irretrievably, *not* as a ground for divorce. Especially if they sacrificed the insistence on an inquest in every case, the Group wanted to emphasize that proof of a matrimonial offence did not necessarily demonstrate that the marriage had broken down; the inference of breakdown was rebuttable.[108] The point was crucial: if the inference could not be denied, then divorce based on a matrimonial offence would basically remain in effect. At a meeting on 17 February, the Law Commissioners accepted these recommendations, and representatives of both groups 'agreed that there appeared to be no difference in principle between the Group and the Commission'.[109] Apparently, in a relatively short period of time, the gap had been bridged.

In May of 1967, Lord Chancellor Gardiner encouraged the hopes of reformers when he publicly declared support for reform. In a speech to the annual conference of the National Marriage Guidance Council at Brighton, he said that divorce should be available on the single ground of irretrievable breakdown. The matrimonial offences that were currently grounds for divorce could be indications that the marriage had broken down rather than the bases for dissolution. Although Gardiner was careful to note that he was stating his personal views and not the position of the Government, Norman Fowler wrote in *The Times* that he understood that the Cabinet would soon consider whether to sponsor a bill or leave divorce reform to a private member. At any rate, Gardiner's public statement, which a *Times* editorial called 'courageous and right', represented an influential and effective call for reform of the divorce laws.[110]

116 *Divorce Reform in the 1960s*

On 17 February 1967, the day after the Church Assembly's significant meeting, representatives of the Law Commission and the Archbishop's Group reached agreement on their proposals. In late July the recommendations were released to the press, and *The New Law Journal* published the proposals in full on 3 August.[111] The two groups recommended that irretrievable breakdown should be the only ground for divorce. In place of an inquest, the court was directed to infer breakdown on the basis of at least one of four situations: (1) the respondent's adultery, which the petitioner found intolerable so that the marriage could not be maintained; (2) the respondent's intolerable conduct (cruelty) that made it unreasonable to expect the petitioner to continue cohabitation; (3) a separation of two years if the respondent had deserted the petitioner, or if neither party objected to the divorce; (4) a separation of five years. The matrimonial offences that had previously been grounds for divorce could now serve as evidence that the marriage had broken down. As safeguards, the two groups agreed that a spouse could not petition for divorce within three years from the date of the marriage. Additionally the solicitor representing the petitioner would be required to certify that the petitioner had discussed the possibility of reconciliation and received the names of agencies and persons who could help to facilitate reconciliation.

The two groups had agreed to abandon the doctrine of matrimonial offence, but they had not agreed on the necessity of a judicial inquest to determine breakdown. Norman Anderson later wrote that 'they accepted from us that breakdown of marriage should be the sole ground of divorce, while we accepted from them that it would not be practicable to hold a full inquest in every case'.[112] Since the lack of an inquest had been identified with divorce by consent, a principle consistently rejected by the Archbishop of Canterbury, Ramsey was in a difficult position. When Bishop Mortimer asked if he would like for the two groups' proposals to be submitted to him formally, the Archbishop responded that 'a public submission of the document to me would put me in a wrong position, as the document will not have been produced by a body appointed by me and awkward questions might be asked about my place in the matter'.[113] The point was that Ramsey could not wholeheartedly endorse the recommendations that had emerged from the negotiations that he had encouraged. When the two groups' Report was published, Hume Boggis-Rolfe, the secretary and chief administrative officer of the Law Commission, telephoned Robert Beloe to ask what the Archbishop's position would be. Beloe said that Archbishop Ramsey had not approved the Report and that he did not agree with all of the recommendations.[114] Thus, the consensus that had been reached did not have the approval of one of the most significant figures in the debate.

An Unacceptable Compromise: The Divorce Act of 1969

Despite the lack of unqualified support from Archbishop Ramsey, divorce reformers proceeded to draft legislation. Although Lord Chancellor Gardiner had publicly declared his support for reform of the divorce laws, the

Government would not formally sponsor the Bill. In the past British Governments had refused to sponsor divorce legislation because of its controversial nature. Even a reforming Labour Government was reluctant to arouse the hostility that such a Bill would provoke. On 12 October the Cabinet did agree to Gardiner's proposal that Parliamentary Counsel in the Law Commission should draft the legislation,[115] but it was clear that a private member must be the sponsor.

William Wilson (Labour, Coventry South) was the member who decided to sponsor what *The Sunday Times* called 'the most important and controversial private member's Bill of the session'. As a solicitor, Wilson understood the legal technicalities and difficulties of the divorce laws; he also said that he had 'an abiding interest in human beings and their problems'.[116] Not surprisingly, it was Leo Abse rather than Wilson who took the lead in guiding the Bill through Parliament. In his earlier attempt to reform the divorce laws, Abse had not had the advantage of assistance from the Law Commission, which did draft Wilson's Bill.[117] This expert assistance, reflecting the tacit support of the Government, augured well for the legislation.

The reforms, however, did not have the full support of the Church of England, a point that was not widely understood in late 1967. Since the proposals that represented a compromise between the Law Commission and the Archbishop's Group formed the basis for Wilson's Bill, there was a general assumption that both of those groups would support the legislation. In a *Sunday Times* article entitled 'Divorce: How a Marriage of Interests was Arranged', Murray Sayle described meetings between Leo Abse and Bishop Mortimer and said that more formal negotiations between the Law Commission and the Archbishop's Group had led to a 'Consensus'. A picture of Abse and Mortimer engaged in an apparently amicable conversation reinforced the perception of agreement between the reformers.[118]

The illusion of a complete consensus was shattered when the Archbishop of Canterbury commented publicly on the proposals. After Wilson's Bill was published on 15 January 1968, in a statement issued from Lambeth, Ramsey said that he was glad that the new Bill contained proposals for reconciliation and for 'more honest and humane processes'. He continued:

> But I am sorry that, in its proposals for grounds of divorce, it differs from those made in the 1966 report, *Putting Asunder*. Instead of one comprehensive ground, the new Bill proposes to retain and enlarge existing grounds.
>
> I specially deplore the proposal for divorce by consent and the shortening of the period for desertion. I think it is not clear that the Bill would give enough protection to the interests of a faithful party and to his or her children.[119]

Leo Abse considered this statement to be 'outrageous', and he publicly accused the Archbishop of 'a breach of faith'.[120] Abse thought that Ramsey had agreed to the compromise reached by the Law Commissioners and the

118   *Divorce Reform in the 1960s*

Archbishop's Group. In response to Abse's charge, Ramsey said, 'I told the Law Commission that there were parts of the proposed compromise that I could not undertake to support'. He continued, 'The Bill that appeared this week is a kind of compromise. As usually happens in a compromise it contains bits that are very good and bits that are very bad. I think it is rather muddled'.[121] When he realized that Ramsey had not formally approved the compromise and thus had not breached an agreement, Abse said, 'The wily prelate evidently decided to keep his options open, and to retain complete freedom of manoeuvre'.[122] This exchange did not reflect well on the participants, and it certainly did not help the cause of divorce reform. Wilson's Bill, which had appeared to have such strong support, now seemed to be based on no more than what *The Times* called 'an uneasy compromise'.[123]

Despite the controversy, the House of Commons voted to give Wilson's Bill a Second Reading by a vote of 159 to 63 on 9 February 1968.[124] Two days later, in an article in *The Sunday Times* entitled 'My Doubts About the Divorce Bill', Archbishop Ramsey publicly stated the reasons why he could not wholeheartedly support the legislation.[125] He repeated the Church's definition of marriage as a lifelong union and stated that divorce based on the breakdown principle, as proposed by *Putting Asunder*, did not contradict that understanding. Even the Church Assembly had accepted the breakdown of marriage as a basis for divorce. The Divorce Bill, however, did not include the inquest that had been critical to the proposals in *Putting Asunder*. Instead, it appeared to Ramsey that the 'matrimonial offence is virtually retained and two new grounds are added'. The Archbishop was especially concerned about the clause that provided for divorce after a five-year separation, even if one of the spouses objected. Once again Ramsey raised the figure of the deserted wife who could not support herself and her children.

Ramsey's article evoked a response from Norman Anderson a week later.[126] Although he expressed regret that he must disagree with the Archbishop of Canterbury, Anderson pointed out what he considered several misperceptions in Ramsey's objections to the Divorce Bill. He stated that the proposals on which the Bill was based did not come from the Law Commission alone but rather represented a compromise between the Law Commissioners and the Archbishop's Group. He objected to the statement that the matrimonial offence had been 'virtually retained' because the Bill viewed the matrimonial offence as 'rebuttable evidence' of the breakdown of a marriage, *not* as a ground for divorce. Anderson also questioned Ramsey's statement that under the new legislation, 'A marriage could be entered into by parties who agreed that it would be a temporary marriage'. In Anderson's opinion, Wilson's Bill did not make that possibility any more likely than it was under the current laws. Anderson's article highlighted disagreements that would become even more evident in the following months.

Among those voicing opposition to Wilson's Bill, the conservative *Church Times* called the proposed legislation 'a bad bill', and said of *Putting Asunder*, 'Bad though the report was, it was not quite as bad as the Bill', since the

Divorce Reform in the 1960s 119

report insisted on proof of the breakdown of a marriage.[127] But the editors remained critical of *Putting Asunder*, claiming that 'most Christians must feel quite unable to approve these . . . changes [in the divorce laws], in spite of the fact that the whole proposed "reform" owes much to that unfortunate report of the Archbishop's commission, with its grotesquely inappropriate title "Putting Asunder"'.[128] The editors were dismayed that a report of a Group appointed by the Archbishop of Canterbury might be viewed as an official statement of the Church's position on marriage and divorce. In January 1968, they wrote, 'For evidence of the Church's view the Prayer Book matters a good deal more than the pronouncement of any unofficial group appointed by an Archbishop, without the authority to declare a change in the Church's belief and practice'.[129] To address the problem, the *Church Times* called for a clear statement of opposition to Wilson's Bill from the Church. On 16 February 1968, the editors stated: 'If the Church remains silent, or nearly silent, in this situation, it will be a betrayal of Christian principles. . . . This bad Bill may become law. It must never be allowed to do so under cover of the pretence that it has the backing of the Church of England'.[130]

Meanwhile, Wilson's Bill lapsed for a lack of time, but Alec Jones (Labour, Rhondda, West) agreed, with Abse's encouragement, to sponsor a new Bill in the next Parliamentary session. That Bill appeared in the midst of other significant reforms. Under a Labour Government elected in 1966 with a substantial majority, Parliament had already passed a Homosexuality Bill in 1966 and an Abortion Bill in 1967.[131] The Divorce Bill had the tacit support of the Government, and Wilson's Bill had paved the way for a successful journey through Parliament. On the other hand, the slow progress of the earlier legislation indicated some of the problems. Thirteen committee meetings were held in the Commons on Wilson's Bill, demonstrating the complexity of the issues and the variety of opinions on both sides. Divorce reform was more complicated than other social issues in the 1960s in that the debates involved legal procedure, child welfare, social security, and property law, as well as divorce laws. Private Members' Bills were allotted only a limited amount of time, and it was difficult to navigate complicated and controversial reforms through Parliament in such a short period.[132] Division within the Church of England was not the only impediment to divorce reform.

Despite these difficulties, the House of Commons approved the Third Reading of the Jones Bill by a vote of 109 to 55 on 13 June, and the Bill proceeded to the House of Lords.[133] In introducing the Bill on 30 June 1969, Lord Stow Hill said that the legislation was based on the agreement between the Archbishop's Group and the Law Commission, which had been published in 1967. Lady Summerskill took exception to that characterization, saying that Lord Stow Hill's frequent references to the Archbishop's Group seemed to imply that 'the Church in this country is wholly behind this Bill'. On the contrary, Lady Summerskill said that her mail from the clergy indicated that the Church was definitely *not* united in support of the Bill. Lord

120 *Divorce Reform in the 1960s*

Chancellor Gardiner also noted religious differences when he said that one of the reasons that the Government could not sponsor the Bill was that it involved 'questions of conscience and of religious conviction'. The presence of Roman Catholics in the Cabinet necessarily meant that the Government could not unite in support of divorce reform.[134]

Against this background of religious differences regarding the Bill, the Archbishop of Canterbury publicly repeated his support for the proposals in *Putting Asunder*. He did not believe, however, that the Bill under consideration sufficiently reflected those proposals. Confirming the Church's definition of marriage as a lifelong union, he also voiced concern about the effect that the Bill would have on the community's acceptance of that definition. He emphasized what he called 'the educative effect of the law' in strengthening the institution of marriage. Ramsey ended his speech by saying, 'I cannot vote for the Bill as it stands, as the things which I have criticized are, for me, matters of justice and principle'.[135] In the end he abstained.

The Bishop of Exeter took a different position. Before Mortimer's speech, Lord Longford, who identified himself as the first Roman Catholic speaker in the debate, vehemently denounced the proposal that a spouse would be able to end a marriage unilaterally after a five-year separation. Longford reminded the House that, six years earlier, Bishop Mortimer had also opposed such a change in the divorce laws. He accused Mortimer of 'ratting' on his previous view.[136] In the debate in the House of Lords on Abse's Bill, on 21 June 1963, Mortimer had indeed referred to the possibility that an 'ageing wife' might be divorced against her wishes. He had denounced the injustice of what he called 'compulsory divorce'.[137] Subsequently, however, he had come to accept the conclusions expressed in *Putting Asunder*. While the Archbishop's Group had sympathized with the faithful wife who did not want to end her marriage, they had concluded that the desire of one spouse to maintain the legal bond could not justify the denial of a divorce.[138] The question in a divorce case was the state of the marriage, not the desires of the spouses.

In the debate on the Jones Bill in 1969, Mortimer responded to Longford's charge by describing the evolution of his views regarding divorce. In 1947 he had declared that marriage was 'indissoluble by natural law'. Twenty years later he said:

> I still believe . . . that the best ordered society is that one of which all the members observe a strict rule of monogamy; and I still believe, if not in the metaphysical doctrine of the indissolubility of marriage, at least that the obligations of a marriage, duly contracted, are lifelong, and that it is wrong and cynical for either party to ignore or evade them or seek by means of a civil divorce to be totally rid of them.[139]

Despite those beliefs, Mortimer reflected that the law alone cannot guarantee the maintenance of a marriage. Even in Roman Catholic countries, such as Spain or Italy, marriages break down. Accordingly, Parliament would have to design laws that both supported the institution of marriage and allowed for divorce. Since Mortimer felt that the current Bill achieved those goals, allowing marriages to end with 'dignity, mutual respect and honesty', he would vote for the Second Reading.

The Lords voted 122 to 34 to approve the Second Reading of the Divorce Bill. While the Archbishop of Canterbury abstained, the Bishops divided. The Bishops of London (Stopford), Chester (Ellison), Coventry (Bardsley), and Southwark (Stockwood) voted for the Bill; Bishop Mortimer served as a teller for the ayes. The Bishops of Chichester (Wilson), Leicester (Williams), and Blackburn (Claxton) voted against the Bill.[140] The debate in the House of Lords on the Jones Divorce Bill shattered any illusion that the Church of England was officially united in support of divorce reform. The lack of official support from the Church of England did not, however, prevent Parliament from accepting divorce reform. On 22 October 1969, the Divorce Bill received the Royal Assent.

The Law in Practice

Archbishop Ramsey had opposed the 1969 Act in part because he believed that it maintained the matrimonial offence principle. The actual implementation of the new divorce law tended to support that argument. Reformers insisted that, under the new legislation, matrimonial offences served as 'rebuttable evidence' of the breakdown of a marriage rather than grounds for divorce. The court could infer breakdown on proof of a matrimonial offence, but the evidence of an offence was 'rebuttable', not definitive. If the court determined that an offence had been proven, then 'unless it is satisfied on all the evidence that the marriage has not broken down irretrievably', the judge was to grant a divorce.[141] The burden, then, was on the respondent to prove that the marriage had *not* broken down, despite the proof of one of the listed offences. Proving that a marriage had not broken down would be extremely difficult.[142] The description of proof of a matrimonial offence as 'rebuttable evidence' of the breakdown of a marriage was illusory. Ramsey's statement that the matrimonial offence had been retained was more accurate.[143]

Ramsey and the Group that he appointed had argued that a judicial inquest was necessary to prevent divorce by consent. Although courts attempted to review the evidence carefully to determine if a marriage had irretrievably broken down, the hearing of undefended divorce cases tended to be brief and rather perfunctory. With the introduction of the 'special procedure' in undefended divorces in 1973, the parties could file printed forms that would be examined by a District Judge in private, which meant that the spouses did not need to be present to obtain a divorce.[144] In practice, the distinction between breakdown of marriage and divorce by consent proved difficult to maintain.

122 *Divorce Reform in the 1960s*

Although Ramsey and the Group that produced *Putting Asunder* were not entirely successful in achieving their goals, they helped to create the new view of divorce that had emerged by the end of the 1960s. Early in their deliberations, the Group had decided, 'If a marriage is broken and dead from the sociological point of view, it is not upholding the sanctity of marriage to say that it still exists'. The belief that maintaining a 'dead' marriage served neither the Church nor the community as a whole represented a significant departure from the traditional opposition to divorce reform. The Group proceeded to reject the matrimonial offence in favor of the breakdown principle as the sole ground for divorce. Both the Archbishop of Canterbury and the Church Assembly accepted that recommendation, which became law with the passage of the 1969 Divorce Act. Gordon Dunstan had written of the Archbishop's Group's task:

> We are so accustomed to starting with the disputed words of the Lord and following the now deeply worn grooves which lead through the Reformation to 1857 and the matrimonial offence that any recommendation like the breakdown principle is going to look very much like apostasy to many good Christians. It will be our duty, if we propose it, to help the godly as well as the politic to accept it.[145]

Although the law in practice did not fulfill their hopes or completely implement their recommendations, Archbishop Ramsey and the Group that he appointed largely achieved the goal of persuading the godly as well as the politic to accept the breakdown principle. On the basis of that new understanding of divorce, the Church of England confronted the task of developing policies and guidelines regarding remarriage in church.

Notes

1. 'The Economist Interviews: The Archbishop of Canterbury', *The Economist* (13 June 1964):1245.
2. O. Chadwick, *Michael Ramsey: A Life* (Oxford: Clarendon Press, 1990), pp. 148–149.
3. *The Economist* (13 June 1964):1249. Chadwick writes, 'In an interview of 1971 Ramsey was asked whether the Church could bless a marriage between persons of the same sex. Ramsey replied: "I don't see the Christian Church ever giving its blessing to that. Because the Christian Church gives its blessing to the best and perfect use of sex, which is the union of a man and a woman in marriage. We confine our blessing to that"' (p. 149).
4. 'The Archbishop of Canterbury on Civilisation, Sex and Morals', *The Times* (17 February 1963):25.
5. *Ibid.*
6. E. James, *A Life of Bishop John A.T. Robinson* (London: Collins, 1987), p. 92.
7. *Ibid.*, p. 115. Bernard Levin remarked that 'the numbers sold suggest that many who would not otherwise have ventured to tread upon the thin ice of theology may have bought it to find out what he [Robinson] was up to now, and perhaps in a few cases because they were sufficiently confused to believe that

Divorce Reform in the 1960s 123

he was the author of *Lady Chatterley's Lover* and that this might be a sequel'. *The Pendulum Years: Britain and the Sixties* (London: Jonathan Cape, 1970), p. 105.

8. J. Robinson, *Honest to God* (Philadelphia: Westminister Press, 1963), p. 47.
9. R. Lloyd, *The Church of England, 1900–1964* (London: SCM Press, 1966), p. 604.
10. P. Welsby, *A History of the Church of England, 1945–1980* (Oxford University Press, 1984), p. 113.
11. Levin, p. 107.
12. Robinson, pp. 108–109, 118.
13. *The Economist* (13 June 1964):1248.
14. D. Rhymes, *No New Morality: Christian Personal Values and Sexual Morality* (New York: Bobbs-Merrill Company, Inc., 1964), pp. 30–31, 123.
15. Levin, p. 49.
16. D. Sandbrook, *Never Had It So Good: A History of Britain from Suez to the Beatles* (London: Little, Brown, 2005), pp. 645–657.
17. G. Machin, *Churches and Social Issues in Twentieth-Century Britain* (Oxford: Clarendon Press, 1998), p. 195.
18. M. Sayle, 'How a Marriage of Interests was Arranged', *The Sunday Times* (12 November 1967):11 and S. Cretney, *Family Law in the Twentieth Century* (Oxford University Press, 2003), p. 777.
19. Letter from Archbishop Ramsey to Lord Hawke, dated 13 June 1963. Ramsey Papers, Vol. 43, ff 184–185. Lambeth Palace Library.
20. *Ibid.*, Vol. 43, ff 121, 137, 203. Abse described van Straubenzee as 'the voice of the bishops', and Eric Fletcher as 'an undistinguished deputy speaker'. *Private Member* (London: Macdonald, 1973), p. 163.
21. Abse, p. 163.
22. *Parliamentary Debates* (Commons), 5th series, 671 (8 February 1963):874.
23. Ramsey Papers, Vol. 43, ff 128–129.
24. *Private Member*, p. 159.
25. 'The Dangers of Divorce by Consent', *The Times* (8 April 1963):6. Abse was angry about Simon's speech. He told the House of Commons that the President of the Divorce Court had apparently 'forgotten that he ever quit this House and has become a judge whose duty it is to interpret the law and not to usurp the function and duty of the House'. *Parliamentary Debates* (Commons) 676 (3 May 1963):1558.
26. *Private Member*, p. 170.
27. *Ibid.*
28. *Parliamentary Debates* (Commons) 676 (3 May 1963):1561. In a note to the file on a meeting with van Straubenzee, Beloe confirmed Abse's statement. Ramsey Papers, Vol. 43, f. 137.
29. Letter from the Archbishop of Canterbury to the Archbishop of York, dated 27 March 1963. Ramsey Papers, Vol. 43, f. 116.
30. Note from Beloe to the Archbishop, dated 31 May 1963. Ramsey Papers, Vol. 43, f 171.
31. *Parliamentary Debates* (Lords) 250 (21 June 1963):1544–1545.
32. *Ibid.*, 1546–1547.
33. *Ibid.*, 1547.
34. *Private Member*, p. 171.
35. *Parliamentary Debates* (Lords) 250 (21 June 1963):1578.
36. *Ibid.*, 1547.
37. Ramsey Papers, Vol. 43, f 178.
38. B. Skinner, *Robert Exon* (Bognor Regis, Sussex: New Horizon, 1979), pp. 55, 57–59; and J. Porter, 'Mortimer, Robert Cecil (1902–1976)', *Oxford Dictionary*

124 Divorce Reform in the 1960s

of *National Biography*, Oxford University Press, 2004 [http://www.oxforddnb.com/view/article/31472].

39. Chadwick, *Michael Ramsey*, p. 151.
40. T. Lacey, *Marriage in Church and State* (1912); rev. R. Mortimer (London: SPCK, 1947; rpt. 1959), pp. 208, 212.
41. E. Norman, *Church and Society in England, 1770–1970* (Oxford: Clarendon Press, 1976), p. 442.
42. Letter dated April 10, 1961. Ramsey Papers, Vol. 43 (1963), f 10.
43. *The Family Is Not Broken* (London: SCM Press Ltd, 1962), pp. 66, 68, 71.
44. *Ibid.*, pp. 72, 76–77.
45. J. Lewis and P. Wallis, 'Fault, Breakdown, and the Church of England's Involvement in the 1969 Divorce Reform', *Twentieth Century British History*, Vol. 11, No. 3 (2000):319.
46. G. Dunstan, 'Morality and the Matrimonial Law' (Unpublished paper in the collection of Helen Oppenheimer).
47. Letter from Helen Oppenheimer to Beloe, dated February 13, 1964. Ramsey Papers, Vol. 62, f 46.
48. H. Oppenheimer, *Law and Love: A Study in Practical Christian Ethics* (London: Faith Press, 1962), pp. 72–73.
49. G. Bentley, 'Foreword', in *Law and Love*, p. 6.
50. Lewis and Wallis, p. 319.
51. Helen Oppenheimer has said of Rubinstein's service that it was 'useful to have somebody who knew, from her variegated professional experience of divorces, where the shoe pinched. People often asked, "Have you, in such a churchy group, anybody who truly understands marriage failure?"' Comments in email to author (17 January 2010).
52. Note to file from Robert Beloe, dated 7 October 1963, Ramsey Papers, Vol. 43, f 24, and Letters from Robert Beloe to Edwin Barker, dated 17 and 23 January 1964, Ramsey Papers, Vol. 62, ff 33, 40.
53. *Minutes of Eighth and Twelfth Meetings*, 9 April and 19–20 November 1965, pp. 70, 124.
54. Dunstan wrote to the Bishop of Exeter on 17 May 1966 that he had pursued MacRae to the extent of calling him seven times a day. The publishers were insisting that the material be sent to the printer, and thus MacRae's chapter could not be included. Ramsey Papers, Vol. 102, f 199. Ultimately MacRae's report appeared as a separate appendix signed only by its author. It included no statistics or other data and consisted mainly of generalities.
55. *Putting Asunder: A Divorce Law for Contemporary Society. The Report of a Group Appointed by the Archbishop of Canterbury in January 1964* (London: SPCK, 1966), pp. 3–4.
56. *Ibid.*, p. 11.
57. *Ibid.*, p. 7.
58. *Ibid.*, pp. 8–12.
59. *Archbishop's Group on Reform of Divorce Laws*, MS 3460, Lambeth Palace Library, Minutes of Second Meeting on 28 July 1964, p. 7.
60. *Ibid.*, Minutes of First Meeting on 26 May 1964, p. 2.
61. *Putting Asunder*, p. 41.
62. Minutes of Third Meeting on 5 November 1964, p. 19.
63. Minutes of Tenth Meeting on 31 July 1965, p. 95.
64. *Putting Asunder*, pp. 65, 67. In testimony before the Group, Sir Jocelyn Simon used the terms 'accusatorial' and 'inquisitorial'. Minutes of Fourth Meeting on 12 December 1964, p. 33.
65. *Putting Asunder*, pp. 57, 59.
66. Minutes of Ninth Meeting on 24 May 1965, p. 87 and Minutes of Eighth Meeting on 9 April 1965, p. 75.

Divorce Reform in the 1960s 125

67. *Putting Asunder*, p. 45.
68. Minutes of Third Meeting on 5 November 1964, p. 17.
69. *Putting Asunder*, p. 50.
70. *Parliamentary Debates* (Lords) 250 (22 May 1963):397 and (21 June 1963):1558.
71. *Putting Asunder*, pp. 49, 54–55.
72. *Ibid.*, pp. 60–61.
73. *Ibid.*, p. 34.
74. Minutes of the Tenth Meeting, 30–31 July 1965, p. 113.
75. Minutes of the Twelfth Meeting, 19–20 November 1965, p. 127.
76. *Putting Asunder*, pp. 63–65, 70–72.
77. *Private Member*, p. 175.
78. 'A New Light on Divorce', p. 13, and 'New Basis for Divorce is Recommended', p. 12.
79. M. Paulsen, 'Divorce—Canterbury Style', *New Society* (August 1966):187.
80. O. McGregor, 'Well Asunder', *Sunday Times* (31 July 1966):9.
81. *Private Member*, p. 172.
82. S. Cretney, *Law, Law Reform and the Family* (Oxford: Clarendon Press, 1998), pp. 4–5, 57.
83. Minutes of Sixth Meeting on 19 February 1965, pp. 60, 62.
84. Cretney, *Family Law in the Twentieth Century*, pp. 789, 799.
85. Ramsey Papers, Vol. 102, f 185.
86. Minutes of the Seventeenth Meeting, 18 and 19 March 1966, p. 168.
87. The Law Commission, *Reform of the Grounds of Divorce: The Field of Choice* (London: HMSO; rpt. 1967).
88. *Ibid.*, pp. 5, 10.
89. *Ibid.*, p. 27.
90. *Ibid.*, pp. 32–33, 54.
91. *Ibid.*, p. 36.
92. *Ibid.*, pp. 41–42.
93. *Parliamentary Debates* (Lords) 278 (23 November 1966):243.
94. *Ibid.*
95. *Ibid.*, 257.
96. *Ibid.*, 251, 262.
97. *Ibid.*, 291.
98. *Ibid.*, 298.
99. *Ibid.*, 274.
100. *Ibid.*, 346–347. According to Stephen Cretney, the other member of the Archbishop's Group was Canon Bentley, and the other Law Commissioner was Gower. *Law, Law Reform and the Family*, p. 64, notes 220 and 221.
101. *Church Assembly Proceedings*, Vol. 47, No. 2 (16 February 1967):239, 253, 257.
102. *Ibid.*, 253, 257, 267.
103. *Ibid.*, 267, 271.
104. *Parliamentary Debates* (Lords) 278 (23 November 1966):270–271.
105. *Ibid.*, 272–274.
106. Letter from the Bishop of Exeter to Gordon Dunstan, dated 8 December 1966. Papers of Gordon Reginald Dunstan as a member of the Archbishop's Group on the Reform of the Law of Divorce, MS4503 in Lambeth Palace Library, f 214.
107. *Ibid.*, Document entitled 'Reform of Grounds of Divorce: Basis for discussion between the Archbishop's Group and the Law Commission' (56–70–01), ff 229–231.
108. *Ibid.*, Letter from Bishop of Exeter to Leslie Scarman, dated 30 January 1967, f 225.
109. 'Minutes of a Meeting between Representatives of the Archbishop's Group on Divorce and the Law Commission, Held on Friday 17th February', Dunstan Papers, f 235.

126 *Divorce Reform in the 1960s*

110. N. Fowler, 'Lord Gardiner Urges Divorce Reform', *The Times* (6 May 1967):1 and Editorial, 'Breakdown of Marriage', p. 11.
111. 'The Grounds of Divorce', *The New Law Journal* (3 August 1967):827.
112. 'Ending Humbug on Divorce', *Sunday Times* (18 February 1968):17.
113. Letter from the Archbishop of Canterbury to the Bishop of Exeter, dated 22 May 1967. Ramsey Papers, Vol. 117, f 323.
114. Note from Robert Beloe entitled 'Marriage and Divorce', dated 26 July 1967. Ramsey Papers, Vol. 117, f 337.
115. Cretney, *Law, Law Reform and the Family*, p. 68.
116. 'The Bill Pushers', *Sunday Times* (3 December 1967):8.
117. B. Lee, *Divorce Law Reform in England* (London: Peter Owen, 1974), p. 74. The Law Commission was not established until 1965 and thus could not have helped Abse with the earlier bills.
118. M. Sayle, 'How a Marriage of Interests was Arranged', *Sunday Times* (12 November 1967):11.
119. 'Statement by the Primate', *Church Times* (19 January 1968):20.
120. *Private Member*, p. 182.
121. 'Archbishop Denies Breach of Faith', *Times* (20 January 1968):3.
122. *Private Member*, p. 182.
123. 'Breakdown or Offences', *Times* (16 January 1968):9.
124. P. Richards, *Parliament and Conscience* (London: George Allen & Unwin Ltd, 1970), p. 148.
125. *Sunday Times* (11 February 1968):10.
126. 'Ending Humbug on Divorce', *Sunday Times* (18 February 1968):17.
127. 'A Bad Bill', *Church Times* (2 February 1968):12.
128. 'Blow at Marriage', *Church Times* (27 December 1968):3.
129. 'Divorce Bill', *Church Times* (19 January 1968):3.
130. 'Still a Bad Bill', *Church Times* (16 February 1968):12.
131. C. Gibson, *Dissolving Wedlock* (London: Routledge, 1994), p. 106.
132. Richards, pp. 148, 158.
133. *Ibid.*, p. 154.
134. *Parliamentary Debates* (Lords) 303 (30 June 1969):296, 307, 314. Gardiner referred specifically to Lord Longford, who was present and who agreed that he would have resigned from the Government if it had officially sponsored a divorce reform bill.
135. *Ibid.*, 338, 342.
136. *Ibid.*, 373.
137. *Parliamentary Debates* (Lords) 250 (21 June 1963):1572–1573.
138. *Putting Asunder*, p. 49.
139. *Parliamentary Debates* (Lords) 303(30 June 1969): 375.
140. *Ibid.*, 441–442; Lee, p. 195.
141. 1969 c. 55, §2(1)(3).
142. In 1998 Stephen Cretney wrote that there was no reported instance of a respondent's successfully persuading a court that a marriage had not broken down. *Law, Law Reform and the Family*, p. 70.
143. Cretney has written that when Norman Anderson objected to Ramsey's statement that 'the matrimonial offence would be "virtually retained", . . . it appears that on this occasion at least the Archbishop understood the principles of statutory construction better than did the legal experts he had appointed to advise him'. *Family Law in the Twentieth Century*, p. 366, note 302.
144. *Ibid.*, pp. 381–382.
145. Letter to Helen Oppenheimer in private collection of recipient.

5 Remarriage in Church after Divorce
In Pursuit of Consensus

The Debate

In 1966, in a letter to the innocent party in a divorce suit who wanted to be remarried in church, Archbishop Ramsey maintained the Church's official position, as stated in the 1957 Act of Convocation. He said that divorced persons whose former spouses were still living could not be married in church but that the clergy could offer help in the forms of prayers in church for the couple. Ramsey added that the sacraments need not be denied to divorced and remarried spouses if they wished to ask for them.[1] Ramsey's letter reflects a central concern for the Church in the debate over the remarriage of divorced persons: Whether or not the Church of England officially denied remarriage in church to those who had legally ended their marriages, the bishops and the clergy still had to respond to Anglicans who were divorced and remarried. The clergy frequently found themselves caught between two competing obligations. They should maintain the discipline of the Church, but they should also administer pastoral care to their parishioners.

A significant aspect of that pastoral care was admission to Communion. The presumption, as indicated by Archbishop Ramsey's letter, was that the sacraments would be denied to remarried divorced persons. Current Church policy, based on the 1957 Act of Convocation, required the clergy to submit such cases to the bishop of the diocese. Only with the bishop's approval should remarried divorced persons be admitted to Holy Communion. The excommunication of remarried divorced persons posed a problem for the clergy because the Prayer Book authorized the exclusion from Communion of only those who were 'open and notorious evil livers'. Earlier in the century, Archbishop Randall Davidson had stated, with regard to the marriage of a man and his deceased wife's sister, that the words 'open and notorious evil liver' could not be properly applied to a spouse in 'a marriage expressly sanctioned by English law'.[2] In 1966 Hugh Montefiore, the Vicar of Great St Mary's, Cambridge and later Bishop of Birmingham, addressed a similar question with regard to second marriages for divorced persons by writing, 'I have never heard any official statement emanating from the Church of England that those who remarry are merely co-habiting and therefore living

128 *In Pursuit of Consensus*

in open sin'.[3] Regarding the practice of requiring a bishop's approval for the admission of remarried divorced persons to Holy Communion, Montefiore stated, 'How any bishop can use a means of grace as a means of discipline I have never begun to understand'.[4] Helen Oppenheimer agreed with Montefiore when she wrote of the sanction of excommunication: 'A Sacrament is a means of grace, not a good conduct prize or a health certificate, and nobody should think to come to it on a basis of merit'.[5]

There were also disagreements on the subject of remarriage after divorce in church, as evidenced by the response of Bishop Mervyn Stockwood of Southwark to the recommendations in *Putting Asunder*. If, as the Group had suggested, a marriage could be declared 'dead', Stockwood said, 'then it is illogical to pretend that for Church purposes it is still alive. No, the Church must screw up its courage and take another look at the difficulty. If a marriage is dead—absolutely and irrevocably—then surely the persons concerned should be free to marry again'.[6] Stockwood recognized that the current marriage service might not be suitable for divorced persons, but he believed that, with a revised service, Christians who had been divorced could be remarried in a public ceremony in church.[7]

Those within the Church who wanted to allow remarriage in church after divorce found an ally in A.R. Winnett, who had studied the issues extensively. In 1958 Winnett had published *Divorce and Remarriage in Anglicanism*, a thorough survey of the subject from the Reformation to the present. G.B. Bentley called this work 'indispensable to anyone wishing to understand Anglican attitudes to divorce'.[8] After describing the historical debate regarding the doctrine of indissolubility, Winnett had concluded that the prohibition against remarriage in church after divorce, as stated in the Act of Convocation in 1957, represented 'the nearest approach to a common mind which the Church is likely to reach'.[9] A decade later, in a discussion of recent developments in the debate over divorce and remarriage, Winnett stated that 'there is a movement in the Church of England away from the doctrine of the absolute indissolubility of marriage'.[10] About his own views, Winnett said, 'I have come to attribute greater importance to the actual personal relationship in marriage as distinct from a bond or *vinculum* believed to exist independently of this relationship'. He added:

> Though I have in my pastoral practice always observed the Resolutions of Convocation out of loyalty both to Episcopal direction and to the mind of the Church as expressed in those Resolutions I have come increasingly to question the basis on which they rest, and to feel that the time has come for a reconsideration of the Church's position in respect of divorce and remarriage.[11]

Winnett's conclusion, after years of research on the historical debate within the Church of England, represented a significant questioning of the traditionally accepted prohibition against remarriage in church.

In Pursuit of Consensus 129

Adding to the Church's problems in clarifying doctrine and establishing appropriate policies were the theological debates of the 1960s. Alec Vidler, the Dean of King's College Cambridge and the editor of *Theology*, was a distinguished theologian whom the church historian Roger Lloyd described as 'one of the most stimulating and original thinkers of the Church'.[12] Vidler saw the 1950s as a time of complacency in theological studies, and he thought that it was time to reconsider fundamental questions.[13] To respond to that need, some of the younger theologians at Cambridge approached Vidler to ask if he would be willing to meet with them 'to discuss their dissatisfaction with the state of English, or at least of Anglican, theological thought and to consider what might be done about it'. Howard Root, then Dean of Emmanuel College, was the first to propose the discussions that eventually produced a volume entitled *Soundings*.[14] In the Introduction to this collection of essays, Vidler explained the title in terms of the current atmosphere regarding theological works: 'It is a time for ploughing, not reaping; or, to use the metaphor we have chosen for our title, it is a time for making soundings, not charts or maps'.[15] These theologians were questioning and postulating, not proclaiming or defining. They admitted that they were asking questions that they could not answer, and their essays reinforced the perception of the 1960s as a time of uncertainty, both in morality and theology.

Evidently the uncertainty was widespread. According to Vidler, *Soundings* 'had a much larger circulation and received much more attention than we could have anticipated'.[16] *Honest to God*, published the same year, had an even wider impact. As the 'new morality' of John Robinson challenged the 'old morality' of the Church of England, the demand for an official clarification of the Church's position on remarriage in church after divorce became more insistent. On 29 July 1966, partly in response to the publication of *Putting Asunder* on that day, the Reverend Evelyn Garth Moore wrote in the *Church Times* that it was time for a group of theologians to review the theology of marriage.[17] In February of 1967, when the Church Assembly accepted breakdown as the only ground for divorce, that body also passed a motion asking the Convocations 'to give fresh consideration to the question of the marriage in Church of persons who have been divorced'.[18] After a debate on the issue in October of 1967, the Convocation of Canterbury passed a Resolution asking the Archbishop to appoint a group to study the Church's doctrine of marriage. Under the chairmanship of Howard Root, who had been appointed to the new chair of theology at the University of Southampton in 1966, that group met for the first time in the summer of 1968. Thus began a new attempt to move through confusion and debate to consensus.

The Root Commission: Social Changes and Moral Reasoning

The purpose of the Commission on Marriage that reported in 1971 was not to recommend changes in the secular laws of divorce, as the Archbishop's Group had done, but rather to study the Christian doctrine of marriage.

130   *In Pursuit of Consensus*

Accordingly, no representatives of the legal profession served on the Commission. The Chair was Howard Root, an American who had studied theology at Oxford. After ordination in 1953, he held an assistant lectureship in the Cambridge Divinity School, where he joined the group that produced *Soundings*. Although his essay, 'Beginning All Over Again', called for a re-examination of Christian theology, Root was not closely associated with the upheaval in the Church during the 1960s that was identified with *Honest to God*. Indeed, the subject of Root's 1972 Bampton Lectures was 'The Limits of Radicalism'.[19]

In Cambridge in 1962, Root delivered a lecture, later published as 'Ethical Problems of Sex', in which he said:

> In sexual matters, as elsewhere, a dry and static moralism is the enemy of ethical understanding. It is a sad but uncontrovertible fact that the Church has often failed to grasp this fact and has betrayed its ethical insight in the interests of a tidy moralistic respectability. It has sometimes dealt with sexual problems as though they could be settled and resolved by black and white rules. It has appeared more censorious than compassionate. And, in so doing, it has been infected by that kind of pharisaic hypocrisy which is the ultimate betrayal of Christian or of any moral life.[20]

Root encouraged an examination of the Christian perception that 'the ideal fulfillment of our sexual nature is found in monogamous marriage'. He argued that any interpretation of Christian principle as an understanding that 'all sex outside monogamous marriage is wrong and all sex inside that relationship is right' is unacceptable. According to Root, 'If the life-long marriage union can provide the right context, so also can it provide its own occasions of wrong. There is nothing magical about the rites of holy matrimony. They are no automatic guarantee of the profundity and integrity of a human relationship'.[21] Root clearly rejected the proposal that the marriage ceremony created a metaphysical bond that could not be broken. In his view, marriages could break down, and the Church had a responsibility to those who suffered as a result of broken relationships: 'Pastorally, Christianity is concerned not with judgement or condemnation but with reconciliation and, in the widest sense, understanding and guidance'.[22] Such statements reveal that the man chosen as chair of the group appointed to study the Church's doctrine of marriage recognized both the reality of the breakdown of marriages and the importance of pastoral care for the divorced.

By 1968 Gordon Dunstan had emerged as a leading moral theologian in the Church of England. He had succeeded Alec Vidler as the editor of *Theology* in 1965, and he was appointed the first F.D. Maurice Professor of Moral and Social Theology at King's College, London, in 1967. Early in his career Dunstan had become interested in the relationship between theology and social questions. He recognized the value of combining evidence from

In Pursuit of Consensus 131

the social sciences with theological considerations to explore those questions and resolve ethical difficulties. Dunstan later said of the approach that '[t]he theology is, in a sense, given. The ethics has to be worked out, by moral reasoning upon the given'.[23] According to Dunstan, the theologian could collaborate with professionals such as doctors, lawyers, and sociologists as 'a man among men, bringing with him as much theology as he can carry in his head, but laying down in advance no theological blueprint or pattern within which the answer must be found'.[24] Evidence from the social sciences, more than Scriptural passages, had encouraged the *Putting Asunder* Group to reject the matrimonial offence and adopt the principle of breakdown.

Dunstan's work with the Church of England Moral Welfare Council provided a pattern for this type of reasoning. In preparing the report *The Family in Contemporary Society* for the Lambeth Conference of 1958, representatives of the Council reviewed demographic, economic, social, and cultural factors, while a subcommittee of theologians and moralists examined the data in the light of established theological traditions.[25] On the basis of the Council's report, the Lambeth Conference reversed the Church's position on contraception.[26] Having theologians interpret evidence collected from the social sciences enabled the Church to look beyond traditional doctrines to accept a radical change in its teachings. Dunstan described the Council's work as 'formulating a method of moral reasoning appropriate to an era of rapid social change'.[27] This method would be influential in the debate over divorce.

The Root Commission's first formal meeting was on 19 June 1968. An immediate problem for the group stemmed from an ambiguity in the terms of reference.[28] The debate in the Convocation of Canterbury in October of 1967 indicated that members of the Upper House felt that the Church should examine the doctrine of marriage before considering changes in discipline related to divorce. Accordingly, they accepted a motion to request the Archbishop of Canterbury 'to appoint a group of theologians to present a statement on the Christian doctrine of marriage'.[29] The members of the Root Commission had a general impression upon appointment that 'their central task was to deal with the disciplinary and pastoral question about re-marriage after divorce'. When they realized that they were being asked, instead, to prepare a major theological statement on the Christian doctrine of marriage, they were 'somewhat alarmed' because that assignment 'seemed an entirely too formidable task for a body of our size and resources'. After consultation with the Doctrine Commission, the group decided to attempt to combine the two interpretations of their terms of reference. They would review the Anglican doctrine of marriage, specifically as represented in the Marriage Service of the Book of Common Prayer, and they would also consider the pastoral and disciplinary questions connected to divorce.[30]

To review Biblical injunctions and Anglican teachings related to the Christian doctrine of marriage, Hugh Montefiore, who had been appointed Bishop of Kingston-upon-Thames in January of 1970, wrote an essay entitled 'Jesus

132 *In Pursuit of Consensus*

on Divorce and Remarriage'. The essay appeared as an *appendix* to the Commission's Report, indicating that the group did not emphasize the topic. Although Montefiore concluded that scholars cannot attain absolute certainty about the sayings of Jesus regarding divorce and remarriage, he also stated, 'All will agree that Jesus taught that in the purposes of God marriage was meant to be permanent'.[31] The Commissioners quoted Canon B30 to confirm the Church's position: 'The Church of England affirms, according to our Lord's teaching, that marriage is in its nature a union permanent and lifelong'.[32]

Yet Montefiore and the other Commissioners acknowledged that marriages, although intended to be permanent, do break down. In such cases, the Commissioners concluded, 'This does not mean that marriage is not permanent in nature, only that a particular marriage has failed to attain the fullness of that nature'.[33] Regarding those instances where marriages do not prove to be permanent, Montefiore wrote that 'divorce and remarriage cannot be ruled out as an authentic response to God's will for particular people, the way in which they can best know and experience the recreative and healing grace of God'. He added, 'When Jesus asserted the permanence of marriage, he did not thereby rule out of court the propriety of all divorce and remarriage'.[34] The Root Commissioners, while acknowledging permanency as a characteristic of marriage established by Jesus, recognized that divorce could be an appropriate Christian response to the breakdown of a marriage.

Montefiore moved beyond evidence in the New Testament when he stated that answers to the questions that the Commission had been called to consider 'must be found by an evaluation of factors other than purely biblical considerations'.[35] Dunstan agreed with this conclusion, explaining that the Commissioners should provide 'an empirical basis for theological speculation, to move from human narrative to God'.[36] In the second appendix to the Root Report, 'The Correlation of Theological and Empirical Meaning', J. W. Bowker argued that the Commission should consider social changes:

> Theologically the Church is committed . . . to a constant relating of the mind and spirit of Christ to circumstances which themselves change and vary from one generation to another. . . . The ways of knowing and of understanding the nature of marriage have been vastly extended in recent generations; the social and economic circumstances in which many marriages are now lived have changed.[37]

Just as the Moral Welfare Council had studied evidence from the social sciences in preparing their report for the Lambeth Conference of 1958, the Root Commissioners recognized the necessity of considering social changes in their study of marriage and divorce. They agreed that 'the perennial task of Christian theology is to interpret God and the things of God to every generation of men'.[38]

In a series of notes for the Commission's consideration, Howard Root reviewed the current generation's emphasis on the personal relationship

In Pursuit of Consensus 133

in marriage.[39] He described the rejection of traditional marriage by many young people who evidently longed for deeply meaningful and fulfilling personal relationships that did not seem characteristic of the marriages that they saw around them. Such young people were horrified by dead marriages maintained purely for social, legal, or religious reasons. For them a loveless marriage could be immoral while a meaningful sexual relationship outside of marriage was not. As Root wrote, 'They tend to preserve the language of moral censure for things which, to them, are the real moral obscenities of our time: nuclear war, racism, poverty in the midst of affluence. . . . By comparison the matter of who sleeps with who looks rather paltry'.[40] Following this line of thought, the Commissioners wrote in their Report that 'the revulsion felt by some young people against the whole institution of marriage . . . [may be] a protest against loveless unions seen in their homes and elsewhere, in which sex is devoid of affection or personal significance'. In assessing that perception of marriage, the Root Commission emphasized the personal nature of the marriage bond as related to social changes:

> Many of the economic and social functions of the household and the family have now passed outside it, some few to the State, others to the network of economic, social, and educational systems of our developed society. Marriage has therefore come to be thought of, less in terms of its function, what it is for, than in terms of what it is. Thus many people have felt that, child-rearing apart, the only bond left to the married pair is their personal bond. . . . If this bond fails, then there is 'irretrievable breakdown' of the marriage; there is no reason why it should not be dissolved, for it is without social function either.[41]

To support this emphasis on the personal bond, the Commissioners cited the Eastern Orthodox tradition. In 'The Sacrament of Marriage in Eastern Christianity', the third appendix to the Root Report, A.M. Allchin quoted the Russian theologian Paul Evdokimov on the point: 'Orthodox doctrine affirms that the first purpose and final end of marriage is to be found in conjugal love, in the fullness of the unity of husband and wife. . . . Marriage may be useful in society, but its own autonomous value remains royally in itself'.[42] While the Western Church emphasized the marital contract, 'in the East the stress is laid on the union of bride and bridegroom, in the image of Christ and the Church'. Although lifelong fidelity remained the goal in a marriage, the Eastern Church recognized that marriages did break down and permitted both divorce and remarriage after divorce. Allchin believed that an emphasis on the freedom and transcendence of God accounted for this difference between East and West in marriage discipline. In Eastern theology God could not be limited by human concepts:

> God . . . is a God of order and of faithfulness. But he is also a God of many plans, of infinite possibilities, who is not defeated by man's

134 *In Pursuit of Consensus*

sin, nor bound even by laws which express his will. His wisdom is many-sided, and we do not comprehend it. In his dealings with men he constantly reveals himself as redeemer and life-giver, and it is forgiveness and redemption which lie at the heart of his relationship with man.[43]

That view of God provided theological support for the reconsideration of the Church of England's prohibition of remarriage after divorce in church.

Dunstan felt that the Commission should address the question of remarriage in church. They did not have the resources to draft a canon, but Root asked Dunstan to present suggestions for the Commission to consider.[44] In a memorandum entitled *In Both Worlds Full*, Dunstan noted, 'Neither the Archbishops nor the Convocations have explicitly asked us to work on the question of the re-marriage of the divorced in Church, but we must assume that this was their implicit intent. . . . I proceed on the assumption that we have to face this difficult question'. That difficult question required the Church 'to apply its powers of moral reasoning in devising a discipline for its members which respects, on the one hand, the clear will of the Lord, and, on the other, the perennial need to deal with imperfection in human relationships'.[45] For a pattern of that type of reasoning, Dunstan looked, once again, to *The Family in Contemporary Society*, the Report prepared by the Moral Welfare Council in 1958. Dunstan had cited and the Root Report had referred to an article by Bishop Ian Ramsey of Durham, who had said that the 1958 Report 'marked a watershed in the Anglican approach to moral problems'. Ramsey had argued that in the 1958 Report's validation of the practice of contraception within marriage, 'the status of the theology used in the argument was subordinate to the moral claim which, in one way or another, it was endeavouring to articulate'.[46] The Root Commissioners accepted that view when they stated in their Report that 'at times the Church may have moral insight prior to and at least as fundamental as the theological insight necessary to explain it'.[47] Moral acceptance could precede theological ratification.

Following this pattern, Dunstan formulated a crucial question regarding the Church's consideration of remarriage, which the Root Commission posed in its Report:

> Is there a growing consensus among Christian people, both clerical and lay, first, that some marriages, however well-intentioned, do break down; secondly, that some divorced partners enter into new unions in good faith and that some of these new unions show such evident features of stability, complementarity, fruitfulness, and growth as to make them comparable with satisfactory first marriages; and thirdly, that Christian congregations are not scandalized, in the theological sense of the word, by the presence of such persons in their midst or by their participation in the Holy Communion?[48]

In Pursuit of Consensus 135

The corollary question was, 'Is there also a growing moral consensus that such persons, with due safeguards, may properly have their marriages solemnized according to the rites of the Church?' The Root Commission answered this question with a striking conclusion: '*It is the unanimous conviction of this Commission*' that 'a moral consensus in favour of remarriage in church (with due safeguards) does exist'.[49] Having reached that conclusion, the Root Commission addressed the question of theological validation for the claim. They stated, 'An adequate doctrine of grace can loose as well as bind, forgive as well as bless, create again as well as create at the first'.[50]

If the Church could confirm that a consensus in favor of remarriage in church did exist, then proper authorities would have to establish procedures for such services. Dunstan recognized the difficulties in using the Prayer Book service for a second marriage. He described a procedure that the Root Commission later proposed in its Report. Before any divorced person could be remarried in church, 'discreet inquiry' should be made into the circumstances of the previous divorce. Specifically, a competent authority should review three crucial factors:

1. 'the discharge of all possible obligations remaining from the first marriage', including financial responsibilities to the former wife and children;
2. 'the character and dispositions of the two persons seeking solemnization of their marriage in church', such as any part played by the prospective spouse in the breakdown of the previous marriage; and
3. 'the same intention of lifelong fidelity that is required by any two persons who come to be married in this country'.[51]

In their Report the Root Commissioners adopted Dunstan's suggestion that the parish priest should meet privately with the couple who wanted to be married in church. At that meeting the divorced party (or parties) could express 'penitence for past faults' and 'right intention in the new marriage'.[52] After the private meeting, there could be a public marriage ceremony that reinforced the understanding that marriage is a lifelong union. For that ceremony the Root Commissioners offered an example of a preliminary declaration by the priest before the service.

> I am to declare that of the two persons now coming to be married, one has (*or* both have) had a previous marriage dissolved by due process of law. . . . I declare further that the competent Church authority has been satisfied that he (she) has (they have) discharged, or bound himself (herself) (themselves), to discharge, such obligations as remained from the former marriage as fully as possible, and that this proposed marriage may now properly be solemnized in Church.[53]

After the preliminary declaration, the traditional service could proceed.

136   *In Pursuit of Consensus*

Another member of the Root Commission who had also served on the Archbishop's Group that produced *Putting Asunder*, Helen Oppenheimer, had previously been reluctant to accept remarriage in church after divorce because, as she later wrote:

> According to Christ's teaching, it appeared, there could simply be no such thing as divorce for Christians: 'Whoever divorces his wife and marries another, commits adultery against her, and if she divorces her husband and marries another, she commits adultery'. On this simple understanding of the data, attempted remarriage is really living in sin.[54]

Dunstan's reasoning helped persuade her to reconsider this position. In response to *In Both Worlds Full*, Oppenheimer briefly described the evolution of her views and reviewed the choices for remarriage after divorce:

> I began (about 1956) by believing in the *logical* position (which I subsequently discovered was the official Anglican view) . . .
>
> a. No excommunication (People's lawful rights valid—Repentance always possible)
> b. No official service for what Christ wished not done.
>
> But I have become convinced in the course of our discussions and definitely by G.R.D.'s paper [*In Both Worlds Full*] that this is not wrong but over-simple. A second marriage is *something* . . . and *needs* blessing.
>   Therefore possibilities in *ascending order of preference*:
>
> 1. Full church service in suitable cases without distinction made*
> 2. Refusal of blessing (logical but proving itself inadequate)*
> 3. Penitential second wedding*
> 4. Service of blessing after registry office wedding
> 5. G.R.D.'s proposal—I think much the best.
>
> *These I positively dislike.[55]

The path that Oppenheimer followed from rigorism to acceptance of the possibility of remarriage in church exemplified the type of reasoning that Dunstan encouraged.

While the Root Commission was collecting evidence and preparing a report, the passage of the 1969 Divorce Act evoked questions and debate about the remarriage of divorced persons in church. On 8 July 1970 the Church Assembly considered the following motion:

> In view of the new Divorce Reform Act (which becomes law in January next) this Assembly requests the bishops, as a matter of urgency, and for the guidance of Church people, to re-assert the Church of England's

In Pursuit of Consensus   137

adherence, without equivocation, to the doctrine contained within the Statement of Canon B.30.

The Reverend David Stevens of Peterborough, who would continue to play a public role in the opposition to remarriage in church, introduced the motion. He said that 'the idea is abroad that after January 1971 almost anybody will be able to get a divorce, and that the Church is beginning to hold weaker beliefs about the marriage bond and re-marriage after divorce'.[56] The clergy needed advice on how to respond to parishioners who believed that the passage of the 1969 Act meant that remarriage in church would be accessible. When Stevens insisted that only the bishops could issue the definite statement on the permanence of marriage that was needed, Archbishop Ramsey responded:

> It would be possible for the bishops next week to pass a resolution reaffirming what is stated in the Canon just as a statement. But if the bishops were to do that, it would be widely said, 'You make a dogmatic statement but it does not tell us in a helpful way how we are to answer the very complex questions that people will be asking about matters of conscience in relation to the problems of the new Divorce Reform Act'.

Evidently interpreting Stevens's demand for a statement as a challenge, Ramsey rather sharply told the Church Assembly that 'the Church has got two Archbishops who do not need to give assurance about their faithfulness to the gospel, nor are they in this matter asleep'.[57]

Instead of merely reaffirming the doctrine stated in Canon B30, the two Archbishops circulated a Pastoral Letter in November 1970.[58] They reassured the clergy that the Church had not abandoned the view of marriage as a lifelong union, and they addressed certain misunderstandings that they believed had developed from the perception that the 1969 Divorce Act was based on the recommendations in *Putting Asunder*. Although both the Act and *Putting Asunder* used the concept of irretrievable breakdown, the statute had introduced changes in the law that concerned the Church. Specifically the Archbishops mentioned the provision that would enable one spouse to divorce the other after a five-year separation, even without the other spouse's consent. Individuals in that situation would need sensitive pastoral attention, and the Archbishops urged the clergy to work with local social agencies to provide that care. They ended the Pastoral Letter with a statement balancing the competing claims that the clergy continued to encounter: 'It is for us . . . to help conserve the stability of marriage as a life-long union and to show compassion for those to whom suffering has come'.

Graham Leonard, the Bishop of Willesden and later Bishop of London, told Archbishop Ramsey that the clergy continued to confront pastoral difficulties related to different interpretations of marriage. Leonard was the

138   *In Pursuit of Consensus*

Chairman of the Commission on the Mothers' Union, and the evidence that the group had received indicated to him that some Anglicans believed that marriage was indissoluble while others did not. As an example of the confusion, Leonard referred to a communicant who had been divorced and remarried. When the man sought readmission to communion and was told of 'Our Lord's teaching', he responded that he thought 'Our Lord was wrong'.[59] Clearly the Church of England needed to establish definite guidelines regarding remarriage after divorce.

The questions and debates surrounding the implementation of the Divorce Act put pressure on the Root Commission. The Convocations urged the group to issue its report as soon as possible, and the Commissioners felt that they were 'working against the clock'. They shared the sense of urgency, however, and were able to complete their work earlier than they had expected.[60] The Report was published as *Marriage Divorce and the Church* on 22 April 1971. Although the Commissioners concluded unanimously that there existed a theologically sound moral consensus in favor of the remarriage of divorced persons in church, they did not definitely recommend that the Church change its policies. Instead they stated:

> We do not presume to tell the Church of England what it ought to do. Our proposal is more modest. We ask the competent authorities to discover, by appropriate means, whether there now exists within the Church of England a moral consensus about the propriety, in certain circumstances, of the marriage in church of divorced persons. It came to be our unanimous conclusion, after prolonged discussions, much heart-searching, and in some cases a conscientious change of mind, that, if the Church of England reached such a moral consensus, it would be compatible with reason, the word of God in Scripture, and theological tradition.[61]

The Commission left to the Church the task of determining if a consensus existed.

Responses to the Root Report: No Consensus

A week before the publication of *Marriage Divorce and the Church*, an article in the *Sunday Telegraph* indicated how controversial the Root Report would be. Bishop Ronald Williams of Leicester was quoted as saying of the Report, 'It's full of dynamite', while Bishop Cyril Eastaugh of Peterborough said, 'It will be much contested'. The Report did not even receive the full support of the Prelate who had appointed the Commission. A spokesman for the Archbishop of Canterbury told the *Telegraph*, 'Just because we set up the commission it does not mean to say we have to accept what it recommends'.[62] The consensus that the Root Commission had predicted was not immediately apparent.

In Pursuit of Consensus 139

Strong differences of opinion were evident in the days following the Report's publication. The Executive Committee of the Church Union, noting that 'the report at the moment represents no more than the opinions of the people who have written it', issued the following statement:

> What is most needed is a clear declaration of Christian doctrine and duty in this matter and encouragement for those who are trying to live by them. To alter the present practice so as to allow re-marriage in church for those who are divorced would greatly weaken such witness, and make it appear that the Church had changed one of its fundamental tenets.[63]

In an editorial, the *Church Times* took issue with the Root Commission's proposal that the Church seek a 'moral consensus': 'Is not this tantamount to an abdication of moral responsibility to the shifting opinions of the majority at any given moment? Can questions of right and wrong be settled by counting heads?' Despite that antagonistic tone, the editors concluded that 'when all that can be said has been said against it, the fact remains that this commission has produced a very strong case for a reversal of the Church of England's present rule and practice to which immediate and sympathetic consideration ought to be given'. While they cautioned against excessive haste in the consideration of the report, the editors also wrote that there was no need for long delay.[64] Even observers who disagreed with the recommendations in the Root Report thought that the Church should consider the proposals.

Some commentators believed that the Root Report would be welcomed by many of the clergy in the Church of England. Hugh Montefiore optimistically said that he thought the Church would follow the Commission's recommendations because bishops were constantly receiving requests for remarriage in church after divorce.[65] An editorial in the *Church of England Newspaper* agreed with that assessment in the statement that there was little doubt that the Commission's recommendations 'are in line with the thinking of most clergy and laity in the Church of England except those on the Anglo Catholic wing'.[66] Harry Arnold wrote of the Root Report in *The Sun*, 'It is almost certain to go through, for the report was prepared against a back ground of growing revolt—particularly among the younger clergy'.[67] These predictions of wide and early acceptance proved overly optimistic.

The debate moved to the pages of *Theology* in May of 1971. Gordon Dunstan, the editor, had been a signatory of the Root Report and wanted to submit that document 'to the strictest examination, in order that the case against it could be fairly opened'.[68] He invited J.R. Lucas, Fellow and Tutor in Philosophy of Merton College, Oxford, to put the case against the Commission's recommendations. Lucas recognized 'the difficulty of reconciling the Church's pastoral concern for those whose marriages have come unstuck with its witness to Christian truth', but argued that, by proposing

140 *In Pursuit of Consensus*

the acceptance of remarriage in church after divorce, the Commission had put the accommodation of human frailty ahead of adherence to Christ's teachings. Comparing marriage to the relationship between siblings, Lucas wrote, 'In the Christian view, the marriage bond is even closer than that of blood'. Accordingly, the Church could not sanction a second marriage after divorce and remain 'faithful to our Lord'. Lucas acknowledged that some second marriages seemed 'successful', and he stated that 'it is not for the Church to say that [such] unions are not blessed in the eyes of God'. Yet he opposed remarriage in church. Second marriages could be successful and happy, and even blessed by God, but they could not be solemnized in church.

In the June 1971 issue of *Theology*, Helen Oppenheimer responded to Lucas by expressing regret that the Church appeared caught between the extremes of rigorism and liberalism.[69] Lucas insisted that Christ had forbidden divorce and the Church must uphold that standard, but Oppenheimer stated that the Commission's position was more subtle: 'The Lord had a very high doctrine of marriage and taught that in its nature it is permanent, but to say that in all circumstances he "forbade divorce" is to go beyond the evidence'. She cited the tradition of the Eastern Orthodox Church as more open to possibilities than the Western insistence that Christians must be either legalistic *or* permissive. Oppenheimer noted that Jesus had tended to repudiate dichotomies; his followers should not feel trapped by such a sharply defined distinction.

Oppenheimer also responded to Lucas's comparison of remarriage after divorce to the adoption of a child. He had written that 'the adoptive relationship may blossom and be blessed with every happiness, and may replace, so far as is humanly possible, the natural one: but still the natural one remains'.[70] Oppenheimer responded, 'Like an adoption, a second marriage after divorce is evidently something. It is not fair to say that people "mouth the marriage vows a second time in Church" any more than they mouth the words "my son" or "my daughter" about an adopted child'.[71] Christians should be open to the reality of the new relationship.

In calling upon the Church of England to determine if a consensus regarding remarriage in church after divorce existed, the Root Commission looked to the General Synod as the appropriate body to explore the issues. The body on which the Commissioners pinned their hopes had only been opened in November of 1970. Replacing the Church Assembly established in 1919 by the Enabling Act, the General Synod consisted of three houses of bishops, clergy, and laity.[72] Although the General Synod was to be the supreme authority on matters of worship and doctrine, it proved difficult for such a new representative assembly to issue a definitive statement or establish a consensus on the controversial question of remarriage in church after divorce.

Herbert Waddams, the only member of the Root Commission who was also a member of the General Synod, presented the Commissioners' Report to that assembly on 10 February 1972. With regard to evidence from the New Testament, Waddams described the moral reasoning that the Commission had followed:

> The Commission . . . came to the conclusion that there were no simple definitive answers to be found in the text of the New Testament to the personal questions which arise for us today, but that the teaching of the New Testament, as expressed by Jesus, had to be taken in conjunction with the examination of moral, theological, and practical issues, and a choice made in the light of all these.

Waddams expressed the concern that the Church's current policy regarding remarriage 'has created a widespread belief among people outside the Church that the Church has no use for those who have been divorced'. This perception made it difficult for the clergy to extend pastoral care to large numbers of people. Stating that 'the most important question is whether a change in practice would help or hinder the Church's witness to Christian marriage', he urged the Synod to commend the Root Report to the dioceses for consideration.[73]

The parish clergy figured prominently in the opposition to the Report in the Synod. One of the strongest opponents was the Reverend David Stevens, who believed that there was a 'moral consensus' within the Church *against* reconsideration of the policy regarding the remarriage of divorced persons. He had recently collected 118 signatures from parish clergy who supported the Church's current policy. He claimed that 'ordinary clergymen' had not been represented on the Commission, and thus their views had not been considered. Stevens wondered if the Commissioners had discerned a consensus about allowing remarriage in church after divorce because that change was the policy that they favored.[74] Other speakers also expressed concern for the parish clergy who would have to decide if a particular couple could be married in church. Responding to the implication that the Commissioners were theologians who would not have to confront the practical difficulties of implementing the policy changes that could result from their recommendations, Waddams told the Synod:

> I cannot claim the honour of having been a parish clergyman all my life, but I have done parish work in South-East London, in the West End of London, and in Canada, and others on the Commission have also had experience in parish work, so we were not completely out of touch with what is going on.[75]

That Waddams felt compelled to defend the Commissioners in such terms did not augur well for the Root Report.

In response to the motion of Canon Waddams 'That this Report be commended for study in the dioceses', Canon J.H. Jacques of Lincoln moved to

142   *In Pursuit of Consensus*

delete the words following 'be' and insert the following amendment: 'sent to the dioceses for study, the Synod emphasizing that the report has no authority other than that of the Commission which produced it'. The Synod, according to Canon G.O. Morgan of Manchester, 'always' commended reports. To change the word to 'sent' indicated a lack of support that the recipients would surely note. Those who opposed the recommendations in the Root Report felt that the division of opinion that was evident in the Synod debate necessitated the change. The amendment was carried by a vote of 184 to 180, a narrow margin that implied that the Synod was almost evenly divided on the questions.[75]

Responses to the Synod's debate focused on the amendment. The *Church Times* headline proclaimed 'Marriage Report is "sent"—but not "commended"—to Dioceses for Study', and an editorial predicted, 'This amendment was a straw in the wind of which the diocesan synods will take due note'. *The Times* headline noted 'Backing for Report on Divorce Lukewarm'.[77] In an editorial in *Theology*, Gordon Dunstan was scornful in writing that the amendment had been passed 'lest the Synod should be tainted with guilt by association with the Commission'. Yet, he continued, although '184 members voted thus to preserve their innocency, 180 would have taken the risk. If the vote is a fair representation of the divided attitude of the Church of England, there may be something to be said for the Commission's analysis after all'.[78] The Synod's reception of the Root Report may not have been as positive or as supportive as the Commissioners had hoped it would be, but the close vote indicated that there was considerable support for the Report's recommendations.

Dunstan was harsh in his analysis of the Synod's deliberations. A power cut had plunged the hall into darkness during the debate, and the proceedings had continued by candlelight.[79] Dunstan referred to the setting as 'a suitable symbolic darkness' before he disparaged the speakers who used the term 'compassion' to describe the Church's current treatment of those who had remarried after divorce: 'The issue to be decided is the theological and ecclesiastical status of those who in good conscience have taken this step, not whether it is "compassionate" to invite them to prayer and sacrament as means of God's blessing on their continuance in a union already declared *a priori* adulterous'. Dunstan's criticism of the speakers who had expressed concern about the parish clergy's difficulties in deciding which couples could be married in church was even more severe:

> To decide whether any such people should be re-married in church would oblige the bishops and clergy to exercise judgment, and this would be abhorrent to them, virtually impossible, they said. By what process, then, do they now exercise their fictitious discretion whether or not to admit the re-married to communion? It is fictitious because they have no legal power to exclude them; and if they repudiate *judgment*, then the process is as pretended as the claim to operate it is false.[80]

In Pursuit of Consensus 143

Dunstan saw the root of the problem as a lack of leadership:

> Headship . . . rules, governs, directs action, dominates thought. Today it shews itself in reticence: it sits back; it leaves the lesser fry to talk and have their way. And in this debate on a theological and moral question, while those with authority and competence sat silent, the General Synod of the Church of England displayed symptoms of its acephaly.[81]

Dunstan's harshness may have stemmed from the frustration that he must have felt when the recommendations to which he had devoted over a decade of thought were rejected by those who had not considered the questions as thoroughly as he had. Surely the initial response of the General Synod to the Root Report was discouraging to the Commissioners who had produced it.

After sending the Root Report to the dioceses for study, the General Synod appointed a working party to review diocesan responses and prepare a report.[82] As the Chairman of the General Synod Committee responsible for appointing the working party, Bishop Gerald Ellison of Chester wrote to Dunstan that the group's purpose would be to produce a document clearly outlining the issues and stating the questions that the General Synod must consider.[83] Dunstan agreed to serve on the working party, as did Helen Oppenheimer; they represented the Root Commission. Bishop Ronald Williams of Leicester was the Chair, and the Reverend Peter Boulton, a member of the General Synod, was the other member.[84]

When the Root Report was sent to the dioceses for study, the General Synod did not provide clear instructions about responses. Not surprisingly, then, the Working Party did not receive a decisive mandate from the dioceses regarding the recommendations in the Report. Out of 43 bishops who received the Report, only 26 responded. Only 8 of the diocesan synods that responded to the circulation of the Root Report passed clear resolutions.[85] On the basis of this patchy evidence, the Working Party was asked to prepare a report.

Before the debate in the General Synod on the Working Party's Report (GS 156), Hugh Montefiore published an article in the *Church Times* expressing his dismay at the fate of the Root Report.[86] He lamented the lack of guidance given to the dioceses when the Synod sent them the Report, which had resulted in a lack of uniformity among the responses. The responses, according to Montefiore, consisted of 'a straggling list of miscellaneous points, without apparent sequence and unconnected with the considered arguments of the Commission—hardly the basis for a balanced judgment'. With regard to the Root Commissioners' recommendation that the Church seek to ascertain if a moral consensus existed, Montefiore wrote that the responses were so 'varied and haphazard' that it was impossible to determine if such a consensus existed. Dunstan blamed the confusion on those who wanted to rush the matter to the Synod for a decision. He wrote to Helen Oppenheimer that the procedure should have been 'first to formulate proper questions to put to dioceses and bishops, secondly to digest their replies properly, and thirdly to

144   *In Pursuit of Consensus*

draft a succinct report and proper resolutions for the General Synod accordingly'. Dunstan added, 'Haste denied us all these steps'.[87]

When the General Synod convened on 7 November 1973 to discuss issues related to remarriage in church after divorce, Bishop Ronald Williams, the Chair of the Working Party, moved to maintain the existing discipline regarding remarriage in church because the evidence supporting change was 'insufficient'.[88] Robert Runcie, the Bishop of St. Albans and later Archbishop of Canterbury, wanted to obtain such evidence. He asked that the Synod return to the dioceses with the specific question of 'whether they believe that an alteration in the present marriage discipline of the Church of England in order to permit remarriage in church (under certain conditions and with due safeguards) is theologically defensible and pastorally desirable, so that the matter may be further considered in the life of this Synod'. Runcie told the Synod that the Root Commission had sent them 'one clear and unambiguous recommendation, namely, that we should try to discover whether a moral consensus exists for the remarriage in church of certain people, with due safeguards'. In response, the Synod, after a confused debate (which Runcie characterized as 'not one of our brightest moments'), sent the Report 'to the dioceses for study without any guidance or questions to be answered'. Without that guidance, in Bishop Runcie's opinion, the Synod had been unable to gather sufficient evidence to determine whether or not a moral consensus for change in the Church's marriage discipline existed.[89]

Several other speakers also argued that the Synod had not properly sought the views of the bishops and the dioceses. Canon J.C. Docker of Chichester claimed that more bishops and dioceses had not responded to the survey of opinions regarding the Root Report because 'they have been waiting for a more specific request from the General Synod'. He urged the Synod to agree to Bishop Runcie's motion and return to the dioceses with clearer questions. John Habgood, the Bishop of Durham and later Archbishop of York, said that his diocese had not yet responded to the Root Report because the late Bishop Ramsey 'considered that there was no clear mandate from the Synod to discuss this and no clear terms given to the diocesan synods in which it could be discussed'. Bishop Oliver Stratford Tomkins of Bristol described a similar reaction in his diocese, saying that 'we understood . . . that there would be further guidance before we were asked to make any definite commitment of diocesan opinion'.[90] Such misunderstandings added to disagreement to create division within the Synod.

Formal votes in the Synod revealed the depth of the division.[91] On Bishop Runcie's motion to refer the questions to the dioceses again, the vote was: 18 *ayes* and 14 *noes* in the House of Bishops; 100 *ayes* and 100 *noes* in the House of Clergy; and 106 *ayes* and 72 *noes* in the House of Laity. The bishops and the laity wanted to return to the dioceses for clearer guidance, but the clergy were evenly divided on the question. Since the approval of all three houses was required for a motion to pass, Bishop Runcie's motion failed by a small margin.

In Pursuit of Consensus 145

The next vote, on the motion of Bishop Robert Woods of Worcester to change the Church's discipline to allow the remarriage of some divorced persons in church, produced larger majorities and thus a more explicit result: 12 *ayes* and 16 *noes* in the House of Bishops; 68 *ayes* and 121 *noes* in the House of Clergy; and 50 *ayes* and 126 *noes* in the House of Laity. Finally, on the Bishop of Leicester's motion to maintain the existing discipline with regard to remarriage in church, the vote was: 16 *ayes* and 14 *noes* in the House of Bishops; 118 *ayes* and 80 *noes* in the House of Clergy; and 117 *ayes* and 58 *noes* in the House of Laity. Five years after the appointment of the Root Commission, the Synod appeared to repudiate their Report by voting to maintain the Church's current marriage discipline. The Commissioners' efforts had ostensibly been in vain.

Two bishops stepped forward to ask the General Synod to reconsider the question of remarriage after divorce in church. One was Bishop Graham Leonard of Truro, whose Anglo-Catholic reputation was confirmed when, after his retirement, he converted to Roman Catholicism and was ordained as a priest in that Church in 1994.[92] In the summer of 1974, the Truro Diocesan Synod had passed a resolution that noted

> with concern the change in understanding of the nature of marriage expressed in the Divorce Reform Act 1969 and therefore asks the General Synod to examine again the Christian doctrine of marriage and only after such examination to consider the marriage discipline in the Church of England or refer the matter to the dioceses.[93]

In an amended form, Bishop Leonard introduced this resolution as a motion to the General Synod on 8 November 1974. He favored sending questions regarding marriage after divorce to the dioceses, but not on the basis of the Root Report. He was especially critical of the Commissioners' recommendation 'that if the moral decision is made for remarriage it will be theologically well founded'. That, for Leonard, was 'putting the cart before the horse'. He told the Synod, 'What we need to do is to get the theological principles straight . . . not to make the moral decision first and then to see whether it is theologically acceptable'.[94] According to Leonard, only after an examination of those theological principles had enabled the Synod to define the doctrine of marriage more clearly should questions be sent to the dioceses.

A year and a day after his motion to send the question of remarriage after divorce to the dioceses had narrowly failed in the General Synod, Bishop Runcie of St. Albans returned to argue again on behalf of the Root Commission.[95] He opened the debate on 8 November 1974 by introducing the following motion:

> That this Synod resolves that the diocesan synods should be asked . . . whether they consider that an alteration in the present marriage discipline of the Church of England in order to permit remarriage of

146   *In Pursuit of Consensus*

divorced persons in church . . . is theologically defensible and pastorally desirable.[96]

Runcie argued that a year earlier 'a sizeable overall majority in the Synod . . . wished the question of remarriage to be referred as a direct question to the dioceses as envisaged by the report *Marriage Divorce and the Church*'. He was now providing the Synod with another opportunity to accomplish that goal. With regard to remarriage in church after divorce, Runcie told the Synod, 'It is not that God cannot bless such a second marriage but that men may be scandalized and confused to hear the same service done a second time'. Deeming this problem 'soluble', he asked the Synod to seek a consensus from the dioceses on the question.[97]

One of the speakers in the General Synod on 8 November 1974 opposed Runcie's motion by questioning the authority of synodical government itself. Donald Coggan, Archbishop of York and Archbishop-designate of Canterbury, opposed sending questions to the dioceses because 'there is a danger coming to us in the early stages of the government of the Church by General Synod that our Church of England shall lapse, almost without realizing it, into government by consensus'. Arguing that diocesan synods might be inclined 'to give answers which are based far more on emotion than they are on sound theological and ethical reasoning', Coggan said the House of Bishops should advise the General Synod on the questions.[98] As the editors of the *Church Times* commented, the argument that any 'important question of theology must be reserved to the bishops alone as the sole guardians of doctrine in the Church' had serious implications for the future of synodical government.[99] The argument was especially significant since it was presented by the next Archbishop of Canterbury.

When the Chairman ordered a division by Houses on Bishop Runcie's motion, the result was: 15 *ayes* and 12 *noes* in the House of Bishops; 94 *ayes* and 79 *noes* in the House of Clergy; and 70 *ayes* and 92 *noes* in the House of Laity.[100] Both the bishops and the clergy favored referring the questions to the dioceses. Only the laity rejected the motion. The vote of 179 *ayes* to 183 *noes* indicates how closely divided the General Synod remained on the issue of remarriage in church after divorce. After the failure of Runcie's motion, it is not surprising that Bishop Leonard's motion passed. Runcie himself had told the Synod that 'if my motion fails, I shall be voting for the Bishop of Truro's motion, because at least something will then be done'.[101]

The three debates in the General Synod revealed not just disagreement about the questions but confusion and uncertainty about the proper procedure to follow. The Synod, designed to maintain a balance in decision-making between episcopal direction and lay participation, had been opened only in November of 1970. In one of its first tests, this national assembly failed to provide strong leadership on a theological and moral question. Criticism of the Synod's deliberations and decisions regarding the recommendations in the Root Report was conspicuous in the press. After the second debate

In Pursuit of Consensus 147

in November of 1973, Canon Paul Welsby wrote, 'In my judgment the way in which this matter has been handled has been the biggest blow that synodical government has yet experienced'.[102] In December of 1974, after the third debate, Clifford Longley, the Religious Affairs Correspondent for *The Times*, wrote, 'The general synod showed itself to be unsure in its relationship with diocesan synods; the House of Bishops showed itself to be unsure in its relationship with the general synod; and the church showed itself to be unsure in its relationship with society'. Longley speculated that there might be a 'silent rebellion' among the clergy, many of whom were evidently willing to remarry divorced persons in church but not eager to talk about it.[103]

Those clergy would not receive support from the Archbishop of Canterbury. Michael Ramsey had appointed the Root Commission but did not choose to support their recommendations or to present their Report formally to the Church. He did not even officially express his appreciation to the Commissioners for their efforts until, evidently at the insistence of Howard Root, he sent them letters over a year later.[104] According to Owen Chadwick, Ramsey strongly opposed remarriage in church after divorce:

> Ramsey was willing to bless with prayers a couple after a civil wedding and did so more than once. The difference between a blessing and prayers on the one hand and a marriage service on the other needed subtle distinctions. He maintained to the end that the distinction mattered.[105]

Neither the Archbishop of Canterbury nor a majority of the General Synod endorsed the Root Commission's recommendation that the Church should seek to determine if there existed a moral consensus about the propriety of the marriage in church of divorced individuals. Instead the questions remained to be addressed by yet another commission appointed to consider the marriage doctrines of the Church of England.

The Lichfield Commission Divides

The bishop who was asked to chair the new General Synod Marriage Commission was no stranger to controversy. Bishop Kenneth Skelton of Lichfield had earlier served as Bishop of Matabeleland in Rhodesia from 1962 until 1970. During those years, Ian Smith, the Prime Minister of Rhodesia, had established white minority rule in that country. Skelton's fearless and active opposition to Smith's government earned him the hatred of many whites. One MP in the Rhodesian Parliament 'asked who would rid the country of this turbulent priest', while a telephone caller threatened, 'If Mr Smith doesn't shoot you, I will'. Michael Ramsey's strong support of Skelton led some of the Bishop's enemies to burn their Bibles and send the ashes to the Archbishop, who was also cursed in the corridors of the House of Lords.[106] A hero to the black African community, Skelton would have stayed in Rhodesia

148   *In Pursuit of Consensus*

to continue the fight, but he had a wife and three children. Pressures on his family led him to return to England, where he was appointed CBE in 1972.[107]

Remarriage in church after divorce was controversial, but surely death threats were not part of the debate. In 1975, when the Archbishop of Canterbury, Donald Coggan, asked the Bishop of Lichfield to serve as Chair of a new Marriage Commission, Skelton did not shrink from the responsibility. He did, however, note a possible objection to his appointment. During the late 1960s, he had helped to draft a proposal for the marriage of divorced persons in church. The Provincial Synod of central Africa had accepted the proposal in 1969, but the measure was controversial. Skelton asked the Archbishop if his known support for remarriage in church might bring the impartiality of the Commission into question. Coggan responded that Skelton's stated position on the question did not disqualify him from serving as the chair of the Marriage Commission.[108] The Commission began its deliberations, then, with a chair who supported reform.

Whereas the Root Commission had been dominated by theologians, the Lichfield Commission was more broadly representative. Archbishop Coggan thought that many critics felt that the members of the Root Commission did not have extensive experience in the parishes.[109] The Lichfield Commission included not only parochial clergy (the Reverend Brandon Jackson, the Reverend M.E. Adie, and the Reverend M.G. Whittock) but also a sociologist (Professor Kathleen Jones, who had been unable to serve on the Root Commission), a marriage guidance counselor (Mrs. M.I. Allen, who was also a solicitor), a psychiatrist (Dr. Kenneth Soddy, a former Chairman of the Institute of Religion and Medicine whose professional focus was children from broken families), and a gynaecologist (Dr. Morgan Williams). Members with professional legal experience included Mrs. Allen and Sheila Cameron, a barrister who served as a Chancellor of Chelmsford Diocese.[110]

Selecting theologians to serve on the Marriage Commission was a bit more complicated. Bishop Skelton had identified himself as favoring reform before accepting the Chairmanship of the Commission. One member who was clearly on the other side in the debate was John R. Lucas, who had taken the side of the indissolubilists in his response to the Root Report in the pages of *Theology* in May of 1971. When Skelton asked that the Archbishops appoint another theologian to the Commission, he suggested Peter Baelz, who was a Canon of Christ Church and Regius Professor of Moral and Pastoral Theology at Oxford. Baelz was regarded as a liberal theologian.[111] The Business Sub-Committee of the Synod suggested the appointment instead of Canon David Stevens,[112] who had spoken against the Root Report in the General Synod debates mainly on the ground that the Root Commission had not sufficiently considered the views of parish clergy. The perception that 'liberal' theologians favored allowing remarriage in church after divorce, while the parish clergy opposed the change, had been evident in the responses to the Root Report and resurfaced in the process of selecting members for the Lichfield Commission. Other observers believed that a majority of the parish clergy *supported* reform. The Root Commission had hoped that the Church could determine a consensus on the question, but divisions persisted.

One of the terms of reference of the Lichfield Commission was 'to consider the understanding by contemporary people of the place of marriage as an institution'.[113] In their Report, which was published in 1978, the Commissioners addressed the implications of such social changes as the increase in employment opportunities for women. Social and economic roles for husbands and wives were no longer clear-cut. The institution of marriage no longer enjoyed the strong social support that had buttressed unions in the past. Few couples had a strong extended family network to help them. Economic pressures that had previously made the breaking up of the home unthinkable had diminished in significance. Without those sources of reinforcement, the Commissioners concluded, 'The institution of marriage now stands or falls on the quality of the interpersonal relationship between the couple'.[114] That conclusion echoed the Root Commission's understanding that the meaning and purpose of marriage were to be found in the relationship between husband and wife and not in the social function of the institution.

The Lichfield Commissioners believed that Christians could not consider only Biblical sources and ignore the social changes that had produced the current understanding of the institution of marriage. As a result, the Commissioners looked at human experience and insight in describing the marriage bond:

> This bond is made up of many different strands. It is a moral bond, deriving from a promise of fidelity. It is an emotional bond, deriving from shared experiences. It is a physical bond, deriving from sexual union. It is a spiritual bond deriving from allegiance to common values. It is a bond of habit: 'I've grown accustomed to her face'. It is above all a personal bond, weaving together some or all of these various strands.

More difficult to understand was the definition of the marriage bond as a bond of *being*, an ontological bond that cannot be severed. If two individuals theoretically become one in marriage, then no human action could end the union. The Lichfield Commissioners concluded:

> All of us are agreed that, in its perfectness, the marriage bond unites two persons at the centre of their being, that it is in this sense an ontological bond. All of us are agreed that there actually occur such ontological unions between man and wife, unions which, as a matter of fact, nothing can dissolve. We are not all agreed, however, how we are to describe those unions which, to all outward appearances, have broken down.[115]

In this interpretation, the ontological bond was not necessarily established by the marriage ceremony but rather was identified with the strength and

150 *In Pursuit of Consensus*

nature of the relationship between husband and wife. The bond 'was not simply a bond of commitment grounded in promise and obligation. It was a relational bond of personal love, a compound of commitment, experience and response, in which the commitment clothed itself in the flesh and blood of a living union'.[116] Not all couples were able to establish such a bond.

All the Lichfield Commissioners agreed that 'marriages *ought* to be indissoluble'. Consistent with their description of the ontological bond, they stated, 'We are all agreed in affirming that indissolubility is characteristic of marriage as it should and can be'. They added, 'Such indissolubility is experienced, not as restriction and constraint, but as liberation and fulfillment'. Despite the 'great joy' that marriage can offer, however, 'marriages can and do break down'. Humans were capable of breaking a bond that God had willed to be unbreakable. Recognizing that humans can put asunder what God has joined together, the Church needed to consider not only how to help couples achieve the deeper bond that cannot be broken but also how to minister to those couples whose marriages had irretrievably broken down. In establishing a discipline for its own members, the Commissioners recommended that 'the Church must not substitute the demands of law for the calling of grace'.[117]

The Lichfield Commissioners had also been asked to report on the courses of action open to the Church. One possibility was to separate the Church's policies from the State's regulation of marriage by introducing universal civil marriage. Earlier the Archbishop of Canterbury had invited two groups to study that possibility. The Archdeacon of Swindon, F.S. Temple, chaired a group of parochial clergy who were primarily concerned with the pastoral aspects of the questions, while Bishop Gerald Ellison of Chester chaired another group that concentrated on legal and administrative matters. Neither of the two groups recommended universal civil marriage. Noting that seven out of every ten marriages in England and Wales were solemnized in churches and chapels and that one out of two marriages in England was celebrated in an Anglican Church, the groups did not want to lose the pastoral opportunities that those numbers represented. The financial implications for the Church represented another consideration. The groups estimated that the abolition of the Common Licence could cause the Church to lose income in the range of £40,000 to £50,000 a year. Additionally, 'if banns were abolished as a preliminary to marriage, and were replaced by a civil preliminary, the loss of income to the clergy would be very considerable indeed—possibly well over £100,000 per annum'.[118] The Lichfield Commissioners did not cite these financial considerations in their opposition to the establishment of a system of universal civil marriage. Instead, they emphasized the importance of maintaining widespread pastoral outreach.[119]

Retaining a primary role in the initiation of marriages in England did not solve the Church's problems regarding remarriage in church after divorce. The Lichfield Commissioners considered various responses to the difficulty. One possibility involved the concept of nullity. Roman Catholics followed

In Pursuit of Consensus 151

a practice whereby an individual who had been divorced by the State could then apply to the Church for a decision that the marriage was null, which meant, in effect, that the marriage had never existed. A divorced individual whose marriage had been declared null was free to marry in church. The Lichfield Commission did not recommend the adoption of this practice.[120] Another possible course of action was to formalize a religious service of prayer and dedication that could follow the civil marriage of a divorced person. The Lichfield Commissioners did not favor adopting this alternative either. They believed that 'there would be a continuing risk of confusion between the service proposed and the marriage service', and stated forcefully, 'We are of one mind in rejecting the suggestion of a public service of prayer and dedication. *We recommend that the present use of such services should be brought to an end*'.[121] The Commissioners were also unanimous in their recommendation that Holy Communion should not be denied to those who had remarried after divorce. Admission to Communion should not be considered a 'seal of approval' but rather a means of grace to those who needed assurance of the love of God. Accordingly, with emphasis, the Commissioners recommended '*that the Convocation regulations requiring that those who marry after divorce should only be admitted to Communion with the permission of the Bishop should be rescinded*'.[122]

While the Commissioners may have been of one mind with regard to services of prayer and dedication and admission to Communion, they were not unanimous in their recommendations regarding remarriage in church after divorce. They stated the choice between two possible courses of action very simply:

a.   To maintain the present official position that divorced persons should in no circumstances be married in church; and
b.   To adopt a system whereby, without conceding a general right of remarriage in church, divorced persons were in certain cases permitted to be married in church following a pastoral enquiry.[123]

Four Commissioners approved the first course of action, which would require an Act of Synod. The existing Convocation regulations had proved unsatisfactory in establishing uniformity of practice regarding the remarriage of divorced persons in church, but the clergy should abide by a formal Act of the General Synod.[124] A majority of the Commissioners recommended that the remarriage of divorced persons in church should be permitted in certain circumstances. In order to maintain a consistent policy, they recommended that the bishop or a small panel appointed by the bishop should make the decision. As the couple's pastor, the incumbent should be involved in the procedure, but the decision should rest with the bishop or his nominees.[125] The division of the Lichfield Commissioners over the question of remarriage in church after divorce demonstrated that, a decade after the appointment of the Root Commission, the consensus that they had hoped the Church might discover had not been found.

152 *In Pursuit of Consensus*

Responses to the Lichfield Report: No Resolution

The Report of the Lichfield Commission, entitled *Marriage and the Church's Task*, was published on 19 May 1978. On that same day Clifford Longley reported, in an article on the first page of *The Times*, that a new membership had been elected to the General Synod since the 1974 debate on the question of remarriage in church after divorce. A third of the current members were new, and those representing Anglo-Catholic and Evangelical views were more numerous as a result. The Lichfield recommendations, based on a divided vote, would face substantial opposition in the Synod.[126] Immediately below Longley's article, a small notice with the title of 'Royal Divorce' announced that Princess Margaret was suing Lord Snowdon for divorce. On the day the Lichfield Commission published its report, the press reported that the Princess who had obeyed the Church's rules regarding divorce was ending her marriage.

Also on the day of the publication of the Lichfield Report, the *Church Times* ran, side by side, two articles responding to the Report. In the article designated 'YES!', Hugh Montefiore, who was at the time the Bishop of Birmingham, wrote, 'The Lichfield Report is a better document than our Root Report'. According to Montefiore, the Lichfield Commission had clearer terms of reference than the Root Commission. Also, the Lichfield Commissioners differed in their views of indissolubility and were thus able to provide 'fairer coverage to opponents of remarriage in church'. Montefiore thought that the Lichfield Report would appeal to the General Synod because it was written 'in a simple pastoral style', while the Root Report had been 'too terse and academic'. Finally, Montefiore believed that the Root Commission had erred in deciding to relegate Scriptural evidence to an appendix. The Lichfield Report 'pays great attention, in the body of the report, to the words of Scripture'. Although he disagreed with the Lichfield recommendation that only a bishop could grant permission to remarry in church after divorce, Montefiore commended the Report as a 'way forward' and wished them well in the Synod.[127]

In the article designated 'NO!' in the *Church Times*, Canon David Stevens noted that a friend had referred to the Lichfield Report as 'a complete sell-out'. Stevens did not think that the characterization was accurate with regard to the main body of the Report, 'which contains many signs of the deep moral integrity of the Commission as a whole'. Specifically he praised the section on the Bible, which 'consistently asserted that what counts for us Christians is what Jesus taught and intended'. But Stevens, who had been one of the strongest opponents of the Root Report in the General Synod, still rejected the Lichfield Commission's majority recommendation that remarriage in church after divorce be allowed in certain cases.[128]

An editorial that also appeared in the *Church Times* on 19 May 1978 referred to the articles by Montefiore and Stevens as representing the deep divisions within the Church of England over the question of remarriage

In Pursuit of Consensus   153

in church after divorce. With regard to the Reports of both the Root and Lichfield Commissions, the editors themselves stated:

> The arguments advanced by the two Commissions are strong; and, whatever the General Synod may or may not decide, after these two reports which have made the same proposal it seems probable that more and more parish priests will conduct such marriages in the years to come. We conclude that the Church's ban ought to be lifted.[129]

The General Synod debate on *Marriage and the Church's Task* in July of 1978 revealed substantial opposition to that recommendation. Kathleen Jones, who had served on the Lichfield Commission, described the atmosphere in the General Synod as 'highly politicized':

> It seemed evident that some groups in Synod, particularly the Anglo-Catholic group and the Evangelical group, whose views on this subject coincided, were organized to take a hard line against remarriage in Church. They had the advantage of a clear and uncompromising position, which appealed to some waverers.[130]

Into that atmosphere the Bishop of Lichfield introduced a motion asking that the Report of the Commission that he had chaired be received. His speech was well organized and clear. In it, he noted the diversity of the backgrounds of the Commissioners, emphasizing their wide range of perspectives and experiences. With regard to the Biblical sources, Skelton told the Synod, 'We are united in our belief that the New Testament insists that marriages should not be dissolved. But most of us are unable to accept that they cannot'. He added, 'Of course the challenge of Jesus' words must be upheld: but we do not believe he wished them to be used to tie round men's necks burdens which they are not able to bear'. Skelton told the Synod that the majority of the Commissioners recommended that the Church should allow some divorced persons to remarry in church. He concluded, 'The one option which is not open to the Church is to stay as we are'.[131]

The first speaker to disagree with that conclusion was Mrs. M. E. R. Holmes, who had been one of the four Lichfield Commissioners who could not accept the majority recommendation. In the speech immediately following Skelton's, Mrs. Holmes raised a point that would be reinforced by Archbishop Coggan. Mrs. Holmes favored maintaining the Church's current discipline, she said, because 'to relax it would appear to the world as a concession to secular pressure'. Coggan told the Synod that he feared that permitting remarriage in church after divorce 'would be to give the impression that the Church was bending to the wind of current laxity in regard to marital faithfulness'.[132] Even though the Church continued to maintain the definition of marriage as a lifelong union, the acceptance of remarriage in church in certain cases might imply to the public that the Church had yielded to secular pressures.

154 *In Pursuit of Consensus*

The Lichfield Commissioners had taken note of the point in their Report. They had written that the argument to prohibit remarriage in church as a means of maintaining the Church's 'clear witness to life-long marriage' had appeared only recently as a result of 'a deep concern at the increasingly high divorce rate'. In response the Commissioners had argued:

> The burden of making the witness falls on those who are least well placed to do so, that is, those whose marriages have already broken down. If the previous marriage has already been dissolved there is no positive witness that they can make to its life-long character. Since they experienced no comparable expression of disapproval from the Church at the point where the earlier marriage was being dissolved they are likely to conclude (however illogically) that the Church is not so much opposed to the dissolution of the shell of the earlier marriage as to their attempt to make a reality of marriage in a fresh union.[133]

The arguments are reminiscent of the familiar emphasis on individual self-sacrifice that had long been central to the debates over divorce reform. By prohibiting remarriage in church, the Church of England was asking divorced individuals whose previous marriages had broken down to sacrifice personal hopes for a church marriage in order to provide witness to the principle of marriage as a lifelong union. The Lichfield Commissioners emphasized the well-being of the individual when they argued that, in permitting remarriage in church after divorce, the Church would not be conceding to 'secular pressure', but rather recognizing that the

> contemporary experience of marriage, with all its stresses and uncertainties, may in some respects represent a deeper understanding of what God intends marriage to be. The emphasis on mutuality and sharing, the belief that in marriage each partner can become more fully himself or herself while contributing to the growth of the other—these reflect a certain convergence between secular expectations and Christian understanding which it should be the job of the Church to nourish.[134]

Social changes could encourage, not 'laxity', but the emergence of a closer marital relationship blessed by God. To deny individuals the opportunity to initiate such a union in church seemed inconsistent with the Church's goals. To argue that 'hard cases make bad laws', or, more to the point, 'hard cases should maintain the Church's principles', seemed counterproductive.

A second point that Mrs. Holmes raised in objection to the majority recommendations of the Lichfield Commission was the difficulty of deciding which couples should be allowed remarriage in church after divorce. Whereas the Commissioners had thought that requiring bishops or their representatives to make the decision would foster the development of consistent policies, Mrs. Holmes argued that the exercise of the discretion would vary from diocese to diocese. Archbishop Coggan told the Synod that having bishops decide which couples could be remarried in church would place a burden on the incumbent, who would be required to enforce the bishop's decision. If one couple in a parish were allowed remarriage in church and another was not, the incumbent would have to cope with the bitter disappointment that the decision caused. Archbishop Coggan said, 'I do care about my priests'.[135]

As this objection suggests, Coggan could not accept the recommendation of the majority of the Lichfield Commissioners. He told the Synod that he had administered the current marriage discipline of the Church for over twenty-two years without making a single exception. He argued that maintaining that discipline, 'difficult and unsatisfactory as it was, has borne public witness to the fact that we take seriously the Christian teaching about the lifelong participation of two people in marriage'. Acknowledging that his position could cause hardship in certain cases, the Archbishop repeated the phrase that had been the basis for opposition to divorce reform for over a century: 'Hard cases make bad law'.[136]

Coggan did have an alternative to offer to those hard cases. In lieu of remarriage in church, he offered 'a service of committal'. In such a service the couple would commit themselves, their children, and their new homes to God 'not as some hole-in-the corner affair but as part of the main Sunday service'. This proposal evoked a negative response in the Synod. The Venerable M.E. Adie, the Archdeacon of Lincoln who had served on the Lichfield Commission, said that his initial reaction as a parish priest was that 'to single out those who have been remarried in a way quite distinct from those who have been married for the first time and, so to speak, to draw particular attention to them in the context of the Christian congregation' would be very embarrassing. The Reverend G.B. Austin was unhappy with the word 'committal', explaining, 'If the Archbishop of Canterbury will forgive me, I do not think he does crematorium duty—it has other connotations'.[137]

The Lichfield Commissioners had an advantage over the Root Commissioners when presenting their Report to the General Synod because several of them were members and could participate in the debate. The Bishop of Lichfield himself presented the Report, while Mrs. M.E.R. Holmes and the Venerable M.E. Adie addressed the Synod. Professor Kathleen Jones was yet another of the Commissioners who participated in the debate, telling the Synod how her opinions had changed:

> When I entered on the work of the Marriage Commission I was the wife of a parish priest who had always taken a strong line against remarriage, which I shared with him, and I did not expect that my views would be changed. But one goes into this kind of work to be educated. I learnt a great deal. . . . Out of that came the conviction that the Church dare not stand still.[138]

156 *In Pursuit of Consensus*

Jones recommended that the issues be submitted to the dioceses for further reflection. The Synod had not granted the Root Commission's request to take that step. Now the same possibility was before them.

After Jones had concluded her speech, the Synod voted to receive the Lichfield Report and then proceeded to consider another motion from Bishop Skelton:

> That this Synod shares the view of the majority of the Marriage Commission that the Church of England should now take steps . . . to permit a divorced person with the bishop's permission to be married in church during the lifetime of a former spouse . . . and asks the Standing Committee to bring forward draft regulations to give effect to the Commission's proposals . . . so that these can be referred to diocesan synods for consideration before a final decision is taken by this Synod.[139]

Bishop Graham Leonard of Truro responded negatively to the motion. In 1974 he had played a significant role in the General Synod's decision to defer sending the recommendations of the Root Commission to the dioceses for review until after another examination of the questions could be conducted. The Lichfield Commission's Report represented that examination, yet when Leonard spoke again in the Synod debate in July of 1978, he was still dissatisfied.[140] He had hoped that a new Commission would review all of the options and recommend sending those possibilities to the dioceses for consideration, rather than asking the Synod to endorse one particular course of action. Leonard could support much of the substance of the Lichfield Report but not the recommendations of the majority.

The Synod vote on Skelton's motion to accept the majority view of the Commission that a divorced person should be permitted to remarry in church reflected the continuing divisions within the Church of England: 25 *ayes* and 13 *noes* in the House of Bishops; 92 *ayes* and 112 *noes* in the House of Clergy; and 89 *ayes* and 88 *noes* in the House of Laity.[141] Since all three Houses did not pass the motion, it failed. A decade after the appointment of the Root Commission, the Church's position on remarriage in church after divorce remained unchanged. Not only the Synod but also two Archbishops of Canterbury had refused to accept the Root and Lichfield Commissioners' recommendations that the Church should permit remarriage in church after divorce. Apart from the Church's canonical definition of marriage as a lifelong union, several other obstacles to acceptance of the Commissions' Reports appeared in the debates during the 1970s. The Root Commission's concept of a moral consensus was troubling to those who believed that questions of right and wrong could not be settled by 'counting heads'. Both Commissions had argued that social changes could not be ignored in formulating rules regarding divorce, yet opponents of change feared that permitting remarriage in church would appear to be conceding to secular pressures. Since remarriage in church after divorce would be allowed only in certain cases, there was concern about the clergy who would have to make difficult decisions and who could be subject to pressure from prominent and influential parishioners. While, officially, the Church would not permit remarriage in church after divorce, the debate began to turn to questions of determining which divorced individuals might be allowed a religious service.

Notes

1. Letter from the Archbishop of Canterbury dated 4 January 1966. Lambeth Palace Library, Ramsey Papers, Vol. 102, f 331.
2. G. Bell, *Randall Davidson, Archbishop of Canterbury* (Oxford University Press, 1952), p. 554.
3. 'Church's Attitude to Divorce Criticised', *Church Times* (30 September 1966):15.
4. H. Montefiore, *Remarriage and Mixed Marriage: A plea for Dual Reform* (London: SPCK, 1967), p. 4.
5. H. Oppenheimer, *Law and Love* (London: Faith Press, 1962), p. 76.
6. 'Bishop Writes on Freedom to Re-Marry', *Church Times* (5 August 1966):15.
7. 'Church Must Accept Second Marriages', *Church Times* (28 October 1966):16.
8. 'Marriage Law', *Church Times* (19 July 1968):4.
9. *Divorce and Remarriage in Anglicanism* (London: Macmillan, 1958), p. 248.
10. *The Church and Divorce* (London: Mowbray, 1968), p. 30.
11. *Ibid.*, p. ix.
12. R. Lloyd, *The Church of England 1900–1965* (SCM Press, 1966), p. 598.
13. A. Vidler, *Scenes from a Clerical Life: An Autobiography* (London: Collins, 1977), p. 177.
14. *Ibid.*, p. 176.
15. A. Vidler, ed. *Soundings: Essays Concerning Christian Understanding* (Cambridge University Press, 1963), p. ix.
16. *Scenes from a Clerical Life*, p. 179.
17. 'A New Way to Put Asunder', p. 13.
18. *Church Assembly Proceedings*, Vol. 47, No. 2 (16 February 1967): 267, 271.
19. Obituaries of Canon Howard Root in *Times* (28 November 2007) and *Telegraph* (27 November 2007).
20. D. MacKinnon, H. Root, H. Montefiore, and J. Burnaby, *God, Sex and War* (Philadelphia: Westminster Press, 1965), pp. 34–35.
21. *Ibid.*, pp. 39, 41.
22. *Ibid.*, p. 52.
23. J. Lewis and P. Wallis, 'Fault, Breakdown, and the Church of England's Involvement in the 1969 Divorce Reform', *Twentieth Century British History*, Vol. 11, No. 3 (2000):317, quoting *And What Have the Righteous Done?*
24. *Not Yet the Epitaph: Some Ethical Dilemmas of 1968* (University of Exeter, 1968), p. 41.
25. G. Dunstan, *The Artifice of Ethics: The Moorhouse Lectures 1973* (London: SCM Press, 1974), pp. 46–47.
26. Lewis and Wallis, p. 316. Lewis and Wallis credit the Moral Welfare Council, later the Board for Social Responsibility, for providing 'the intellectual programme and organizational skills needed to produce a new position on divorce reform for the church' (p. 331).
27. *The Artifice of Ethics*, p. 47.
28. *Marriage Commission Minutes, 1968–1970*, MS 4388, f 1, Lambeth Palace Library.

158   In Pursuit of Consensus

29. Memorandum from H.E.R. [Howard Root], dated 6 November 1968, Papers on Root Commission, MS 4666, f 125, Lambeth Palace Library.
30. *Ibid.*, f 127.
31. *Marriage Divorce and the Church: The Report of a Commission Appointed by the Archbishop of Canterbury to Prepare a Statement on the Christian Doctrine of Marriage* (London: SPCK, 1972), p. 94.
32. *Ibid.*, p. 35.
33. *Ibid.*, p. 36.
34. *Ibid.*, p. 95.
35. *Ibid.*
36. *Marriage Commission Minutes*, f 18.
37. *Marriage, Divorce and the Church*, p. 97.
38. *Ibid.*, p. 13.
39. 'Remarks for discussion on questions which might be considered in the final report', MS 4389, ff 11–17. Lambeth Palace Library.
40. *Ibid.*, f 16.
41. *Marriage Divorce and the Church*, pp. 16, 47.
42. *Ibid.*, p. 114.
43. *Ibid.*, pp. 119, 121–123.
44. Minutes January 5–6, 1970 in MS 4389, 'Root Report on Marriage & Divorce', ff 145, 147. Lambeth Palace Library.
45. MS 4389, ff 157–166, Lambeth Palace Library. Dunstan took his title from Lancelot Andrewes: 'To be in both worlds full is more than God was, who was hungry here'. The Root Commission included much of *In Both Worlds Full* in Chapter 4, entitled 'The Strengthening of Marriage', in *Marriage Divorce and the Church*.
46. *Marriage, Divorce, and the Church*, p. 72, citing the article 'Christian Ethics in the 1960s and 1970s', *The Church Quarterly* (January 1970):221.
47. *Ibid.*
48. *Ibid.*, p. 71.
49. *Ibid.*, p. 72. Italics in Root Report.
50. *Ibid.*, p. 73.
51. *Ibid.*, pp. 73–74.
52. *Ibid.*, p. 74. The Commissioners stated that penitence should be expressed privately and not in a public service. They wrote, 'The white robes of those called to the marriage-supper of the Lamb (Rev. 19:9) were the robes not of the innocent but of the forgiven: they were washed before they came' (p. 73). The words were Dunstan's in *In Both Worlds Full*.
53. *Ibid.*, p. 75.
54. *Marriage* (London: Mowbray, 1990), p. 44.
55. 'A further note by H.O. on G.R.D.'s paper,' MS 4666, f 140, Lambeth Palace Library. Allchin's appendix on the Eastern Orthodox acceptance of remarriage in church had also influenced the evolution of Oppenheimer's views. Conversation with author, 13 June 2010.
56. Church Assembly, *Report of Proceedings*, Vol. 50, No. 2 (8 July 1970):417.
57. *Ibid.*, 421, 424–425.
58. 'Pastoral Guidance and the Divorce Act', Ramsey Papers, Vol. 183, ff 291–294.
59. Letter from the Bishop of Willesden to the Archbishop of Canterbury, dated 5 February 1971. 'Memorandum on the present situation in the Church of England regarding marriage and divorce, particularly in the light of evidence received by the Commission on the Objects and Policy of the Mothers Union.' Ramsey Papers, Vol. 207, ff 244–245.
60. Notes on the draft of the Report of the Root Commission, MS 4666, f 112. Lambeth Palace Library.

In Pursuit of Consensus 159

61. *Marriage Divorce and the Church*, p. xii.
62. John Hunt, 'Church Split over Report on Marriage of Divorcees', *Sunday Telegraph* (11 April 1971):1.
63. '"One-sided", says Church Union', *Church Times* (23 April 1971):20.
64. 'Second Marriage?' *Church Times* (23 April 1971):10.
65. 'Disapproval Voiced by Church Union', *Times* (22 April 1971):3.
66. 'In Our View/Editorials: Till death . . . ', *Church of England Newspaper* (23 April 1971):6.
67. H. Arnold, 'Go-ahead Soon for Divorcee Marriages in Church', *Sun* (22 April 1971):14.
68. 'Editorial', *Theology*, Vol. 74 (May 1971):193. Lucas's article, entitled 'Frustration and Forgiveness', is on pages 194–200 of the issue.
69. 'Marriage, Divorce and the Church', *Theology*, Vol. 74 (June 1971):254–258.
70. Lucas, p. 197.
71. Oppenheimer, 257.
72. Adrian Hastings, *A History of English Christianity 1920–2000* (London: SCM Press, 2001), p. 546.
73. *General Synod Proceedings*, Spring Group of Sessions (1972), Vol. 3, No. 1 (10 February 1972):77, 80.
74. *Ibid.*, 82–83.
75. *Ibid.*, 106–107.
76. *Ibid.*, 107–108.
77. *Church Times* (18 February 1972):10, 12 and *Times* (11 February 1972):3.
78. 'Editorial', *Theology*, Vol. 75, No. 622 (April 1972):170.
79. *Times* (11 February 1972):3.
80. *Theology* (April 1972):169.
81. *Ibid.*, 169–170.
82. Letter from the Bishop of Chester, Gerald Ellison, to Helen Oppenheimer, inviting her to serve on the working party. The letter, dated 12 October 1972, is in Oppenheimer's private collection.
83. Letter from the Bishop of Chester to Gordon Dunstan, dated 23 October 1972, in the private collection of Helen Oppenheimer.
84. 'Marriage Discipline: Synod's Two Choices', *Church Times* (19 October 1973):1. Charles Moore, as editor of the *Spectator*, identified Peter Boulton as one of the Anglo-Catholics' 'influential friends in the Synod'. *The Church in Crisis: A Critical Assessment of the Current State of the Church of England* (London: Hodder and Stoughton, 1986), p. 35.
85. K. Jones, 'Divorce and Remarriage', in *Living the Faith: A Call to the Church*, ed. K. Jones (Oxford University Press, 1980), p. 128.
86. 'Remarriage Report: An Issue Confused', *Church Times* (26 October 1973).
87. Letter from Gordon Dunstan to Helen Oppenheimer, dated 6 November 1973. Private collection of Helen Oppenheimer. Dunstan did not sign the Report of the Working Party because he did not think that it was ready for presentation to the General Synod. Letter from Gordon Dunstan to the Bishop of Leicester, dated 22 October 1973. Private collection of Helen Oppenheimer. The Bishop of Leicester repeated Dunstan's objection in the General Synod debate on 7 November 1973.
88. *General Synod Proceedings*, November Group of Sessions (1973), Vol. 4, No. 3 (7 November 1973):774.
89. *Ibid.*, 743–744, 774.
90. *Ibid.*, 747, 753, 764.
91. *Ibid.*, 777, 778, 780.
92. Peart-Binns, 'Leonard, Graham Douglas (1921–2010)', *Oxford Dictionary of National Biography*, Oxford University Press, Jan 2014 [http://www.oxforddnb.com/view/article/102956].

160   *In Pursuit of Consensus*

93. *General Synod Proceedings* November Group of Sessions, Vol. 5, No. 3 (8 November 1974):812.
94. *Ibid.*, 815.
95. Since the death of Herbert Waddams, no member of the Root Commission had been a member of the General Synod. Runcie wrote Root, Montefiore, and Oppenheimer that he would give 'one final heave for the Root Commission'. Letter from the Bishop of St. Albans to Professor Howard Root, the Bishop of Kingston, and Lady Helen Oppenheimer, dated 20 September 1974. Private collection of Helen Oppenheimer.
96. *General Synod Proceedings* (8 November 1974):808.
97. *Ibid.*, 808, 810.
98. *Ibid.*, 816–817.
99. 'Blow to Synod', *Church Times* (15 November 1974).
100. *General Synod Proceedings* (8 November 1974):831–832.
101. *Ibid.*, 811.
102. P. Welsby, 'Letters to the Editor: Re-marriage & the General Synod', *Church Times* (16 December 1973):14.
103. C. Longley, 'Church Puts Aside Issue which Highlighted Weaknesses', *Times* (9 December 1974).
104. J. Peart-Binns, *Bishop Hugh Montefiore* (London: Anthony Blond, 1990), p. 180. In a letter to Helen Oppenheimer, dated 24 March 1972, Ramsey apologized for not thanking her after he had received the Report. Letter in Oppenheimer's private collection.
105. Chadwick, *Michael Ramsey*, p. 153.
106. B. Hopkinson, 'Obituary: The Right Rev Kenneth Skelton', *The Independent* (7 August 2003). Kenneth Skelton, *Bishop in Smith's Rhodesia: Notes from a Turbulent Octave 1962–1970* (Zimbabwe: Mambo Press, 1985), p. 5 and Obituary of the Right Rev Kenneth Skelton in *The Times* (1 August 2003).
107. John S. Peart-Binns, 'Skelton, Kenneth John Fraser (1918–2003)', *Oxford Dictionary of National Biography*, Oxford University Press, Jan 2007; online edn, Jan 2009 [http://www.oxforddnb.com/view/article/92672].
108. Letter from the Bishop of Lichfield to the Archbishop of Canterbury, dated 23 June 1975, and reply from the Archbishop of Canterbury, dated 26 June 1975. Coggan papers, Vol. 17, ff 66, 67. Lambeth Palace Library.
109. Letter from the Archbishop of Canterbury to the Bishop of Newcastle, dated 29 May 1975. Coggan papers, Vol. 17, f 58.
110. The following documents are in Vol. 17 of the Coggan Papers in Lambeth Palace Library: Letters from W.D. Pattinson to the Archbishop of Canterbury, dated 17 April and 2 May 1975, ff 42, 43, and 'Marriage Commission: Suggested Membership [Categories]', f 54.
111. Peter Sedgwick, 'Baelz, Peter Richard (1923–2000)', *Oxford Dictionary of National Biography*, Oxford University Press, 2004 [http://www.oxforddnb.com/view/article/73846].
112. Letter from W.D. Pattinson to Archbishop of Canterbury, dated 16 December 1975. Coggan Papers, Vol. 17, f 75. Lambeth Palace Library. Ultimately Baelz served as a Consultant, rather than a Member, for the Lichfield Commission.
113. *Marriage and the Church's Task: The Report of the General Synod Marriage Commission* (London: CIO Publishing, 1978), p. v.
114. *Ibid.*, p. 22.
115. *Ibid.*, pp. 36–37.
116. *Ibid.*, p. 38.
117. *Ibid.*, pp. 38, 60–61.
118. Report entitled 'Solemnisation of Marriage,' in Ramsey Papers, Vol. 207, ff 327–330. Lambeth Palace Library.

119. *Marriage and the Church's Task*, p. 67.
120. *Ibid.*, p. 80.
121. *Ibid.*, pp. 83–84. Italics in Report.
122. *Ibid.*, p. 77. Italics in Report.
123. *Ibid.*, p. 84.
124. *Ibid.*, pp. 84–85. The members of the Lichfield Commission who supported this course of action were Chancellor Sheila Cameron, Mrs. M.E.R. Holmes, John R. Lucas, and the Reverend M.G. Whittock. P. 100, note 2.
125. *Ibid.*, pp. 85, 89. The members of the Commission who supported this course of action were the Bishop of Lichfield; the Venerable M.E. Adie; Mrs. Susan Aglionby; Mrs. M.I. Allen; Canon Prof. J. Atkinson; Chancellor T.A.C. Coningsby; Mrs. J. Dann; the very Reverend Brandon D. Jackson; Prof. Kathleen Jones; Canon Barnabas Lindars, SSF; Dr. Kenneth Soddy, and Dr. H. Morgan Williams. Peter Baelz voted with the majority as a Consultant. P. 100, note 1.
126. Clifford Longley, 'Call to Relax on Church Remarriage of Divorcees', *The Times* (19 May 1978):1.
127. H. Montefiore, '"Lichfield" Right to Recommend Changing Rules', *Church Times* (19 May 1978):11.
128. D. Stevens, 'A Good Report—But Proposals are a Sell-out', *Church Times* (19 May 1978):11.
129. 'Re-Marriage', Editorial in *Church Times* (19 May 1978):10.
130. Jones, p. 129.
131. *Marriage and the Church's Task: The General Synod Debate in July 1978*, reprint of the General Synod's *Report of Proceedings* for July 1978, pp. 1, 3, 4, 7. Lambeth Palace Library.
132. *Ibid.*, 9, 16.
133. *Marriage and the Church's Task*, p. 99.
134. *Ibid.*
135. *The General Synod Debate* (July 1978):9, 17.
136. *Ibid.*, 15, 17.
137. *Ibid.*, 18, 28, 36.
138. *Ibid.*, 39.
139. *Ibid.*, 43.
140. *Ibid.*, 52–54.
141. *Ibid.*, 60.

6 Remarriage in Church after Divorce
Each Case is Different

The General Synod's Acceptance of Remarriage in Church

In July of 1978 the General Synod voted against accepting the majority recommendation of the Lichfield Commission that, with a bishop's permission, a divorced person could be remarried in church. Later that same year, however, in November, the Synod commended the Lichfield Report to the dioceses for consideration. The Standing Committee that reviewed the diocesan responses was chaired by Robert Runcie, who was enthroned as Archbishop of Canterbury on 25 March 1980. In their Report, dated 13 January 1981, the Standing Committee concluded that a majority of the dioceses approved of the Lichfield Commission's recommendation to rescind the Convocation regulations requiring a bishop's permission for the admission of a divorced person to Communion. Accordingly the Standing Committee asked the Synod to reconsider that recommendation.[1]

When the Synod met in February of 1981, they received the report of the Standing Committee and agreed to two key recommendations regarding marriage and divorce. The Synod approved the rescission of the current rules regulating the admission of divorced persons to Holy Communion and recommended the continuation of services of prayer and dedication after remarriage. During the debate, Archbishop Runcie began his speech by announcing the engagement of Prince Charles and Lady Diana Spencer. When he said, 'Archbishops of Canterbury don't get much opportunity for marrying people', the Synod responded with 'delighted laughter'.[2] Little could those present imagine that one day the remarriage of Prince Charles, after his divorce and the death of his former wife, would be the subject of debate on the very issue under discussion in February of 1981.

Regarding the question of the remarriage of divorced persons in church, the Standing Committee had found that eighteen dioceses favored 'remarriage in church in certain circumstances', while seventeen opposed such services.[3] The lack of strong support for a controversial proposal, or, conversely, the presence of significant opposition, prevented the Standing Committee from presenting a motion in February of 1981.[4] Just as private members of Parliament had stepped forward in 1937 and 1969 to introduce reforms in

Each Case is Different   163

the secular divorce laws, so did a bishop, without the *official* support of the Church, introduce a controversial motion in the General Synod in 1981.

At the Synod meeting at York on 7 July 1981, Bishop John Vernon Taylor of Winchester introduced a motion that would allow a divorced person to be married in church during the lifetime of a former partner.[5] Bishop Taylor was an effective sponsor of the proposal. The high regard in which he was held was evident in 1974, when he became the first priest to be consecrated directly to the see of Winchester in 450 years. One of his biographers described Taylor as 'a respected bishop, known for his reverence for the categories of biblical thought, who had become a liberal theologian, whom no one could accuse of diluting the revealed faith'.[6] Bishop Taylor's experience and reputation made him appropriately qualified to introduce the controversial proposal on remarriage in church.

During the debate in the General Synod, Bishop Graham Leonard of Truro, a consistent opponent of divorce reform, attempted to amend Bishop Taylor's motion by asking for a deferral of any decision until the proposal had been more fully considered. The Synod overwhelmingly rejected Leonard's amendment.[7] Instead, after decades of debate within the Church of England, the General Synod passed the following motion:

That this Synod—

a.   Believes that marriage should always be undertaken as a lifelong commitment;
b.   Considers that there are circumstances in which a divorced person may be married in church during the lifetime of a former partner; and
c.   Asks the Standing Committee to prepare a report setting out a range of procedures for cases where it is appropriate for a divorced person to marry in church in a former partner's lifetime.

The passage of the motion by a vote of 296 to 114 marked a dramatic turnaround.[8] In July of 1978, by a vote of 213 to 206, the General Synod had rejected the Lichfield Commission's recommendation that, with a bishop's permission, divorced persons should be allowed to be remarried in church. Sending the Lichfield recommendation to the dioceses for review had revealed such a close division on the question that the Standing Committee had thought that it would be 'inappropriate' for them to submit a recommendation to the Synod for consideration in February of 1981. Yet in July of that same year, when Bishop Taylor submitted the controversial proposal, the motion passed by a substantial margin.

In a debate in the Synod in November of 1983, Archbishop Runcie provided a possible explanation for the growth in support for the proposal. According to Runcie, the initiative for Bishop Taylor's proposal had come from within the House of Bishops. Runcie said that the bishops 'know better than any in the Church that the existing Regulations are no longer

164　*Each Case is Different*

adequate to the Church's needs. It is not simply that a growing number of clergy are exercising their right in law to marry a divorcee in church. . . . The bishops know that many clergy who have not yet exercised that right want the Regulations changed'.[9] Many of the bishops and clergy, charged with implementing the Church's regulations regarding marriage, favored reform. The motion in July of 1981 had the advantage of the support of the Archbishop of Canterbury, who told the Synod that 'he was not suggesting that the Church should realign its theology, but he believed that the witness to the ideal of lifelong marriage could be strengthened by taking steps to alter the discipline'.[10] On that basis, the Church of England moved forward to design a procedure for the remarriage of divorced persons in church.

Option G and "Endless Wrangling" (1983–1985)

In July of 1981 members of the General Synod not only voted to accept remarriage in church after divorce in certain cases, they also asked the Standing Committee to prepare and submit a list of procedures appropriate for such a service. Archbishop Runcie chaired that Committee, which published their Report, *Marriage and the Standing Committee's Task*, in June of 1983. The Committee considered seven options, including nullity procedures and procedures from the Eastern Orthodox Church and the Scottish Episcopal Church. The possible courses of action were identified by letters of the alphabet, from 'A' to 'G'. The last possibility, which the Committee recommended, became known as 'Option G'. Under that procedure, a couple would consult the incumbent, who would then inquire into the case and complete an application form for submission to the bishop. The applicant couple would sign a Declaration stating their understanding and acceptance of the Church of England's teachings regarding marriage. After receiving the form, the bishop would submit the application to a panel of advisers. The Standing Committee decided that panels with representatives from more than one diocese were preferable to diocesan panels because 'the Multi-Diocesan Panel offers the greatest opportunity for breadth of experience, objectivity of standards, consistency of pastoral decisions and protection from local pressures'.[11] The Committee did not recommend requiring the Panel to interview the applicants personally. If the Panel granted permission for the couple to marry in church, the bishop would issue an affirmative decision, including a statement dispensing the applicants from the obligations of previous marriage vows. The marriage could then be solemnized 'according to one of the currently authorized marriage services without alteration or diminution'. Specifically, the Committee did not recommend the addition of a penitential preface.[12]

Immediately upon publication, the Standing Committee's recommendations encountered negative publicity regarding Option G. In *The Times*, Penny Perrick characterized the reviews of applications for remarriage in church as 'intensely probing interviews', and stated, 'All but the most determined will probably think that the briskness of a register office ceremony

Each Case is Different 165

is preferable to an intrusive inspection into one's past life'. She criticized procedures that would 'serve to remind everyone concerned of past failures, at the very time when it is helpful to be able to concentrate on future happiness'.[13] Privately, Dean Peter Baelz of Durham, who had served as a Consultant to the Lichfield Commission and who was a member of the Synod, wrote to Helen Oppenheimer regarding the Standing Committee's Report that the proposed procedure seemed to be 'both cumbersome and probably insensitive'.[14]

The Synod's debate on the Standing Committee's Report in July of 1983 revealed serious dissatisfaction with Option G. The Reverend Richard Holloway moved to reconsider the proposal because 'this procedure will not [be] sufficiently acceptable throughout the church'. That motion was defeated by a vote of 233 to 211, demonstrating the deep division within the Synod over the question.[15] Archbishop Runcie defended his Committee's recommendations with familiar arguments. He told the Synod that the Church should uphold 'the highest possible view of marriage' while recognizing the reality of divorce; he argued, 'The Church could be strict and merciful at the same time'. Several speakers criticized Option G and said that they favored 'Option F', which would have given the parish priest sole discretion in approving remarriage in church after divorce.[16] Summarizing the debate, Clifford Longley wrote of Option G in *The Times*, 'Heavy criticism was directed at almost every detail of the scheme but the mood of the debate gradually hardened into determination to try it as the best option available, with the possibility of revising it in the light of experience'. The General Synod approved Option G by a vote of 284 to 143, finally approving a procedure for determining which couples could remarry in church after divorce.[17]

Once the Synod had approved Option G, the Church proceeded to develop a detailed description of the procedure, which was published in October of 1983. The procedure for gaining approval of remarriage in church after divorce required a thorough investigation by the incumbent of the circumstances in each case, including several questions that could be considered intrusive. For example, the incumbent would ask the couple if one of them were responsible for the ending of a previous marriage. If so, the incumbent should ask if there were 'true repentance' for the actions that ended the union. Another question would explore whether or not 'sufficient efforts were made to save the previous marriage'.[18] A panel of advisers would review the answers to the questions posed in Option G before sending a recommendation to the bishop, who would make the final decision. There would be no appeals in cases where a petition was refused, and the couple would not be entitled to know the reasons for the refusal.[19]

The description of the new procedure evoked an immediate adverse reaction. Archbishop Runcie felt compelled to rebuke opponents of the proposal, telling Canterbury Synod that some critics had declared the procedure unworkable 'before the documents and directions have been seen'. With regard to Option G, the Archbishop spoke to the heart of the Church's

166 *Each Case is Different*

problem when he said that it was difficult to explain 'how the church has got itself into the situation of agreeing to something in principle which it is either unwilling or unable to do in practice'.[20] The General Synod debate in November of 1983 echoed Runcie's point. The Synod considered over 30 amendments but did not pass any that fundamentally altered the procedures outlined in Option G. The Archbishop of York, John Habgood, expressed the feelings of the reluctant supporters of the proposals when he said, 'We have aroused so many expectations by what I believe were foolish decisions, that we must now go ahead and make it work, and make it work honestly'.[21] Of that statement Charles Moore later wrote, 'To the outside world, it sounds rather alarming that a prince of the Church counsels the Church to press ahead with something that he believes to be mistaken'.[22] Although they may have been unsatisfactory, the proposals embodied in Option G proceeded from the Synod to the House of Bishops.

At their meeting on 18 October 1983, the House of Bishops had asked its members to submit Option G to their dioceses for consideration after the General Synod debate in November of 1983. When the proposals were sent to every diocese for review, the discussions revealed 'strong support for the *principle* that there are circumstances in which a divorced person should be permitted to marry in church during the lifetime of a former partner', but 'the procedures envisaged by "Option G" were not seen as the way forward'.[23] The General Synod had not wholeheartedly endorsed Option G, and a diocesan review of the procedure revealed even less enthusiasm. The House of Bishops reported, 'It is clear that an alternative procedure, less complicated in its operation and seen to be more clearly pastoral and personal in its approach, will be needed if it is to command that degree of support which would enable us to act as a Church'. The House decided by a unanimous vote not to send the proposals in Option G to the General Synod again. Yet the bishops wrote that they were 'impressed by the strong evidence in the diocesan discussions of firm support for some modification in the Church's present marriage discipline'. They asked the General Synod to renew the effort to find 'an acceptable, pastoral procedure'.[24]

The proposal that the House of Bishops sent to the General Synod for consideration at its meeting in February 1984 was referred to as 'the Bishops' Option' in an editorial in *The Times* because it had originated in the House of Bishops and placed the responsibility for decision upon the diocesan bishop.[25] Elsewhere, however, the proposal became known as 'Son of Option G'.[26] The motion that was put to the Synod for a vote noted 'the criticism of Option G expressed in the recent informal consultations in the dioceses' and asked the House of Bishops to introduce a procedure that would

a. Place the responsibility for decision upon the diocesan bishop in consultation with the parish priest;
b. Permit the possibility in appropriate cases of reference by the bishop to a diocesan panel of advisers. . . .

c. Be more evidently pastoral in its application to the couple concerned.
d. Set out guidelines for diocesan bishops, clergy and panels.[27]

Among those who opposed the proposal in February of 1984 were Bishop Graham Leonard of London and Canon David Stevens, both of whom had consistently opposed allowing remarriage in church after divorce. The opposition was not strong enough, however, to prevent the Synod from approving the Bishops' Option by a substantial majority of 295 to 130.[28]

Reluctant to accept that decision, Bishop Leonard organized a group of ten bishops to propose an alternative plan. In a statement circulated to members of the Synod, those bishops argued against remarriage after divorce on theological grounds. They urged the Synod not to abandon the indissolubilists, who could not accept ending a marriage by any means except nullity. In place of the Bishops' Option they proposed a revised nullity procedure followed by a service in church for those who remarried. The existing Service of Prayer and Dedication following a Civil Marriage could serve as a model.[29]

Critics outside of the Synod also argued that the Bishops' Option lacked a sound theological basis. In an editorial entitled 'The Marriage Bond', the editors of *The Times* wrote, 'Important changes in doctrine and practice of this kind are inadvisable unless there is a clear and coherent theological basis for them, and unless there is general consent to this basis. That cannot be said'.[30] In a subsequent letter to the editor, Garth Moore, the Chancellor of the dioceses of Durham, Southwark, and Gloucester, agreed and called the House of Bishops to account:

> If General Synod should now pass legislation permitting second marriages in church to those who have a first spouse living, it will be changing the centuries old doctrine of the Church of England.
>
> This is a grave step to take and it is frightening to know that today General Synod feels free to take such a step, despite the fact so large a number of its members are totally untrained in theology or canon law.
>
> It is still more frightening that the bishops, who are the traditional guardians of sound doctrine, should be content to leave such a decision to so inexpert a body without first seeking clearance from a body of trained theologians and canonists.[31]

The bishops could not ignore these theological arguments. One of the questions that they confronted was whether or not Canon B30, which defined marriage as 'in its nature a union permanent and lifelong', would have to be amended. At the meeting of the House of Bishops on 6 June 1984, Archbishop Habgood reported, 'The General Synod lawyers are agreed in advising that Canon B30 should be amended if the new regulation commends itself to the Synod. They differ on whether such an amendment would constitute a change in the Church's doctrine, or only in its discipline'. If the

168   *Each Case is Different*

matter were disciplinary, a change in the Convocation regulations would be sufficient. A change in the Church's doctrine of marriage would require an amendment to the Canons. Habgood reported that the lawyers were 'unwilling to venture' into the theological dimensions of the question. The bishops did not have a choice. As Habgood said,

> If the whole matter is purely disciplinary, no problem arises. But if the House decides that it is doctrinal or has doctrinal dimensions, we shall need to move very carefully. . . . The method by which the Church decides such issues may have considerable repercussions for the future and will say a lot about our claim to be a theologically responsible body.[32]

In the end, the bishops did not amend the Canons, and the theological questions remained.

Undermining the bishops' attempts to take a decisive stand was the considerable opposition in the dioceses to the proposals contained in the Bishops' Option. The General Synod had voted favorably on the proposals in February 1984, but only twelve of forty-three diocesan synods subsequently approved.[33] By the time the bishops returned to the General Synod in February 1985, they had abandoned the Bishops' Option and proposed a compromise in a new Bishops' Report (GS669). When Michael Adie, who had served on the Lichfield Commission and had become the Bishop of Guildford in 1983, moved that the Report be received, he explained that the bishops did not recommend rescinding either the existing 1957 Convocation regulation prohibiting remarriage in church *or* the July 1981 Synod Resolution accepting remarriage in church in certain circumstances. Both of those directives remained in effect. Since 1857, the laws of the State had allowed clergy the freedom either to marry or to refuse to marry individuals who had been divorced. Adie told the Synod that, in GS669, 'what we are now asking is that clergy should seek the advice of their bishop' in such decisions.[34] By leaving the 1957 Convocation prohibition in effect, however, the Bishops appeared to discourage remarriage in church.

In the debate Archbishop Runcie seemed resigned to the abandonment of the attempts to formulate policies for the implementation of the 1981 Synod Resolution. Admitting defeat, he told the Synod, 'There are clearly those like myself who have argued for a consistent pastoral discipline to allow for some second marriages to be solemnized in Church, and in Synod we have not carried the day'. Runcie enumerated the arguments that he thought had prevented the Church from implementing the 1981 Resolution:

> First, the repetition of the marriage vows in Church is an offence to many people. Second, a belief in days of rising divorce figures and rising unease as to whether recent legislation has seriously undermined the principle of marriage as life-long in intention, the Church should not

even seem to depart from it. Third, the real pastoral problem of discriminating between the deserving and the undeserving by some general rules; and, fourth, reluctance on the part of a majority to go down the road of extended nullity.[35]

Runcie said that he had argued consistently 'that there are exceptions who ought to be allowed to celebrate their marriage in Church with the marriage service', but the arguments against that position had been too strong. He told the Synod that 'there comes a time when I must agree that there is no real consensus in my favour, and that the peace of the Church demands that we cease this endless wrangling over a question on which we are so divided'. For his own part, Runcie said, 'I must continue my existing practice of rejecting the applications from those who already have a partner to a previous marriage' because 'I must not attempt to get round what I cannot achieve by persuasion'.[36] The Archbishop who had argued for years that some divorced individuals should be allowed a second marriage in church could not follow his own inclination to approve such a marriage as long as the Convocation prohibition remained in effect.

Archbishop Runcie's position, however, was not official. The Bishops' Report had left both the 1957 Convocation prohibition *and* the July 1981 Synod Resolution in effect, leaving the decision regarding the remarriage of divorced persons in church to the discretion of the clergy. The Reverend D.N. Gibbs of Sheffield told the Synod that the absence of specific instructions would be especially burdensome to the clergy in the North. He claimed that the clergy in the South and inner city areas had fewer problems with marriage, 'simply because fewer and fewer people are coming to the Church for Christian marriage'. While clergy in the South might have three to six weddings a year, 'many of us in the North have upwards of one hundred weddings a year'. When confronted with the ambiguity inherent in the current proposal, Gibbs said that the clergy in his area had told him:

> If it goes through we shall marry everybody, 'N' number of times, because you cannot make any kind of judgment. There is no backup here, there would be no time, you could not cope with the numbers, you could not keep going to the bishop with all the problems in every case, you would have no instructions on how it was to work and it would be entirely a matter of my principles.[37]

The clergy might achieve the 'uniformity of decision' that Archbishop Runcie sought, not by consulting bishops or following clear guidelines, but rather by succumbing to overwhelming pressure.

After approving the Bishops' motion that the parish priest, in consultation with his bishop, should decide whether a divorced person could marry a second time in church, the General Synod considered the issue of services of prayer and dedication. Bishop Adie moved that the Synod grant 'provisional

170 *Each Case is Different*

approval' to the rescission of the Canterbury Convocation resolution that no public service should be held 'for those who have contracted a civil marriage after divorce'. Despite the Canterbury Convocation prohibition, Adie told the Synod that services of prayer and dedication were widely used. He said that the purpose of his proposal was 'to regularize what has in fact become fairly common practice'.[38] The Lichfield Commission had recommended an end to services of prayer and dedication, yet seven years later the Synod passed Adie's motion and then gave final approval to the rescission of the Canterbury Convocation prohibition on 2 July 1985.[39]

In 1971 the Root Commissioners had asked 'competent authorities' to determine 'whether there now exists within the Church of England a moral consensus about the propriety, in certain circumstances, of the marriage in church of divorced persons'. A decade later, in July of 1981, the General Synod passed a motion stating 'that there are circumstances in which a divorced person may be married in church during the lifetime of a former partner' by a vote of 296 to 114. Reports from two Commissions and a Working Party, numerous debates in the General Synod, and discussions in dioceses throughout the country had not produced a procedure to implement the 1981 Resolution. Instead, the General Synod agreed to leave the decision in each case with the parish priest, who was asked to consult his bishop. In 1985, the Church of England offered a divorced person whose former spouse was still living the *possibility* of a second marriage in church and the alternative of a service of prayer and dedication. 'Endless wrangling' had not produced a decisive result.

Divorce in Church and State: Rules and Exceptions

After the Synod had approved the official use of services of prayer and dedication, the Church returned to the question of remarriage after divorce by appointing a Working Party 'to review and report on the effect of recent and current changes in society and in the Marriage Law and the growing number of divorces on the doctrine of Marriage according to English law'. Specifically the Working Party addressed the question of

> whether developments in the substantive law and the procedure relating to divorce have had such a deleterious effect on the legal view of marriage that it is no longer possible to hold the opinion that this can be recognised as marriage as understood in the rites, ceremonies and the Canon law of the Church of England.[40]

The members of the Working Party established in 1985 to consider that question had varied professional backgrounds. Sir Timothy Hoare, the Chair, came from a prominent banking family. He had been an active lay member of the Church's General Assembly for ten years and then served for thirty more years on the General Synod. Hoare's obituary in the *Telegraph*

Each Case is Different 171

described him as 'one of the Church of England's leading laymen and a life-long representative of its evangelical wing'.[41]

In their consideration of current legal and social views of marriage, the Working Party consulted Professor Brenda Hoggett, a member of the Law Commission. According to Hoggett, in the view of the Law Commissioners:

> There are limits to the part which law can play in moulding social attitudes. . . . Ultimately, it is held, it must be the prevailing views amongst the population at large which influence changes in the law. The law provides the mechanism for contracting and dissolving marriages and makes provision for those within the married state. It does not, of itself, state a 'view' of marriage.[42]

If the laws reflected rather than guided social attitudes, the Working Party concluded that the Church should continue to encourage the entire population to accept a view of marriage based on Christian principles. After analyzing the choice between 'either taking up a doctrine of Christian marriage, and leaving the others to go their own way, or pursuing a Christian understanding of marriage, which is applicable to everyone', they recommended that the Church adopt the latter course of action.[43] In their Report, *An Honourable Estate*, published in 1988, the Working Party stated that 'we wish to say as firmly as we can that in our view there have been no changes in the law which have fundamentally altered the basic legal character of the institution in England as a lifelong and exclusive union'.[44] The Church should continue to support the State actively in maintaining that definition of marriage.

While the Working Party advised the Church that the laws of the State were still based on the definition of marriage as a lifelong union, legal reformers were concerned about marriages that did break down. In their 1966 Report *The Field of Choice*, the Law Commissioners had stated that, when a marriage had broken down, the objective of a 'good divorce law' was 'to enable the empty legal shell to be destroyed with the maximum fairness, and the minimum bitterness, distress and humiliation'.[45] As the number of divorces increased[46] and the Church struggled with a greater demand for remarriage in church, the State contended with laws that did not achieve the goal of ending marriages fairly and amicably. Even though the matrimonial offence was no longer a *ground* for divorce, as long as it remained in the statute as proof of the breakdown of a marriage, the courts found it difficult to alleviate bitterness and distress. Some reformers had hoped that the Special Procedure introduced in 1973, which had made it possible for divorcing couples to avoid court appearances altogether, might help to make divorce suits less acrimonious. Couples had only to submit documentary evidence, which would be examined by a judge in private to determine if the marriage had broken down irretrievably. The Special Procedure, however, did not appear to reduce the 'bitterness, distress and humiliation' in the

172 *Each Case is Different*

proceedings. According to Stephen Cretney, 'The fact that a respondent was in practice denied the opportunity of answering allegations in the petition which he believed to be exaggerated, one-sided or even untrue apparently often engendered a burning sense of injustice'.[47]

Reformers from both the Law Society and the Law Commission addressed problems with the divorce laws in a series of reports. In *A Better Way Out* (1979), the Family Law Sub-Committee of the Law Society confirmed what reformers from both Church and State had concluded more than a decade earlier, namely that restrictive divorce laws do not preserve marriages, and courts should not attempt to force couples to stay together. Instead, the members of the Sub-Committee recommended that evidence of the irretrievable breakdown of a marriage should be proof of a one-year separation rather than proof of a matrimonial offence. The courts should eliminate adversarial procedures and grant a decree of divorce not as 'an award to either party' but rather, simply, as a record of the dissolution of the marriage.[48] In two Reports—*Facing the Future* (1988) and *The Ground for Divorce* (1990)—representatives of the Law Commission issued recommendations that were consistent with the conclusions reached in *A Better Way Out*.[49] The principle of irretrievable breakdown did not appear to be the problem, but the procedures by which breakdown was established continued to cause bitterness and distress.

In responding to the Law Commission's recommendations, Lord Mackay, the Lord Chancellor in John Major's Conservative Government, revealed his Christian perspective. Mackay, an active Presbyterian lay leader, stated, 'I personally believe strongly in the value of the institution of marriage and I believe that it is a divinely appointed arrangement fundamental to the well-being of our community'. Yet, he added:

> However desirable it might be for marriages generally not to be dissolved, some do break down. It would be unrealistic for the law not to recognize this fact and make provision for an orderly process of dealing with it: for example, when the Pharisees said to Jesus that Moses permitted a man to write a certificate of divorce and then to divorce his wife, Jesus replied that Moses permitted it because of their hardness of heart (Mark's Gospel, chapter 10 at verses 4 and 5).[50]

In the last decade of the twentieth century, the influence of Christianity in the formulation of secular divorce laws in Great Britain was still very much in evidence. In April of 1995, based on a report from the Lord Chancellor's Department, the Government recommended that irretrievable breakdown remain the sole ground for divorce. The couple would be required to wait for one year, which was to be a period for 'reflection and consideration'. At the end of a year, with no fault being established by either spouse, the court could grant a divorce.[51] These recommendations became the basis for the Family Law Bill introduced in 1995.

Each Case is Different 173

Representatives of the Church of England responded positively to the Family Law Bill. A favorable editorial in the *Church Times* stated:

> On the whole a diminishing of acrimony would be a good thing: if a couple is determined to bring its marriage to an end, however regrettable that may be, then it is better that it does so with dignity and the minimum of recrimination.[52]

Bishops in the House of Lords were also supportive of the Bill. Bishop Philip Goodrich of Worcester said in the debate on 30 November 1995 that bishops 'uphold the highest possible standard for marriage, but we are also pastors' who must deal with human frailty. Goodrich said, 'You do not improve human marital relationships by making the law more punitive'. While critics viewed the Family Law Bill as liberalizing the divorce laws, Goodrich told the Lords, 'I believe that the Bill has the potential to end quickie divorces and to make the option of divorce harder'. He argued for an end to divorces based on matrimonial offences, not because such offences did not contribute to the breakdown of a marriage, but because 'faults are not justiciable'.[53] Goodrich considered a court an inappropriate forum in which to analyze and evaluate matrimonial offences.

In the debate in the House of Lords, Bishop Richard Harries of Oxford responded firmly to those critics who thought that 'the abolition of fault as evidence of breakdown means that marriage as a legal concept no longer has any meaning'. Harries argued that as long as a court played the central role in divorce proceedings, marriage was not simply a private contract that could be dissolved at the will of the parties. He told the Lords that assessing blame in the breakdown of a marriage is difficult: 'In some marriage breakdowns it may seem glaringly obvious who is at fault, but in a good number of cases the real story is painful, private and confused. A court with an adversarial process is not the best context in which to adjudicate'.[54] In an article in the *Church Times*, Harries argued that the proposed procedure would facilitate the decision in positive ways. Mediation and marriage counseling, with a required full year to reflect on the state of the marital relationship, could possibly help a couple to save their marriage. According to Harries, this procedure was preferable to the current practice of 'an undefended petition on the basis of adultery, which might be handled by post and granted in less than six months'.[55]

The Family Law Act, which received the Royal Assent on 4 July 1996, was never fully implemented. The Government made significant changes in the legislation in order to assuage the fears of those who thought that the legislation made divorce easier. A key concession was a compulsory information meeting for couples who wanted to initiate divorce proceedings. Such meetings were enormously expensive—estimates ranged from £40 million to £50 million to provide information sessions for all couples who wanted a divorce—and research indicated that the meetings did not accomplish the

174   *Each Case is Different*

goal of saving marriages.[56] On 16 January 2001, the Government announced the decision 'not to proceed to implementation of the provisions of the 1996 Act dealing with the ground for divorce'. The Lord Chancellor provided no explanation for the decision, but Stephen Cretney reported that 'the failure of couples to opt for mediation in preference to legal representation on the scale apparently expected was significant'.[57] The hopes that mediation would save marriages, or at least minimize the bitterness and acrimony associated with divorce suits, were not realized.

Concern for divorced individuals was a factor that motivated reformers in both Church and State. Theologians continued to confront the task of reconciling compassion for the individual with clear guidelines for the community. In 1983 Oliver O'Donovan addressed the point in *Principles in the Public Realm*, his Inaugural Lecture as Regius Professor of Moral and Pastoral Theology at the University of Oxford. O'Donovan argued that, in matters of discipline, Christian social thinkers in recent years had tended to emphasize 'a "pastoral" rather than a "juridical" approach to discipline'. The former appeared to emphasize 'a preference for discretionary measures' rather than clearly established procedures; the concern was for the welfare of the individual rather than the community.[58] The Church had thus failed to establish clear regulations and followed instead what O'Donovan termed 'a self-consciously occasionalist approach'. The difficulty continued to be maintaining the permanence of marriage while extending pastoral care to divorced Anglicans. O'Donovan quoted Peter Hinchliff's Bampton Lectures, *Holiness and Politics* (1982), on that point: 'The exception must not prove to *be* the rule. . . . No one has yet found a way of including the exceptions within a formal assertion of the ideal without appearing to deny it. The best anyone can do is to provide pastoral ways of dealing with the exceptions'.[59] From this perspective, while the Church maintained the ideal of lifelong marriage, the clergy could consider the possibility of remarrying divorced persons in church in exceptional cases. The Church continued to search for a process by which those exceptional cases could be identified.

Each Case is Different: The Establishment of Guidelines for Remarriage in Church

While Sir Timothy Hoare's group was producing *An Honourable Estate*, a small working party established under the auspices of the Ecclesiastical Law Society examined the question, 'Can the Church of England have a consistent discipline with regard to those seeking marriage after divorce?' and issued a report in 1992. Sending a questionnaire to all the archdeacons on the General Synod revealed to the working party the variety of practices regarding the remarriage of divorced persons in church:

> One in five dioceses adhere strictly to the Convocation Regulations, 76% encourage clergy who do marry divorced people to refer, in some

way, to the bishops, and 1 in 20 support the clergy in making their own decisions. The overall impression is that it is very difficult for diocesan bishops to provide a consistent policy throughout their diocese, though most provide guidance. In every diocese there are clergy who, whatever the diocesan ruling, choose to exercise their right to marry those who have been divorced and whose former spouse is still living.[60]

The failure of the General Synod to establish uniform procedures to assist the clergy in determining whether or not to allow divorced persons to remarry in church had resulted in confusion and inconsistency. According to the working party, the problem was growing more acute because statistics 'show that the number of weddings taking place each year in Anglican Churches in England and Wales involving at least one person who has been married before and whose previous spouse is still alive, has grown from about 1,200 in 1979 to over 6,000 in 1989'. Clearly the clergy needed guidance, but disagreement within the Church made it impossible to establish uniform practice. The working party concluded, 'While the survey underlined the unsatisfactory nature of the present situation, it failed to reveal a common mind as to the best way of regulating remarriage and providing an intelligible policy for the Church of England and the people of this nation as a whole'.[61]

On 2 December 1994 the General Synod passed a motion requesting the House of Bishops 'to consider the present practice of marriage in Church after divorce and to report'.[62] Despite many references in the debate to the various Church Commissions that had issued recommendations during the past three decades, the Synod once again asked for a report on the issues in the hope that a report from the House of Bishops would be definitive. The response to the Synod's resolution was the appointment of a Working Party chaired by Bishop Michael Scott-Joynt of Winchester. The group presented its findings to the House of Bishops in October of 1998, but the Report was not published until January of 2000. Even before publication, word had spread that the Winchester Report favored allowing remarriage in church after divorce in certain cases. In the *Church Times*, Sarah Meyrick speculated that the delay in publication indicated concern among the bishops that 'the report will be seen as undermining marriage, at a time when the Church should be taking a strongly traditional line'.[63] Apparently those concerns inspired the House of Bishops to issue *Marriage: A Teaching Document from the House of Bishops of the Church of England* in September of 1999, before the publication of the Winchester Report.

The teaching document followed the pattern of earlier reports. While the bishops stated, 'All Christians believe that marriage is "indissoluble" in the sense that the promises are made unconditionally for life', they noted that the Church of England had never taught that divorce was impossible or that subsequent marriages were invalid. For those Anglicans who did believe that second marriages were impossible, the bishops wrote, 'These

176   *Each Case is Different*

convictions demand respect, though they are not those of the Church of England as a whole'.[64]

The problem continued to be the development of guidelines by which the clergy could identify couples who should be allowed remarriage in church after divorce. The bishops wrote:

> In some circumstances to marry again after divorce may compound the wrong that one has done, e.g. when obligations to the partner or children of the first marriage are not being met; or when the marriage causes further hurt to the children of the previous one; or when an act of unfaithfulness which contributed to the breakdown is the basis of the new relationship. It may sometimes be a sign of emotional immaturity; and it may also be imprudent, emotionally and financially. In other circumstances . . . it may be responsible, prudent (e.g. in relation to the care of young children) and emotionally wise.

In deceptively few words, in a sentence that appeared to summarize decades of debate, the bishops identified the obvious difficulty in determining whether the decision to remarry was prudent or imprudent: 'There is no simple rule for discerning this, for each case is different'.[65] The bishops stated that 'a further marriage after divorce is an exceptional act' and said that 'the Church itself, through its ministry, has a part in deciding whether or not a marriage in such circumstances should take place in the context of church worship'.[66] In 1999, then, the bishops confirmed the General Synod's 1981 resolution that 'there are circumstances in which a divorced person may be married in church during the lifetime of a former partner'. By confirming that resolution and indicating that the Church would decide whether or not such second marriages could take place in church, the Teaching Document prepared the way for the publication of the Winchester Report in January of 2000.

The members of the committee that produced the 2000 Report entitled *Marriage in Church after Divorce* came from a variety of lay and clerical backgrounds. The Chair, the Right Reverend Michael Scott-Joynt, had been Bishop of Winchester since 1995. Serving as the Archbishops' liaison with Broken Rites, the self-help organization for deserted clergy wives, he had become acquainted with the consequences of divorce.[67] Oliver O'Donovan, the Regius Professor at Oxford who had studied questions relating to divorce, was also on the committee.[68] All of the lay members were members of the General Synod who could participate in the debates on the report in that assembly. Apparently the bishops had learned an important lesson from Synod debates on the reports of earlier Commissions.

At the beginning of the Winchester Report, the Working Party established what they did and did not recommend. They concurred with the General Synod's 1981 Resolution regarding remarriage in church under certain circumstances, but they did not 'envisage indiscriminate opportunity for further marriage in church', nor did they 'recommend a panel-based mechanism for handling applications for such marriages'. Experiences with the proposals in Option G in the 1980s had indicated that procedures based on panels could be 'overly bureaucratic and pastorally insensitive'. The Working Party favored leaving the decision for remarriage in church after divorce with the incumbent, in consultation with the diocesan bishop. The group recognized the reluctance of some incumbents to distinguish among parishioners as to which couples could and could not be remarried in church. Seeking the advice of the bishop could ameliorate that difficulty and, the Working Party stated, could minimize inconsistencies in practice.[69]

Evidence collected by the Working Party indicated that incumbents were already confronting decisions regarding second marriages in increasing numbers. In 1971, in 16% of all marriages, one or both parties were remarrying after divorce; that number had increased to 40% by 1996. Of that 40%, 7,270 weddings involving a divorced individual were solemnized by clergy of the Church of England and the Church in Wales, constituting 10% of all Anglican marriages in those two Churches.[70] Despite the Convocation Act prohibiting the use of the marriage service for a divorced person whose former spouse was still living, Anglican clergy were performing such services. When the Working Party consulted diocesan bishops about policies regarding remarriages of divorced persons, they found 'considerable variations in practice both between and within dioceses'. The Working Party concluded that 'the present diversity of practice leads to inconsistency which may often be perceived as unfair'. They recommended the establishment of national guidelines to foster consistency.[71]

The Working Party concluded: 'We take the unanimous view that the Church should provide a common procedure authorizing incumbents, where they see fit, to officiate at the further marriage of divorced people with a former spouse still living'.[72] In the Draft Code of Practice included in the Report, the Working Party described the principles, pastoral criteria, and procedures that they recommended incumbents follow. The procedure would include the couple's completion of a national application form, interviews with the priest, and reference of the case to the diocesan bishop. Once the incumbent had received the bishop's advice, he or she would decide how to respond to the couple's application.[73] In order to identify a 'clear mandate from the Church', the bishops asked the diocesan synods to respond to the questions of whether or not they accepted the principle that a divorced person could be remarried in church and whether or not they accepted the Working Party's recommended procedure for such a marriage.[74]

The responses demonstrated continuing division within the Church of England. Although the diocesan synods were almost unanimous in accepting the principle that divorced persons could be remarried in church—only Sodor and Man rejected it—nearly half of the dioceses rejected the Winchester Report's recommended procedure. A major concern was assigning the parish priest the responsibility of deciding which couples could be

178 *Each Case is Different*

remarried in church. Oliver Osmond, a vicar in north London, wrote in the *Church Times* that the clergy felt that it would be difficult to deny some couples, and allow others, a church service. According to Osmond:

> Some priests are saying openly that, if the proposals are accepted, they will simply marry all who request it, because it will be impossible for them to pick and choose. Others have announced that they will still not marry anyone who has been previously married. If this happens, we shall not have made much progress in trying to remove the existing inconsistency of practice.[75]

Having served as a parish priest in the Anglican Church of Canada, Osmond recommended the panel-based procedure used there. The Diocese of London agreed with that approach and gave overwhelming support to a proposal for a system of panels similar to that suggested by Option G in the 1980s.[76] A similar system found favor in the Diocese of Lichfield, which would have based the panels on the family magistrates' court. Other dioceses suggested that every marriage should be instituted in a civil service with a church blessing to follow for those who wished it. The Diocese of York took the extreme position of proposing that divorced persons who wanted to be married in church should be treated no differently from those who had never been married.[77] In light of the variety of diocesan responses to the Winchester Report, the group's goal of establishing a greater degree of consistency in the procedure of remarrying divorced persons appeared as elusive as ever.

Ultimately it was secular laws that provided the answer to the question that had caused so much disagreement within the Church of England over the remarriage of divorced persons in church. In May of 2002, a year after receiving the diocesan responses to the Winchester Report, the House of Bishops issued a report that was also entitled *Marriage in Church after Divorce* (GS 1449). In that Report, the bishops stated that the law required clergy to marry parishioners 'who comply with the necessary preliminaries', unless the incumbent refused to perform the ceremony on the basis of a right that had been established in 1857 and confirmed in 1937 and 1965. That right enabled the clergy 'to decline to solemnize (or allow their church to be used for) the marriage of someone who has been divorced and has a former spouse still living'. The bishops had consulted the Legal Officers of the General Synod, who interpreted the statutory protection provided the clergy to mean:

> Clergy thus have the right to decide under civil law whether to conduct a further marriage or not, and neither a Resolution nor an Act of Synod—or a Canon—can lawfully take that responsibility away from them, either by requiring them to apply certain principles or to accept the decision of a third party (such as the bishop, or a tribunal). Only an Act of Parliament or a Measure could change the position in that respect.[78]

According to this interpretation, the Church could not require the clergy to submit the question of whether or not a divorced person could be remarried in church to either a panel or a bishop, two of the procedures that had been proposed. One of the Legal Officers expressed the opinion that any guidance that the Church attempted to provide the clergy could be considered a 'fetter' on the individual priest's judgment.[79]

With regard to the Church's official statements, the Legal Officers considered the implications of both Canon B30 and the 1957 Act of Convocation. They questioned the validity of the 1957 Act, since 'it purported to prohibit further marriage by precluding the use of the marriage service wherever one of the parties had been divorced and their former spouse was still living'.[80] Such a prohibition appeared as a restriction on the individual priest's decision. In addressing the question of whether permitting remarriage in church would require an amendment to Canon B30, the Legal Officers analyzed the statement, 'The Church of England affirms, according to our Lord's teaching, that marriage is in its nature a union permanent and lifelong'. The Legal Officers unanimously agreed that it was not necessary to amend the Canon because the wording was ambiguous. They noted that the Canon referred to marriage as '*in its nature [emphasis supplied] a union permanent and lifelong*' rather than defining marriage as '*a permanent union*'. In 1978 the Lichfield Commissioners had reached the conclusion that the expression '*in its nature*' did not necessarily mean '*its determinative and invariable essence*' but could mean '*the characteristic and normative nature of marriage*'. In 2002 the Synod's Legal Officers agreed with that assessment.[81]

Amending Canon B30 would be complicated because it would be difficult to find the proper words to clarify the definition of marriage, and 'it would be undesirable to do anything to suggest that the *doctrine* of the Church had changed'. In a parenthetical statement the Legal Officers said that the House of Bishops had determined in 1984 that remarriage after divorce 'was not necessarily incompatible with the Church's doctrine of marriage', an ambiguous statement, which the Legal Officers did not clarify when they added that they 'were not aware of any change in that position'.[82] The reluctance to change or clarify doctrine was evident. In 1984, when the House of Bishops considered the possibility of amending Canon B30, the Archbishop of York, John Habgood, had said that the General Synod lawyers were 'unwilling to venture' into the theological dimensions of the question. In 2002 the Legal Officers demonstrated a similar reluctance, and Canon B30 was not amended.

In July of 2002 both the Lower House of the Convocation of Canterbury and the General Synod discussed the House of Bishops' recommendation that the clergy alone should make the decision about whether or not a divorced person should be remarried in church. In both debates the clergy once again expressed concern about leaving the decision solely with the parish priest. Echoing arguments heard many times in the past, speakers said that the decision was burdensome because it was difficult to allow some

180 *Each Case is Different*

divorced persons remarriage in church while denying the service to others. Other speakers objected to the idea that the State could dictate Church doctrine. The Reverend Robin Ward of Rochester said:

> Theologically there is a problem with proceeding with the legal advice as we now have it. If we have a General Synod, then General Synod ought to be able to make doctrinal decisions and teach the Christian faith. . . . I do not think that we can simply throw up our hands and say that, because the lawyers have said we cannot, we have to leave this in limbo. This has ecumenical consequences. If other Churches come to us and say, 'What is your discipline on further marriage after divorce?' we cannot really say with credibility, 'We are not allowed to have one, because the lawyers say it interferes with an Act of Parliament'.

In many regards secular laws had determined Church doctrine and practice for centuries, yet it was still difficult for some of the clergy to accept that reality.[83]

For a century and a half, Parliamentary statutes had provided protection for the consciences of the clergy who could not recognize remarriage in church after divorce. When in 2002 that protection was deemed legally conclusive in that *only* the clergy could make the decision, some among the clergy resisted that interpretation. The Reverend Simon Pothen of London said, 'My concern, in an increasing litigious society, is that there are people who will try to use [legal means] to try to overturn a decision that has gone against them, and that will prove extremely costly'.[84] The concern about providing protection for the clergy found expression in the Reverend David Houlding's proposal in the General Synod to return to the plan of establishing panels 'to review all applications for the remarriage of divorced people in Church'.[85] Such panels could provide protection for the clergy, but Bishop Scott-Joynt and others questioned their use from a pastoral perspective. As the Reverend Robert Key of Oxford said in Convocation, 'I would be happy to share my cure of souls with the bishop; I do not want to share my cure of souls with a tribunal'.[86] Houlding's proposal failed.

On 9 July 2002, by a vote of 269 to 83, the General Synod recognized 'that there are exceptional circumstances in which a divorced person may be married in church during the lifetime of a former spouse' and that 'the decision as to whether or not to solemnize such a marriage in church after divorce rests with the minister'.[87] By a substantial majority, then, the Synod confirmed the 1981 decision approving remarriage in church after divorce; the assembly also resolved the endless wrangling over how the decision would be made. The Church's position was further clarified on 14 November 2002, when the Synod voted to rescind the provision in the 1957 Marriage Resolutions of the Convocation of Canterbury that had prohibited the marriage in church of a divorced person whose former spouse was still living. The vote was 27 *ayes* and 1 *no* in the House of Bishops; 143 *ayes* and 44 *noes* in the House of Clergy; and 138 *ayes* and 65 *noes* in the House of Laity.[88] At long last the Church's rules no longer prohibited what the secular laws had clearly allowed since 1857.

The fourth provision of the motion passed by the Synod in July of 2002 invited the House of Bishops to issue the advice that had been included in Annex I of *Marriage in Church after Divorce* (GS1449) to assist the clergy in determining which divorced persons could be remarried in church. The bishops had derived those recommendations largely from the Winchester Report, and the Bishop of Winchester made it clear to the Synod that the clergy should view the suggestions as *advice* 'rather than anything that sounds stronger, in recognition of the legal view that the cleric's discretion in civil law whether or not to solemnize such marriages should not be fettered'.[89] In the 'Advice to Clergy' that the Synod accepted in 2002, the bishops had included the following questions that the priest 'may wish to consider in the light of the Church's doctrine of marriage':

> **Would the effects of the proposed marriage on individuals, the wider community and the Church be such as to undermine the credibility of the Church's witness to marriage?**
>
> • Would the new marriage be likely to be a cause of hostile public comment or scandal?
>
> **Would permitting the new marriage be tantamount to consecrating an old infidelity?**
>
> • While it would be unreasonable to expect that the couple should not even have known each other during the former marriage(s), was the relationship between the applicants—so far as you can tell from the information made available to you—*a direct cause of the breakdown of the former marriage?*[90]

These questions became especially significant when Charles, the Prince of Wales, and Camilla Parker Bowles decided to marry in the spring of 2005.

The Marriage of Prince Charles and Camilla Parker Bowles

On 9 April 2005, Charles, the Prince of Wales, married Camilla Parker Bowles, a divorced woman whose former husband was still living. Almost seventy years after the abdication of Edward VIII, the Church of England once again confronted questions relating to the marriage of an heir to the throne to a divorcée. A comparison of the Church's responses in 1937 and in 2005 illuminates changes in the interpretation of doctrine and discipline that had occurred during the intervening decades. Although Prince Charles and Mrs. Parker Bowles were not married in church with the Prayer Book service, the public approval of the Church of England distinguished their wedding from that of the Duke and Duchess of Windsor.

182　*Each Case is Different*

The marital history of Prince Charles differed significantly from that of his great uncle, Edward VIII. Charles had married Lady Diana Spencer on 29 July 1981, in what was termed a 'fairy-tale wedding' that was broadcast live to a worldwide audience of 750 million. The union produced two sons, Princes William and Harry, but the marriage was not a happy one. Both spouses took lovers; the relationship of Charles and Camilla Parker Bowles, which had begun before he met his wife, was a key factor in the disintegration of the marriage. In the summer of 1996, the Prince and Princess of Wales were divorced. A year later, on 31 August 1997, Diana was killed in an automobile accident in Paris.[91] Camilla Parker Bowles and her husband, Andrew, had divorced in 1995, and he had remarried. Whereas Edward VIII had never been married when he met Wallis Warfield Simpson, Charles had been married, divorced, and widowed. Both men, nevertheless, wanted to marry divorced women whose former spouses were still living.

The public knowledge that the relationship of Charles and Camilla Parker Bowles had contributed to the failure of two marriages placed the Church of England in a difficult position when the two wished to wed. After Diana's death, the couple appeared together in public for the first time in 1999 and lived openly together at Highgrove, Prince Charles's estate.[92] More than one member of the clergy had been critical of the relationship. The incumbent at St. Mary's Church in Tetbury, Gloucestershire, the parish church for Highgrove, had referred to the Prince as an 'unrepentant adulterer'. Charles did not attend services at the church for five years, until a new incumbent told him that he would be very welcome at St. Mary's.[93] When Rowan Williams was enthroned as Archbishop of Canterbury on 27 February 2003, the question of the marriage of Prince Charles and Mrs. Parker Bowles was among the controversial issues that confronted him. When Christopher Morgan interviewed Williams in early 2003, he wrote of the newly designated Archbishop, 'On divorcees remarrying in church he is conservative'. Morgan phrased his question about the possible marriage of the Prince of Wales, and Williams's answer, in the following terms:

> Draft guidelines that are before bishops proscribe anyone from remarrying before God if they were the cause of the previous marital breakup. Wouldn't that oblige him [Williams]—happily married with two children— to refuse Charles permission to marry Camilla Parker Bowles? 'It is possible to say no,' he replies with unusual bluntness.[94]

Morgan was incorrect in saying that the draft guidelines would 'proscribe' anyone from remarrying in church. The bishops had been careful to emphasize that the guidelines they suggested for interviewing couples constituted advice and not strict rules. Williams, of course, was certainly correct in saying, 'It is possible to say no'. It would also have been possible to say 'yes', but that was not the position of the Archbishop of Canterbury.

Each Case is Different 183

Archbishop Williams opposed the remarriage in church of a divorced person whose former spouse was still living, but the policies established by the Church of England during the past two decades provided other options. The compromise that was negotiated for the marriage of Prince Charles and Mrs. Parker Bowles was a civil ceremony in the Guildhall at Windsor followed by a service of prayer and dedication in St. George's Chapel. The couple had originally planned to marry in a civil ceremony at Windsor Castle. If they had done so, however, the Castle would have become an official civil wedding venue open to the public for three years. The ceremony was moved to the Guildhall.[95] Other difficulties with the civil service arose when critics noted that the Marriage Act of 1836, which had introduced civil marriages in England, excluded the Royal Family from such unions. The Marriage Act of 1949, which repealed the 1836 Act, had stated, 'Nothing in this Act shall affect any law or custom relating to the marriage of members of the Royal Family'. Lord Chancellor Falconer finally issued a formal statement to respond to the objections:

> The government is satisfied that it is lawful for the Prince of Wales and Mrs. Parker Bowles, like anyone else, to marry by a civil ceremony in accordance with Part III of the Marriage Act 1949. . . . The provisions on civil marriage in the 1836 act were repealed by the Marriage Act 1949. . . . No part of the 1836 act therefore remains on the statute book. . . .
>
> We also note that the Human Rights Act has since 2000 required legislation to be interpreted wherever possible in a way that is compatible with the right to marry [article 12] and with the right to enjoy that right without discrimination [article 14].[96]

Prince Charles had the same rights as other citizens and could be married in a civil ceremony.

The combination of a civil ceremony with a service of prayer and dedication found favor with the Church of England. Following the announcement of the impending marriage, an editorial in the *Church Times* stated, 'There have been relatively few protests from within the Church'.[97] Confirming the approval of the Church, the Archbishop of Canterbury had issued a formal statement from Lambeth Palace on 10 February 2005: 'I am pleased that Prince Charles and Mrs. Camilla Parker Bowles have decided to take this important step. I hope and pray that it will prove a source of comfort and strength to them and to those who are closest to them'. The Archbishop had agreed to preside at the service of prayer and dedication following the civil ceremony, and he added:

> These arrangements have my strong support and are consistent with Church of England guidelines concerning remarriage which the Prince of Wales fully accepts as a committed Anglican and as prospective Supreme Governor of the Church of England.[98]

184 *Each Case is Different*

The Church of England guidelines had clearly changed since 1937. Archbishop Lang had refused to approve a church service for the marriage of the Duke and Duchess of Windsor. After the couple had been married in a civil ceremony, an Anglican clergyman, the Reverend Robert Anderson Jardine, did read the religious service, but the Church of England had not authorized him to do so. Archbishop Lang had made it clear that the marriage did not have the Church's blessing.

Prince Charles and the Duke of Windsor were similar in that their mothers did not attend their weddings. King George VI had written to his brother that no member of the family could be present when the Duke married Wallis Simpson, saying, 'I can't treat this as just a private family matter'. Queen Mary's absence became more poignant when Lady Alexandra Metcalfe reported that during the religious service her husband had held for the Duke the prayer book inscribed 'To darling David from his loving Mother', which had been a gift when he was ten. When Prince Charles told his mother that he planned to marry Camilla Parker Bowles, the Queen made it clear that, if the couple married in a civil ceremony, she would not be present.[99] After the public announcement of the forthcoming marriage, the Queen said, in a statement issued on her behalf by Buckingham Palace, 'The Duke of Edinburgh and I are very happy that the Prince of Wales and Mrs Parker Bowles are to marry'.[100] Yet she decided not to attend the civil ceremony. Andrew Alderson wrote in *The Telegraph:*

> The Queen has let it be known that the reason she will not be attending the wedding of the Prince of Wales is because she is putting her duties as the head of the Church of England before family feelings. She has told a friend that she feels it incompatible with her role as Supreme Governor of the Church to attend a civil marriage ceremony, particularly one involving the heir to the throne. She does not want to set a precedent that could damage the Church of England. 'I am not able to go. I do not feel that my position [as Supreme Governor of the Church] permits it,' the Queen told her friend. . . . 'The Queen feels she has to put her role with the Church before her role as a mother,' said the friend.[101]

Although the Queen and the Duke of Edinburgh were not present for the wedding, the sister, two brothers, and two sons of the Prince of Wales attended the ceremony in the Guildhall. The Queen and Prince Philip, as well as the rest of the Royal Family and several hundred guests, were present for the Service of Prayer and Dedication in St. George's Chapel, and the Queen hosted a reception following the service. Prince Charles was surrounded by his family on his wedding day in a way that would have been impossible for the Duke of Windsor in 1937.

During the twentieth century, the Church of England sought to reconcile its definition of marriage as a lifelong union with the legal and social realities of divorce. After 1857, while the State had the authority both to end

Each Case is Different 185

a marriage and to marry individuals who had been divorced, representatives of the Church attempted to influence the Government to restrict the grounds for divorce. After the 1937 Act extended the grounds, the Church then sought to maintain its own doctrines by a strict discipline that prohibited remarriage in church after divorce. Gradually, however, both Church and State recognized that strict rules do not preserve marriages. The growing emphasis on marriage as a personal relationship, rather than an institution defined by Christian principles or by its social value, contributed to changes in views of divorce. The Church began to acknowledge that, when the personal relationship failed, there was no useful purpose in maintaining the marriage. As the group appointed by Archbishop Michael Ramsey stated in 1964, 'If a marriage is broken and dead from the sociological point of view it is not upholding the sanctity of marriage to say that it still exists'.[102]

The Archbishop's Group's statement reflected a new understanding of divorce. In the past, when divorce was viewed solely from the perspective of Biblical injunctions or social utility, it could appear as a 'sin', or even a 'crime', to be punished. The Church's strict rules prohibiting remarriage in church seemed to reflect that view. Yet marriages sometimes failed despite each spouse's best intentions and through no one's fault; divorce might be unavoidable. To penalize someone simply because that person's marriage had failed, no matter what the circumstances, seemed unfair. The legal maxim 'hard cases make bad laws' had discouraged both Church and State from taking individual experiences into account in the regulation of divorce. Yet maintaining strict discipline while ignoring human misery had sometimes prevented the clergy from extending pastoral care to those who had suffered what could be one of life's most painful experiences. The view that divorced individuals deserved sympathy rather than condemnation served to guide the Church of England to develop more flexible guidelines regarding remarriage in church.

This new understanding of divorce was consistent with changing perceptions of the indissolubility of marriage. In the strictest sense to say that a marriage is indissoluble means that the two individuals are joined by an ontological bond that no human action can sever. The Lichfield Commissioners challenged that understanding in their Report in 1978. They agreed that 'marriages *ought* to be indissoluble', but that not all marriages could be so characterized. Marriages that could be identified as indissoluble were based on a 'relational bond of personal love, a compound of commitment, experience and response, in which the commitment clothed itself in the flesh and blood of a living union'.[103] In other words, indissolubility was not necessarily established at the altar in a marriage ceremony but rather was identified with the strength of the personal bond between spouses. From that perspective first marriages could break down, while second marriages could be indissoluble. The Church could offer the 'survivors' of a failed marriage an opportunity to form a new, perhaps indissoluble, union through a ceremony in church.

186 *Each Case is Different*

Recognition of the reality of human experience helped to enable the Church of England to adopt more lenient policies with regard to divorce. Finally, in 1981, the General Synod voted to accept remarriage in church in certain cases. Yet a procedure for identifying those cases remained problematic. Some wanted strict rules to guide the decision, while others, especially those who were concerned with the clergy's pastoral responsibilities, favored what they considered to be a more compassionate approach. In the end English statute law determined the procedure. Since 1857, Parliament had granted parish priests the right to decide whether or not a divorced individual could be married in church. In 2002, the bishops acknowledged that the Church could not interfere with that statutory right.

For years the Church of England had sought an elusive clarity in the debate over divorce by maintaining rigid rules. At the end of the twentieth century, the bishops conceded that the decision about which divorced individuals could be remarried in church was so complex that an inflexible discipline was unrealistic because 'each case is different'. By confirming the parish priest's authority to judge each case according to the circumstances, the Church enabled the clergy to offer remarriage in church to those whose early marriages had not proved to be indissoluble. The ideal of lifelong marriage would not take precedence over human needs. Permission for a divorced person to remarry in church was consistent with words attributed to Jesus: 'I desire mercy, and not sacrifice' (Matthew 9:13). After a century and a half of debate, what the Church offered at last to the divorced was not inflexible rules but grace.

Notes

1. *General Synod Papers 1980–1981*, Vol. I: 'GS 469: Marriage and the Church's Task: Follow-up of the Reference to the Diocesan Synods 1979–1980' (13 January 1981):1, 4, 8. Lambeth Palace Library.
2. 'Marriage Discipline: Synod Helps to Clear the Air—But Avoids Key Issue', *Church Times* (27 February 1981):4.
3. *Marriage and the Standing Committee's Task: The Standing Committee's Response to the Motion, Carried by the General Synod in July 1981, Requesting a Report Setting Out a Range of Procedures for Cases where It Is Appropriate for a Divorced Person to Marry in Church During the Lifetime of a Former Partner* (London: CIO Publishing, 1983):3.
4. *General Synod Papers, 1980–1981*, Vol. I, GS 469:5.
5. *Marriage and the Standing Committee's Task*, p. 5.
6. D. Wood, *Poet, Priest and Prophet: The Life and Thought of Bishop John V. Taylor* (London: Churches together in Britain and Ireland, 2002), pp. 134, 178.
7. 'Synod's Green Light for Marriage of Divorcees in Church', *Church Times* (10 July 1981):1.
8. The vote in the House of Bishops was 27 *ayes* to 7 *noes*; the vote in the House of Clergy was 134 *ayes* to 58 *noes*; and the vote in the House of Laity was 135 *ayes* to 49 *noes*. *Marriage and the Standing Committee's Task*, 1.
9. *General Synod Proceedings*, Vol. XII (1983): 10 November 1983: Legislative Business: Draft Marriage Regulation GS587, f 1110.
10. 'Synod's Green Light for Marriage of Divorcees in Church', 20.

Each Case is Different   187

11. *Marriage and the Standing Committee's Task*, pp. 16–17, 41–42, 45.
12. *Ibid.*, pp. 46, 50, 62.
13. P. Perrick, 'Someone Old, Someone New', *Times* (3 June 1983):13.
14. Letter from Peter Baelz to Helen Oppenheimer, dated 21 June 1983. Private collection of Helen Oppenheimer.
15. C. Longley, 'Remarriage in Church Approved', *Times* (15 July 1983):1.
16. 'Church Marriages for Divorcees: Synod Limbers up for the Main Battle', *Church Times* (15 July 1983):4.
17. Longley, 'Remarriage in Church Approved'.
18. C. Longley, 'Synod to Debate Proposal to Allow Remarriage in Church after Full Inquiry', *Times* (21 October 1983):3.
19. *Ibid.*
20. C. Longley, 'Runcie Rebukes Critics of Remarriage Rules', *Times* (24 October 1983):3.
21. C. Longley, 'Synod Split on Choice of Divorcees who could Remarry in Church', *Times* (11 November 1983):3.
22. C. Moore, *The Church in Crisis* (London: Hodder and Stoughton, 1986), p. 41.
23. 'GS 616: Marriage in Church after Divorce: A Report by the House of Bishops', *General Synod Papers, 1983–1984*, Vol. I, Nos. 583–624 (10 February 1984). Lambeth Palace Library.
24. *Ibid.*
25. 'The Marriage Bond', *Times* (25 February 1984):9.
26. 'Remarriage: Return to Square One?' *Church Times* (9 March 1984):1.
27. 'Synod's Initial Green Light for Bishops' New Attempt to Solve Remarriage Issue', *Church Times* (9 March 1984):4.
28. *Ibid.*
29. 'A Statement by Ten Bishops'. Original document in collection of Helen Oppenheimer. Those who signed the statement, in addition to Bishop Leonard, included the Bishops of Salisbury (John Baker); Chichester (Eric Kemp); Europe (John Satterthwaite); Exeter (Eric Mercer); Norwich (Maurice Wood); Peterborough (Douglas Feaver); St. Albans (John Taylor); Sherborne (John Kirkham); and Truro (Peter Mumford). See also 'Remarriage: Split among Bishops', *Church Times* (22 June 1984).
30. *Times* (25 February 1984):9.
31. *Times* (1 March 1984):17.
32. 'Canon B30 and the Proposed Marriage Regulation: Some Deeper Issues in the Marriage Debate'. Report from the Archbishop of York, Dr. John Habgood, to the House of Bishops at the meeting on 6 June 1984.
33. C. Longley, 'Remarriages in Church after Divorce Ruled Out', *Times* (23 January 1985):3.
34. *General Synod Proceedings*, February Group of Sessions, Vol. 16, No. 1 (13 February 1985):204–205.
35. *Ibid.*, 214–215.
36. *Ibid.*
37. *Ibid.*, 222–223.
38. *Ibid.*, 226.
39. *General Synod Proceedings*, July Group of Sessions, Vol. 16, No. 2 (2 July 1985):432–435.
40. *An Honourable Estate: The Doctrine of Marriage According to English Law and the Obligation of the Church to Marry All Parishioners Who Are Not Divorced*, GS 801 (London: Church House Publishing, 1988), pp. 1, 43.
41. 'Sir Timothy Hoare, Bt', Obituary, *Telegraph* (30 January 2008). Other members of the Working Party appointed in 1985 were Professor Peter Bromley, Emeritus Professor of English Law, Manchester University; Mr. John Bullimore,

188   *Each Case is Different*

Barrister, Chancellor of the Diocese of Derby; The Rt Revd Peter Coleman, Bishop of Crediton; The Rt Revd Michael Mann, Dean of Windsor; Mrs. Rachel Nugee JP, Past Central President of the Mothers' Union; and Lady Oppenheimer.

42. *An Honourable Estate*, p. 4.
43. *Ibid.*, p. 9.
44. *Ibid.*, p. 43
45. *The Field of Choice*, p. 10.
46. The number of decrees absolute (in thousands) in England and Wales had grown from 29 in 1951 to 74 in 1971 (just as the 1969 Divorce Act went into effect) to 153 in 1986. *An Honourable Estate*, p. 52.
47. *Family Law in the Twentieth Century*, p. 383.
48. Family Law Subcommittee of the Law Society, *A Better Way Out: Suggestions for the Reform of the Law of Divorce and Other Forms of Matrimonial Relief* (London: Law Society, 1979), pp. 2, 5.
49. The Law Commission, *Facing the Future: A Discussion Paper on the Ground for Divorce* (Law Com. No. 170) (London: HMSO, 1988) and *Family Law: The Ground for Divorce* (Law Com. No. 192) (London: HMSO, 1990).
50. Lord Chancellor's Department, *Looking to the Future: Mediation and the Ground for Divorce: A Consultation Paper* (London: HMSO, December, 1993), Foreword.
51. Lord Chancellor's Department, *Looking to the Future: Mediation and the Ground for Divorce: The Government's Proposals* (London: HMSO, April 1995), 14.
52. 'Nobody's Fault: A Useful Legal Fiction', *Church Times* (5 May 1995):10.
53. *Parliamentary Debates* (online), House of Lords (30 November 1995):715–717.
54. *Ibid.*, 735–736.
55. R. Harries, 'Hard to Find Fault in the Wreckage', *Church Times* (15 March 1996):8. Harries referred to Lord Mackay, 'the architect of the bill', as 'a devout Christian'.
56. F. Gibb, 'Irvine will Scrap "No Fault" Divorce Proposal', *Times* (18 December 2000).
57. *Family Law in the Twentieth Century*, p. 390.
58. O. O'Donovan, *Principles in the Public Realm: The Dilemma of Christian Moral Witness* (Oxford: Clarendon Press, 1984), p. 7.
59. *Ibid.*, p. 17.
60. A. Clarkson, S. Rix, J. Rees, and D. Sherwood, 'Marriage in Church after Divorce: A Working Party Report', *Ecclesiastical Law Journal*, Vol. 2(1992):359.
61. *Ibid.*, 360.
62. *General Synod Proceedings* (2 December 1994):933.
63. S. Meyrick, 'Remarriage Report Stays Under Wraps', *Church Times* (10 September 1999).
64. *Marriage: A Teaching Document from the House of Bishops of the Church of England* (London: Church House Publishing, 1999), pp. 14–15.
65. *Ibid.*, 17.
66. *Ibid.*, 18.
67. A. Thatcher, *Celebrating Christian Marriage* (Edinburgh and New York: T & T Clark, 2001), p. xviii.
68. The other members of the Working Party were Mr. Mark Birchall, General Synod Member and Vice-Chairman of the Evangelical Alliance; the Right Revd Graham James, Bishop-designate of Norwich, formerly Bishop of St. Germans; Mrs. Sarah James, General Synod Member and Trustee of the Mothers' Union; the Revd Canon Peter Lock (from May 1997), General Synod Member and Vicar of SS Peter and Paul, Bromley; the Revd Canon David Lowman, General

Synod Member and Director of Ordinands, Lay Ministry Adviser and NSM Officer for the Diocese of Chelmsford; Mrs. Christine McMullen, General Synod Member, Secretary of Broken Rites, and Director of Pastoral Studies on the Northern Ordination Course; and the Right Revd John Yates, formerly Bishop of Gloucester and Bishop at Lambeth. *Marriage in Church after Divorce: A Discussion Document from a Working Party Commissioned by the House of Bishops of the Church of England*, GS 1361 (London: Church House Publishing, 2000), p. 96.

69. *Ibid.*, pp. xi, 6, 38–39.
70. *Ibid.*, pp. 21–22.
71. *Ibid.*, pp. 37–38.
72. *Ibid.*, p. 45.
73. *Ibid.*, pp. 56–57.
74. *Ibid.*, pp. vi–vii.
75. S. Hillman and B. Bowder, 'More Chaos Ahead as Dioceses Reject Remarriage Plan', *Church Times* (18 May 2001):1; O. Osmond, 'The Second Time Around', *Church Times* (9 February 2001):12.
76. S. Hillman, 'Marriage Panels Mooted Again', *Church Times* (16 March 2001):5.
77. 'How Dioceses Voted', *Church Times* (18 May 2001):5; S. Hillman and B. Bowder, 'More Chaos Ahead as Dioceses Reject Remarriage Plan', *Church Times* (18 May 2001):1; S. Hillman, 'Regard Divorcees as Unwed, says York Diocesan Synod,' *Church Times* (4 May 2001):3.
78. *Marriage in Church after Divorce: A Report from the House of Bishops*, GS 1449 (London: General Synod, 2002), p. 5. The bishops cited Section 8 of the Matrimonial Causes Act of 1965 as confirming the right of the clergy to refuse to marry a divorced person in church.
79. *Ibid.*, p. 31.
80. *Ibid.*, p. 30.
81. *Ibid.*, pp. 26–27.
82. *Ibid.*, p. 27.
83. *The Chronicle of Convocation, Being a Record of the Proceedings of the Convocation of Canterbury* (6 July 2002):13–14.
84. *Ibid.*, 14.
85. *General Synod Proceedings* (9 July 2002):428.
86. *Chronicle of Convocation* (6 July 2002):16.
87. *General Synod Proceedings* (9 July 2002):437–438.
88. *Ibid.* (14 November 2002):278.
89. *Ibid.* (9 July 2002):406.
90. *Marriage in Church after Divorce: A Report from the House of Bishops* (GS 1449), pp. 15–17.
91. K.D. Reynolds, 'Diana, princess of Wales (1961–1997)', *Oxford Dictionary of National Biography*, Oxford University Press, 2004; online edn, Jan 2014 [http://www.oxforddnb.com/view/article/68348].
92. P. Naughton and R. Allen, 'Prince Charles to marry Camilla Parker Bowles', *Times Online* (10 February 2005).
93. S. de Bruxelles, 'Vicar will Welcome "Adulterer" Prince', *The Times* (3 December 2002).
94. 'Interview: Christopher Morgan meets Rowan Williams', *The Sunday Times* (2 February 2003).
95. P. Naughton, 'Lord Chancellor Rules that Royal Wedding is Legal', *The Times* (23 February 2005).
96. 'Lord Chancellor's Statement in Full', *BBC News* (23 February 2005). www.news.bbc.co.uk.
97. 'Supporting the Royal Wedding', *Church Times* (18 February 2005):8.

190 *Each Case is Different*

98. 'Charles and Camilla—Archbishop's Statement' (10 February 2005). www.cofe.anglican.org/news.
99. A. Pierce, 'One will not be Coming but don't take it Personally, Son', *The Times* (26 March 2005).
100. 'Prince Charles to marry Camilla', *BBC News* (10 February 2005). www.news.bbc.co.uk.
101. A. Alderson, 'I had to put Church before Charles, says the Queen', *The Telegraph* (5 April 2005).
102. *Archbishop's Group on Reform of Divorce Laws*, MS 3460, Lambeth Palace Library. Minutes of Second Meeting on 28 July 1964, p. 7.
103. *Marriage and the Church's Task: The Report of the General Synod Marriage Commission* (London: CIO Publishing, 1978), p. 38.

Index

Abdication Crisis 43–8, 50, 54–5, 75, 78
Abortion Bill of 1967 119
Abse, Leo 95–9, 107, 108, 117–18
Act of Convocation of 1957 84–6,
  127–8, 168–70, 177, 179–80
Adie, Bishop Michael E. 148, 155,
  168–70
adultery: double standard 34–6; as
  ground for divorce 1–2, 5–9, 30,
  38–40, 48, 53, 103, 105, 114; as
  proof of breakdown needed for
  divorce 115–16
Allchin, Arthur Macdonald [Donald] 133
Allen, M. I., Mrs. 148
Anderson, Norman 102, 113, 116, 118
Andrews, Leonard Martin 46
Anson, Sir William Reynell 10–12, 21–2
Archbishops' Commissions on Church
  and State (1914) 36–7; (1935) 37–8
Archbishop's Group on Reform of
  Divorce Laws (1964–66): and
  Divorce Act of 1969 117–22;
  and Law Commission 114–16;
  membership and goals 99–104;
  presentation of report to Church
  Assembly and House of Lords
  111–14; report 104–7; response to
  report 107–11
Armstrong-Jones, Antony, Earl of
  Snowdon 77, 152
Asquith, Herbert Henry 10–12, 13

Baelz, Peter 148, 165
Baldwin, Stanley 44–6, 76–7
Balfour, Frances 11, 14
Banister v. *Thomson* (1908) 41
Barnes, Bishop Ernest William 42
Barnes, Henry Gorell, 2nd Baron Gorell
  see Gorell of Brampton, 2nd Baron
  Gorell

Barnes, John Gorell, 1st Baron Gorell
  see Gorell of Brampton, 1st Baron
  Gorell
Barnes, Ronald Gorell, 3rd Baron
  Gorell *see* Gorell of Brampton, 3rd
  Baron Gorell
Batty, Bishop Basil 47
Beloe, Robert 88n29, 96, 98, 103, 116
Bentley, G. B. 102, 125n100, 128
Birkenhead, Earl of (Frederick Edwin
  Smith) 30–1, 33, 38, 56n14
Bishops' Option 166–8
Bishops' Report on Marriage
  Regulation [GS 669] (1985) 168–9
Boggis-Rolfe, Hume 116
In Both Worlds Full (Dunstan) 134–6,
  158n45, n52
Boulton, Peter 143, 159n84
Bowker, J. W. 132
Bowman v. *Secular Society* (1917) 29
Bray, Jeremy 97
breakdown of marriage: as ground for
  divorce 104–14, 118, 121–2, 131;
  and inquest 110–12, 114–16
Buckmaster, Stanley Owen, first Viscount
  Buckmaster 29–34, 36, 38, 40–1, 53
Buckmaster's Divorce Bill (1920) *see*
  Matrimonial Causes (Buckmaster)
  Bill (1920)

Cameron, Sheila 148
Campbell, Bishop Montgomery 84
Canon B30 132, 167, 179
Charles, Prince of Wales 162, 181–4
Church Assembly 37, 55, 113–14, 118,
  122, 129, 136–7, 140
Churchill, Randolph 78–9
Churchill, Sir Winston 75
Coggan, Archbishop Donald 146, 148,
  153, 155

192 Index

Colville, John Mark Alexander, Viscount Colville of Culross 102
Convocation of Canterbury, Committee on Marriage Laws of Lower House (1910) 23
Convocations of Canterbury and York, Joint Committee (1932) 40–1, 49; Report (1935) 41–4, 46, 49, 51–2
Convocations of Canterbury and York, Resolutions on Marriage (1938) 54–5, 84

Davidson, Archbishop Randall: appointment of Royal Commission on Divorce 9–12, 22, 65, 72; debates in House of Lords 30–2, 34, 36, 39; memorial to oppose divorce reform 28–9; Prayer Book Crisis 37; remarriage in church 40; resignation 38; statement on marriage with a deceased wife's sister 127
Davies, Llewelyn 18–19
Deceased Wife's Sister's Marriage Bill 10, 12
Denning Committee 61
Devlin, Patrick Arthur, Baron Devlin 102
Diana, Princess of Wales 162, 182
Dibdin, Sir Lewis 10–12, 17, 21–2, 41
Divorce Act of 1857 1, 6–7, 10, 13–14, 17, 23, 31, 34, 39, 50, 53, 178
Divorce (2nd Lord Gorell) Bill (1914) 24
Divorce (3rd Lord Gorell) Bill (1921) 34
Divorce Reform Act (1969) 107, 116–22, 136–7
Don, Alan Campbell 46, 48
double standard 34–6, 40
Dunstan, Gordon ix, 86, 100–2, 122, 130–2, 134–6, 139, 142–4, 159n87

Eden, Anthony 76
Edward VIII, King of the United Kingdom (Duke of Windsor) 43–8, 50, 54, 77–8, 181–2, 184
Edwards, Quentin T. 102
Elizabeth, Queen of the United Kingdom, consort of George VI 75
Elizabeth II, Queen of the United Kingdom 75, 184
Ellison, Bishop Gerald 121, 143, 150
Enabling Act (1919) 36–7, 140
Entwistle, Cyril 36

The Family in Contemporary Society (1959) 86–7, 100, 131, 134
Family Law Act (1996) 172–4

Field of Choice (1966) 110–12, 115, 171
Fisher, Archbishop Geoffrey 60–1, 64–70, 75–81, 84–6
Fisher, Rosamond 68
Fletcher, Eric 96, 123n20
Fox, G. R. Lane 33
Furse, Bishop Michael 52–3

Garbett, Archbishop Cyril 64–6
Gardiner, Gerald (Baron) 108–12, 115–17, 120
General Synod: acceptance of remarriage in church (1981) 3, 162–4, 168, 170, 176, 186; and Bishops' Option 166–9; and House of Bishops 175, 179–81; and Lichfield Report 152–6; opened (1970) 140; and Option G 164–6; and Root Report 140–7
George V, King of the United Kingdom 44
George VI, King of the United Kingdom 46–7, 75, 184
Gibbs, D. N. 169
Goodrich, Bishop Philip 173
Gore, Bishop Charles 7–8, 13–15, 19, 22, 26n41, n44, 31
Gorell Commission see Royal Commission on Divorce (1909)
Gorell of Brampton, 1st Baron Gorell (John Gorell Barnes) 11, 20–2, 24
Gorell of Brampton, 2nd Baron Gorell (Henry Gorell Barnes) 24
Gorell of Brampton, 3rd Baron Gorell (Ronald Gorell Barnes) 34, 56n32
Gower, L.C.B. 109, 125n100

Habgood, Archbishop John 144, 166–8, 179
Haldane, Richard Burdon, Viscount Haldane 24
Harries, Bishop Richard 173
Henry VIII, King of England 5
Henson, Bishop Hensley 15–16, 26n41 and n44, 35, 44–7, 52–4, 82
Herbert, Sir Alan Patrick 4n2, 48–54, 81–4
Hoare, Sir Timothy 170–1, 174
Hoggett, Brenda 171
Holmes, (Mrs.) M.E.R. 153–5
Holy Communion 32, 36, 41–2, 63–4, 69, 81, 84–5, 127–8, 142, 151, 162
Homosexuality Bill of 1966 119
Honest to God 93–4, 129–30

Index 193

An Honourable Estate: The Doctrine of Marriage According to English Law and the Obligation of the Church to Marry All Parishioners Who Are Not Divorced [GS 801] (1988) 171, 174
hotel divorce 39–40, 44, 51
House of Bishops (General Synod) 146, 163, 166–7, 175, 178–9, 181

Inge, Ralph 16–17, 86
Inskip, Bishop James Theodore 42

Jackson, Brandon 148
Jardine, Robert Anderson 47, 58n93, 184
Jones, Alec 119
Jones, Kathleen 148, 153, 155–6
Jowitt, Earl (William Allen Jowitt) 61, 65–6

Kirk, Bishop Kenneth 42–3, 62

Lacey, Thomas Alexander 23–4, 62, 71, 100
Lambeth Conference (1867) 8
Lambeth Conference (1888) 13
Lambeth Conference (1908) 12–13
Lambeth Conference (1920) 35, 38–9
Lambeth Conference (1930) 38–9
Lambeth Conference (1948) 62–4, 84
Lambeth Conference (1958) 87, 131–2
Lang, Archbishop Cosmo Gordon: Abdication Crisis 44–8, 54, 78, 184; Archbishop of Canterbury 38, 43; Gorell Bill (1914) 24; Matrimonial Causes Bill (1920) 30, 32, 36; Matrimonial Causes Act (1937) 50–5; resignation 60; Royal Commission on Divorce 10–12, 17, 20–2
Law Commission 108–19, 171–2
Law Society 172
Leonard, Bishop Graham 137–8, 145–6, 156, 163, 167
Lichfield Commission (1975–1978) 147–51; Report 152–6, 162, 179, 185
Loreburn, Earl (Robert Threshie Reid) 11
Lucas, J. R. 139–40, 148

Mackay, James Peter Hymers, Baron Mackay of Clashfern 172
Macmillan, Harold 94–5
MacRae, Donald 103, 124n54

Margaret Rose, Princess 74–80, 152
Marriage and the Church's Task (Lichfield Report, 1978) 152–6
Marriage and the Standing Committee's Task (1983) 164
Marriage: A Teaching Document from the House of Bishops of the Church of England (1999) 175–6
Marriage Divorce and the Church (Root Report, 1971) 138–47
Marriage in Church after Divorce [GS 1361] (Winchester Report, 2000) 176–8, 181
Marriage in Church after Divorce [GS 1449] (House of Bishops, 2002) 178–81
Martin, Andrew 109
Mary, Queen of the United Kingdom, consort of George V 47–8, 184
Matrimonial Causes Act (1857) *see* Divorce Act of 1857
Matrimonial Causes Act (1923) 36
Matrimonial Causes Act (1937) 48–55, 69, 81, 100
Matrimonial Causes Act (1963) 99
Matrimonial Causes (Buckmaster) Bill (1920) 29–33, 36, 53
Matrimonial Causes (White) Bill (1951) 64–5, 67, 95
Matthaean Exception 2, 6–8, 12–13, 15–16, 23, 38, 52–3, 62, 67, 100
McGregor, Oliver Ross, Baron McGregor of Durris ix, 73–4, 102, 108
McLeod, Hugh 3
Merriman, Boyd, Baron Merriman 49
Metcalfe, Edward Dudley ('Fruity') 47
Metcalfe, Lady Alexandra Curzon 47–8, 184
Modern Churchmen's Union 68–9
Monckton, Walter 46–7
Montefiore, Bishop Hugh 127–8, 131–2, 139, 143, 152
Montmorency, J.E.G. de 40
Moore, Evelyn Garth 129, 167
Moral Welfare Council 86, 131–2, 134
Mortimer, Bishop Robert 62, 71–2, 100, 103–4, 109, 111–12, 116–17, 120–1
Morton, Fergus Dunlop, Baron Morton of Henryton 66, 69–70
Morton Commission *see* Royal Commission on Divorce (1951)
Mothers' Union 17–18, 51, 68, 73, 96, 138

Nullity 5, 150–1, 164, 167, 169

194   *Index*

O'Donovan, Oliver 174, 176
Oppenheimer, Helen ix, 102, 128, 136, 140, 143
Option F 165
Option G 164–6, 177–8
Osmond, Oliver 178

Pakenham, Francis Aungier, Baron Pakenham and Earl of Longford 120, 126n134
Parker Bowles, Camilla 181–4
Parliamentary divorces 6
Pastoral Letter from Archbishops of Canterbury and York (1970) 137
Percy, Eustace Sutherland Campbell, Baron Percy of Newcastle 66
Philip, Prince, Duke of Edinburgh 184
Prayer Book Crisis (1927) 36–8
Profumo, John 95
Putting Asunder: *A Divorce Law for Contemporary Society* (1966): debate in Church Assembly 113–14; debate in House of Lords 111–12, 114; purpose of 103; recommendations 104–7; responses to 107–11, 117–20, 128, 137

Quilter, Harry 2, 4n2

Ramsey, Archbishop Michael: Abse Bill 95–9; Archbishop's Group and *Putting Asunder* 99–100, 103, 109, 112–13, 116; Divorce Act (1969) 117–18, 120–2; Kenneth Skelton 147; matrimonial offence 114; 'new morality' 92–4; Pastoral Letter (1970) 137; remarriage in church after divorce 127, 147; Root Report 138, 147
Ramsey, Bishop Ian 134, 144
Rashdall, Hastings 16–17, 86
Rendall, Athelstan 32–3
Rhymes, Douglas 94
Riley, Athelstan 28
Robinson, Bishop John 93–4, 129
Rogers, Guy 40, 42
Root, Howard 129–30, 132–3, 147
Root Commission (1968–1971) 2, 129–36; comparison with Lichfield Commission 148–9, 151–2, 155–6; Report 138–47, 170
Royal Commission on Divorce (1909): appointment of 2, 9–12; comparison with Morton Commission 64–7, 72–3; Majority Report 21, 24, 32,

34–5, 48, 73; Minority Report 12, 21–4, 34–5, 53, 73; testimony presented to 13–20, 34–6, 43, 52, 86
Royal Commission on Divorce (1951): appointment and membership 64–6, 102; comparison with 1909 Royal Commission 64–7, 72–4; Report 71–4, 95, 105; testimony presented to 66–9, 109
Rubinstein, Joan 102, 124n51
Runcie, Archbishop Robert 144–6, 160n95, 162–6, 168–9

Sanday, William 15–16
Scarman, Leslie, Baron Scarman 109, 112, 115
Schuster, Claud 50
Scott-Joynt, Bishop Michael 175–6, 180–1
secularisation 3
Selborne, Earl (Roundell Cecil Palmer) 32
Shepherd, A. P. 84–5
Simon, Jocelyn, Baron Simon of Glaisdale 97, 123n25
Simon, John Allsebrook, Viscount Simon 50
Simpson, Ernest 43–4
Simpson, Wallis Warfield (Duchess of Windsor) 43–8, 50, 181–2, 184
Skelton, Bishop Kenneth 147–8, 153, 155–6
Smith, Frederick Edwin, Earl of Birkenhead *see* Birkenhead, Earl of
Soddy, Kenneth 148
Somervell, Donald, Baron Somervell of Harrow 50
Soundings 129–30
Spencer, Lady Diana *see* Diana, Princess of Wales
Spicer, Eulalie 106–7
Stevens, David 137, 141, 148, 152, 167
Stockwood, Bishop Mervyn 128
Stow Hill, Baron (Frank Soskice) 119
Straubenzee, William van 96, 123n20
Summerskill, Edith Clara, Baroness Summerskill 106, 112, 119
Sumner, Archbishop John Bird 6–7, 35
Sumner, Viscount (John Andrew Hamilton) 29

Tait, Archbishop Archibald Campbell 7, 9
Taylor, Bishop John Vernon 163
Temple, Archbishop William 52, 60

Titmuss, Richard Morris 101, 103
Townsend, Peter 74–80, 89n64

Vidler, Alexander 129–30

Waddams, Herbert 140–1
Walker, James 71
Ward, Robin 180
Waterfield, Reginald 42
White, Eirene 64–5, 67, 95
White's Matrimonial Causes Bill (1951) *see* Matrimonial Causes (White) Bill (1951)
Whittingham, Bishop Walter Godfrey 53

Whittock, M. G. 148
Williams, Archbishop Rowan 182–3
Williams, Bishop Ronald 138, 143–5
Williams, Morgan 148
Wilson, William 117
Winchester Report *see Marriage in Church after Divorce* [GS 1361] (Winchester Report, 2000)
Winnett, Arthur Robert 63, 128
Withers, Sir John 40
Wolfenden Report 92
Women's Co-operative Guild 18–19
Working Party's Report [GS 156] (1973) 143